VOL. 34
VIZ Media Edition

Story and Art by
RUMIKO TAKAHASHI

English Adaptation by Gerard Jones

Translation/Mari Morimoto
Touch-up Art & Lettering/Bill Schuch
Cover and Interior Graphic Design/Yuki Ameda
Editor/Ian Robertson

Editor in Chief, Books/Alvin Lu
Editor in Chief, Magazines/Marc Weidenbaum
VP of Publishing Licensing/Rika Inouye
VP of Sales/Gonzalo Ferreyra
Sr. VP of Marketing/Liza Coppola
Publisher/Hyoe Narita

Printed in the U.S.A.

Published by VIZ Media, LLC
P.O. Box 77010
San Francisco, CA 94107

VIZ Media Edition
10 9 8 7 6 5 4 3 2 1
First printing, July 2008

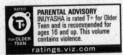

VIZ
MEDIA
www.viz.com

store.viz.com

INUYASHA

VOL. 34

VIZ Media Edition

STORY AND ART BY
RUMIKO TAKAHASHI

CONTENTS

THE STORY THUS FAR

Long ago, in the "Warring States" era of Japan's Muromachi period (Sengoku-jidai, approximately 1467-1568 CE), a legendary dog-like half-demon called "Inuyasha" attempted to steal the Shikon Jewel—or "Jewel of Four Souls"—from a village, but was stopped by the enchanted arrow of the village priestess, Kikyo. Inuyasha fell into a deep sleep, pinned to a tree by Kikyo's arrow, while the mortally wounded Kikyo took the Shikon Jewel with her into the fires of her funeral pyre. Years passed.

Fast-forward to the present day. Kagome, a Japanese high school girl, is pulled into a well one day by a mysterious centipede monster and finds herself transported into the past—only to come face to face with the trapped Inuyasha. She frees him, and Inuyasha easily defeats the centipede monster.

The residents of the village, now 50 years older, readily accept Kagome as the reincarnation of their deceased priestess Kikyo, a claim supported by the fact that the Shikon Jewel emerges from a cut on Kagome's body. Unfortunately, the jewel's rediscovery means that the village is soon under attack by a variety of demons in search of this treasure. Then, the jewel is accidentally shattered into many shards, each of which may have the fearsome power of the entire jewel.

Although Inuyasha says he hates Kagome because of her resemblance to Kikyo, the woman who "killed" him, he is forced to team up with her when Kaede, the village leader, binds him to Kagome with a powerful spell. Now the two grudging companions must fight to reclaim and reassemble the shattered shards of the Shikon Jewel before they fall into the wrong hands...

THIS VOLUME Inuyasha and the gang follow a trail of rumors that lead to a "living mountain." Naraku has awoken the mountain from its 200-year slumber and stolen its sacred stone. To help Inuyasha and his group retrieve the stone, the "living mountain" gives them a gift. What could Naraku hope to achieve with this stone?

CHARACTERS

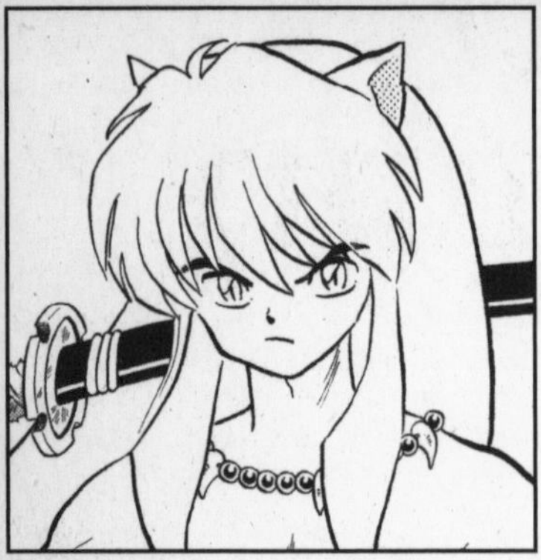

INUYASHA
Half-demon hybrid, son of a human mother and demon father. His necklace is enchanted, allowing Kagome to control him with a word.

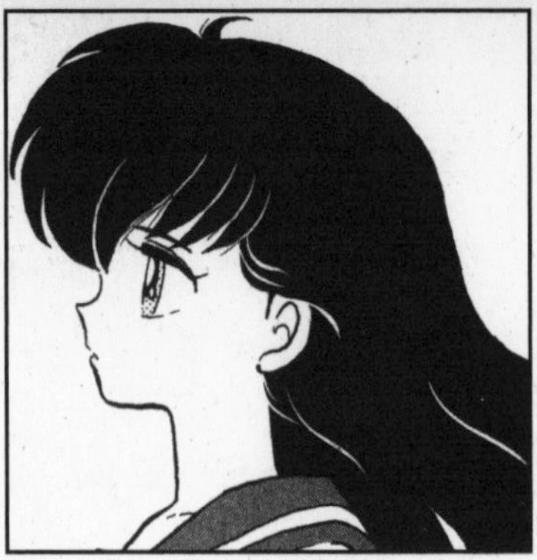

KAGOME
Modern-day Japanese schoolgirl who can travel back and forth between the past and present through an enchanted well.

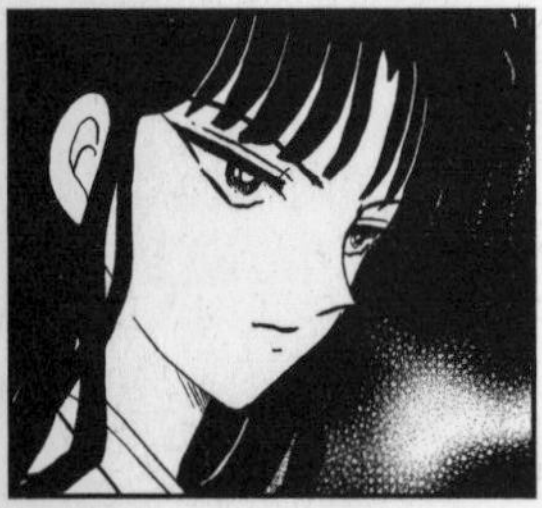

NARAKU
Enigmatic demon-mastermind behind the miseries of nearly everyone in the story.

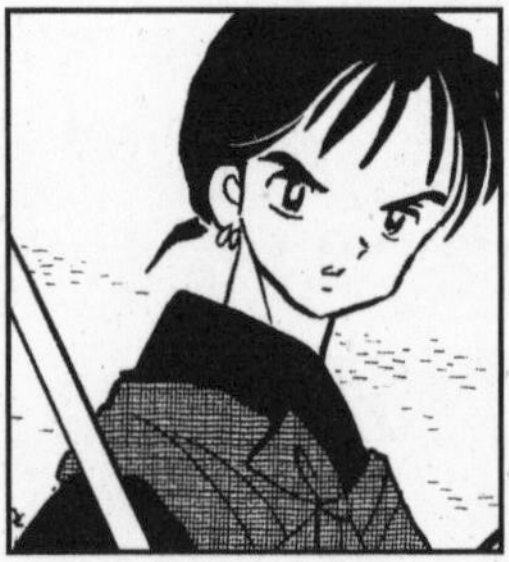

MIROKU
Lecherous Buddhist priest cursed with a mystical "hellhole" in his hand that's slowly killing him.

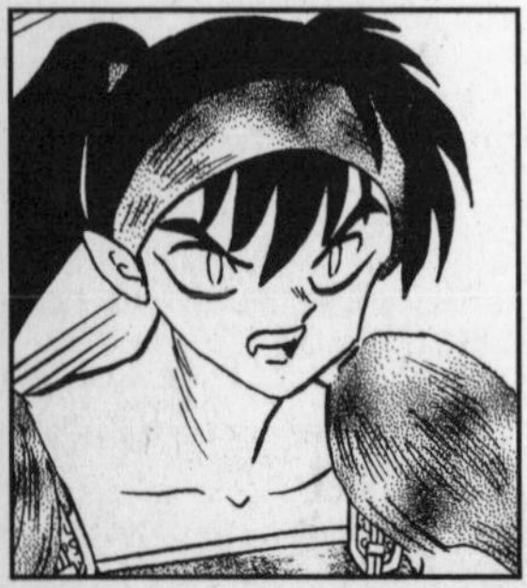

KOGA
Leader of the Wolf Clan, Koga is himself a Wolf Demon and, because of several Shikon shards in his legs, possesses super speed. Enamored of Kagome, he quarrels with Inuyasha frequently.

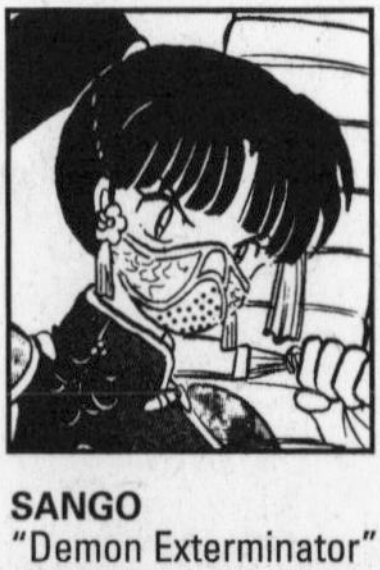

SANGO
"Demon Exterminator" or slayer from the village where the Shikon Jewel was first born.

SCROLL 1
TREE BLIGHT

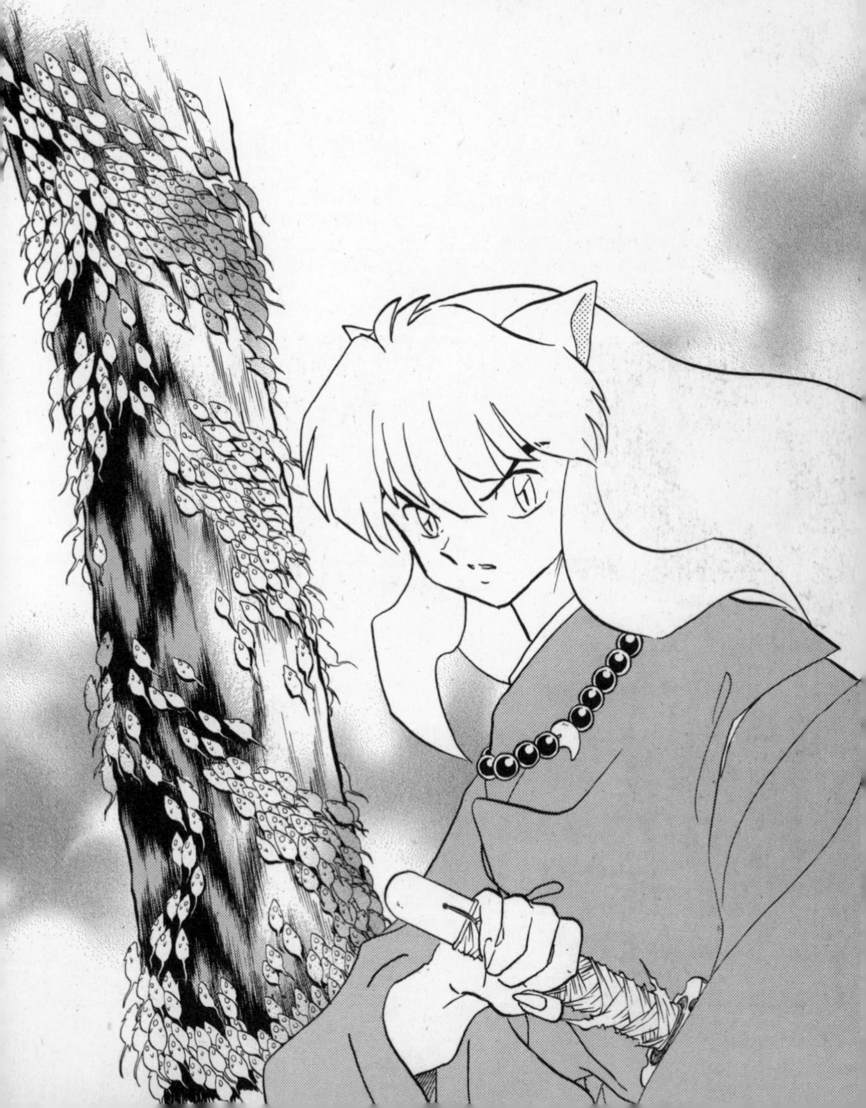

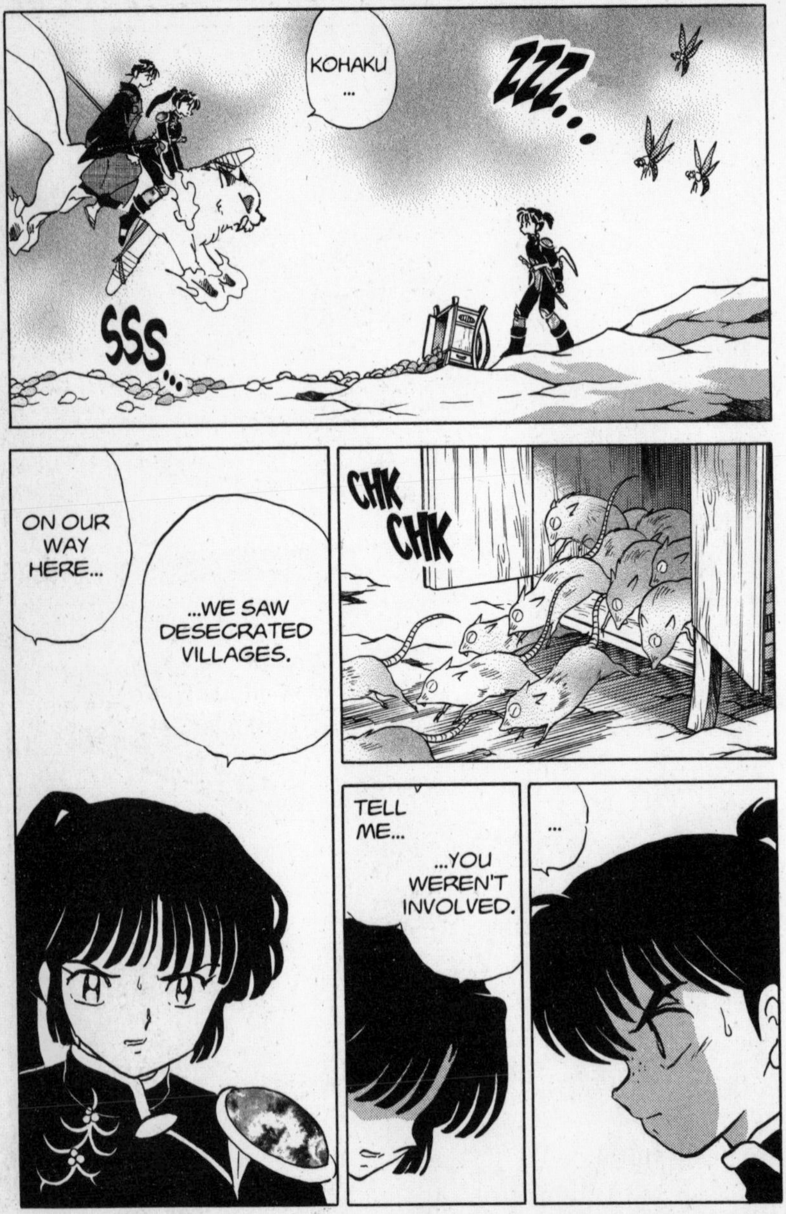

KOHAKU ...
ZZZ...
SSS...
ON OUR WAY HERE...
...WE SAW DESECRATED VILLAGES.
CHK CHK
TELL ME...
...YOU WEREN'T INVOLVED.
...

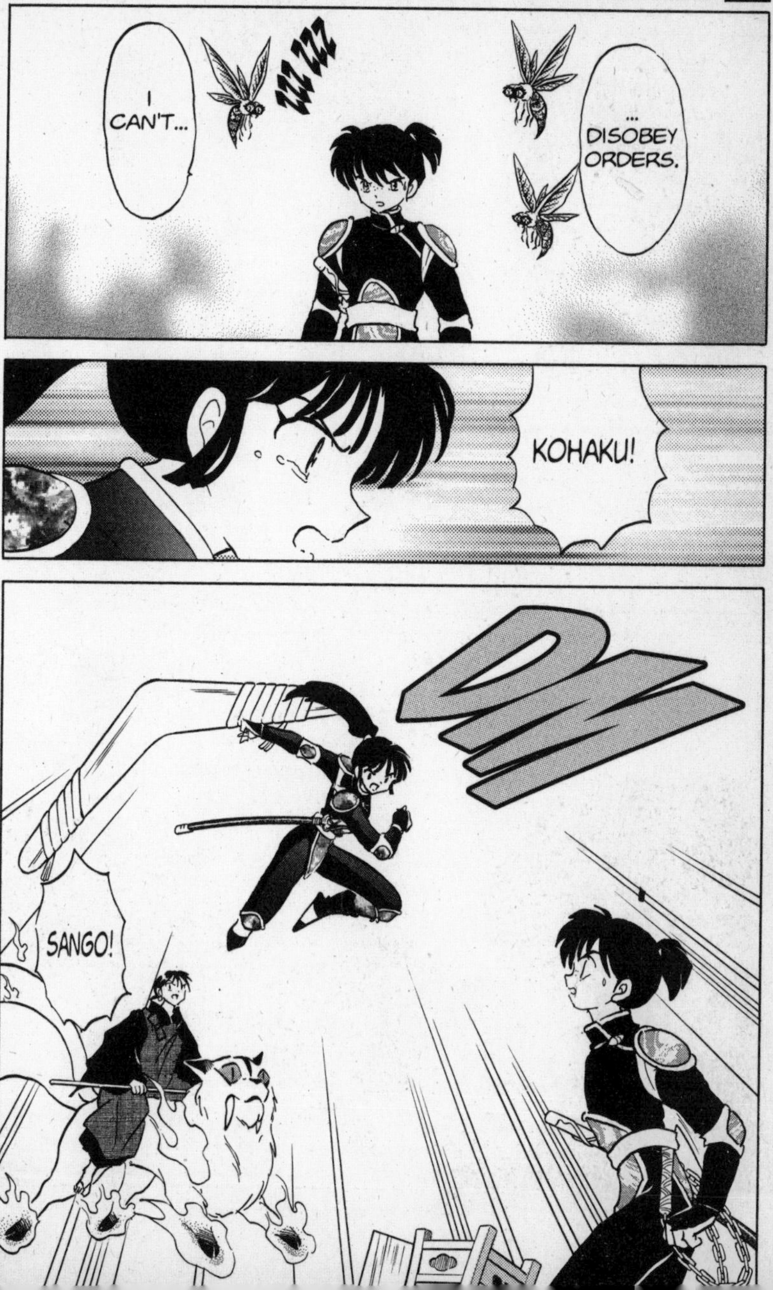
I CAN'T...
ZZZ ZZZ
... DISOBEY ORDERS.
KOHAKU!
DM
SANGO!

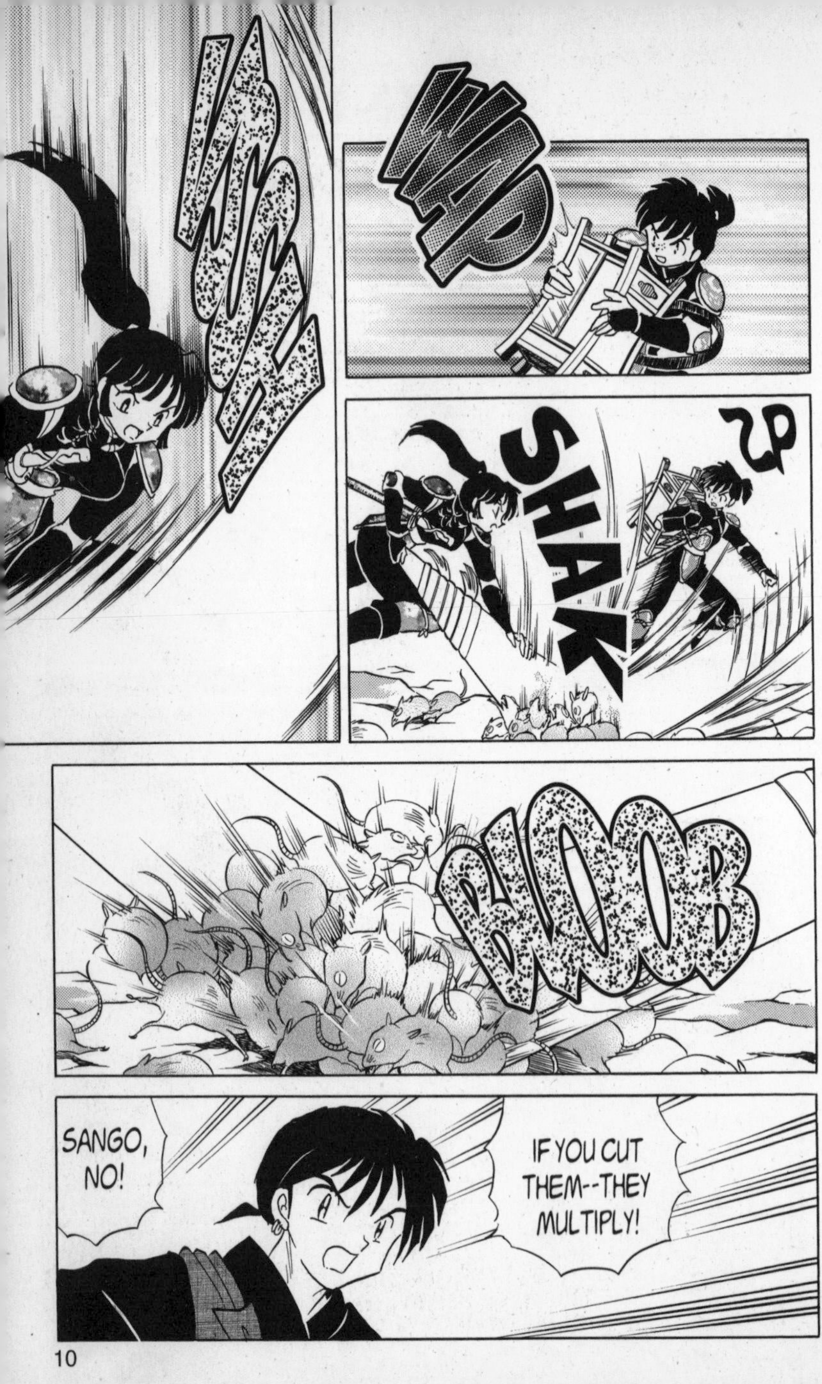
WAP
SHAK
BLOOB
SANGO, NO!
IF YOU CUT THEM--THEY MULTIPLY!

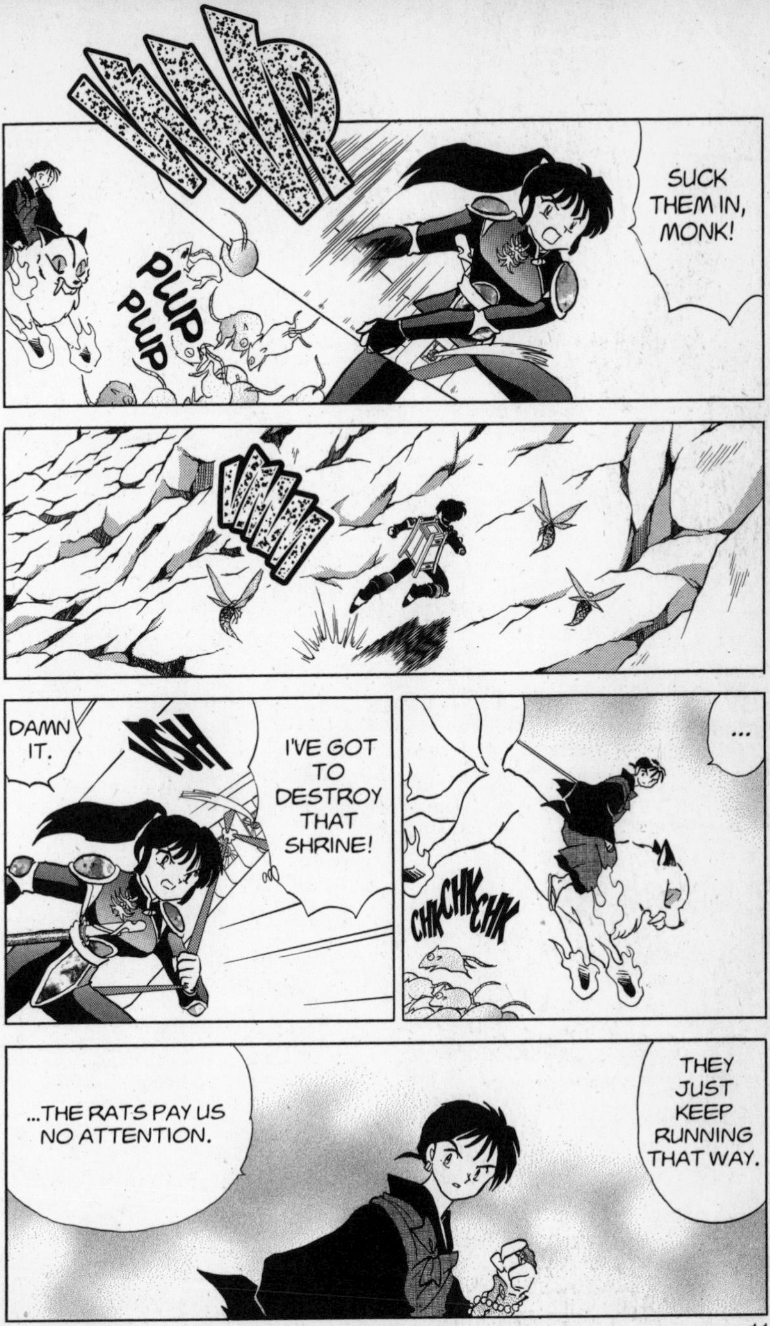
WHIP
SUCK THEM IN, MONK!
PWIP PWIP
VMMM
DAMN IT.
VSH
I'VE GOT TO DESTROY THAT SHRINE!
...
CHK CHK CHK
...THE RATS PAY US NO ATTENTION.
THEY JUST KEEP RUNNING THAT WAY.

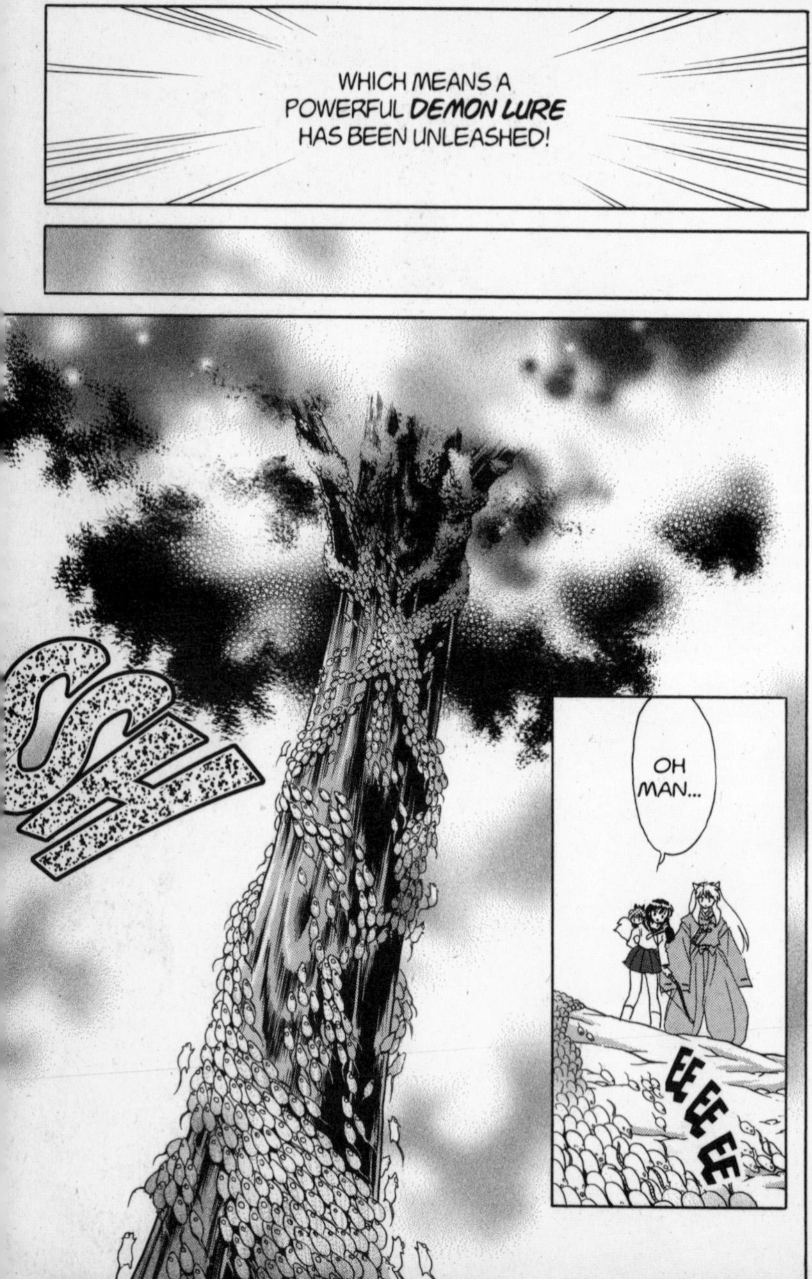
WHICH MEANS A POWERFUL **DEMON LURE** HAS BEEN UNLEASHED!
OH MAN...
EEEEEEEE

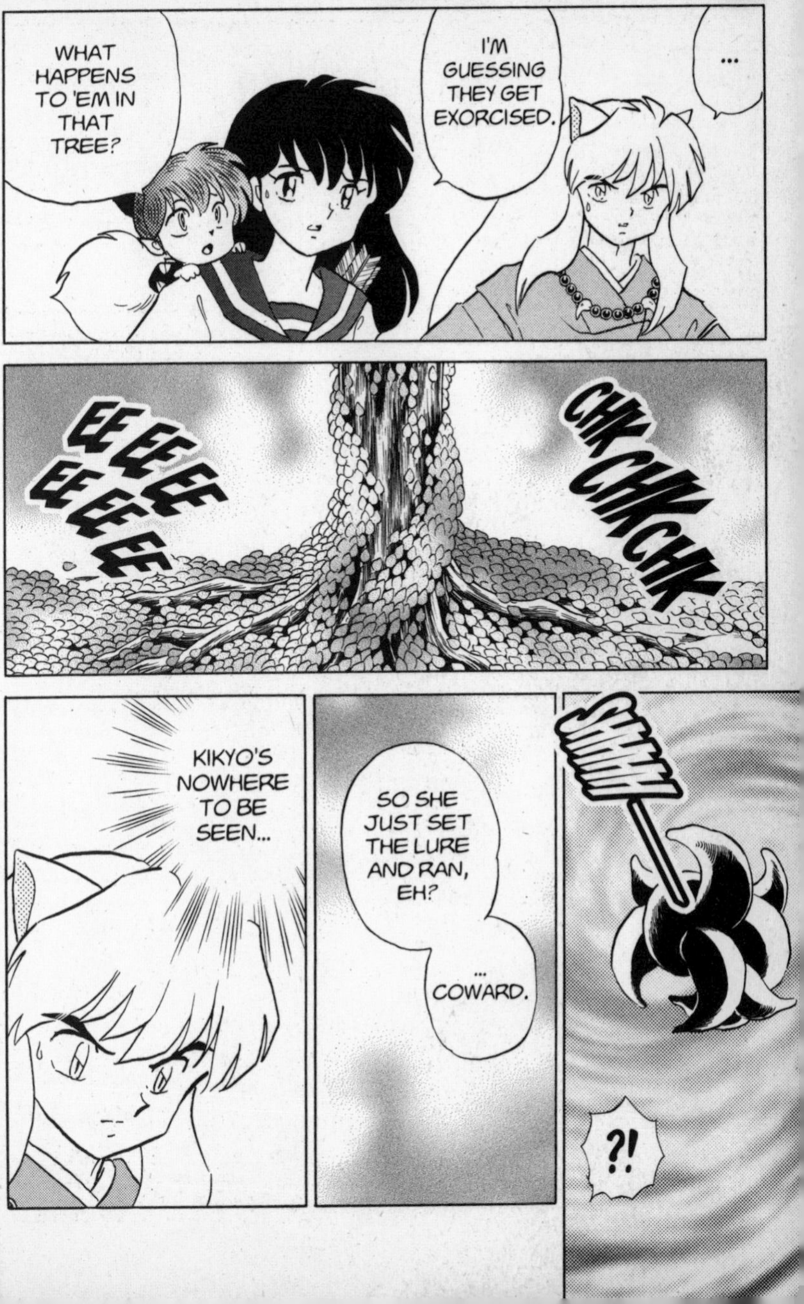
WHAT HAPPENS TO 'EM IN THAT TREE?
I'M GUESSING THEY GET EXORCISED.
...
EE EE EE EE EE EE EE
CHK CHK CHK CHK
KIKYO'S NOWHERE TO BE SEEN...
SO SHE JUST SET THE LURE AND RAN, EH?
... COWARD.
SHHHH
?!

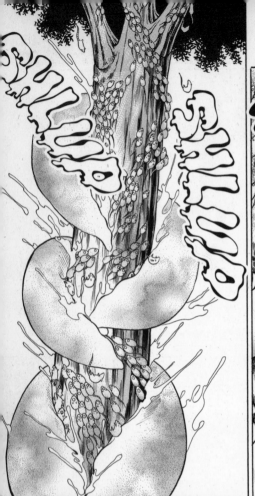

WHAT...?!

MONSTER SLUGS!

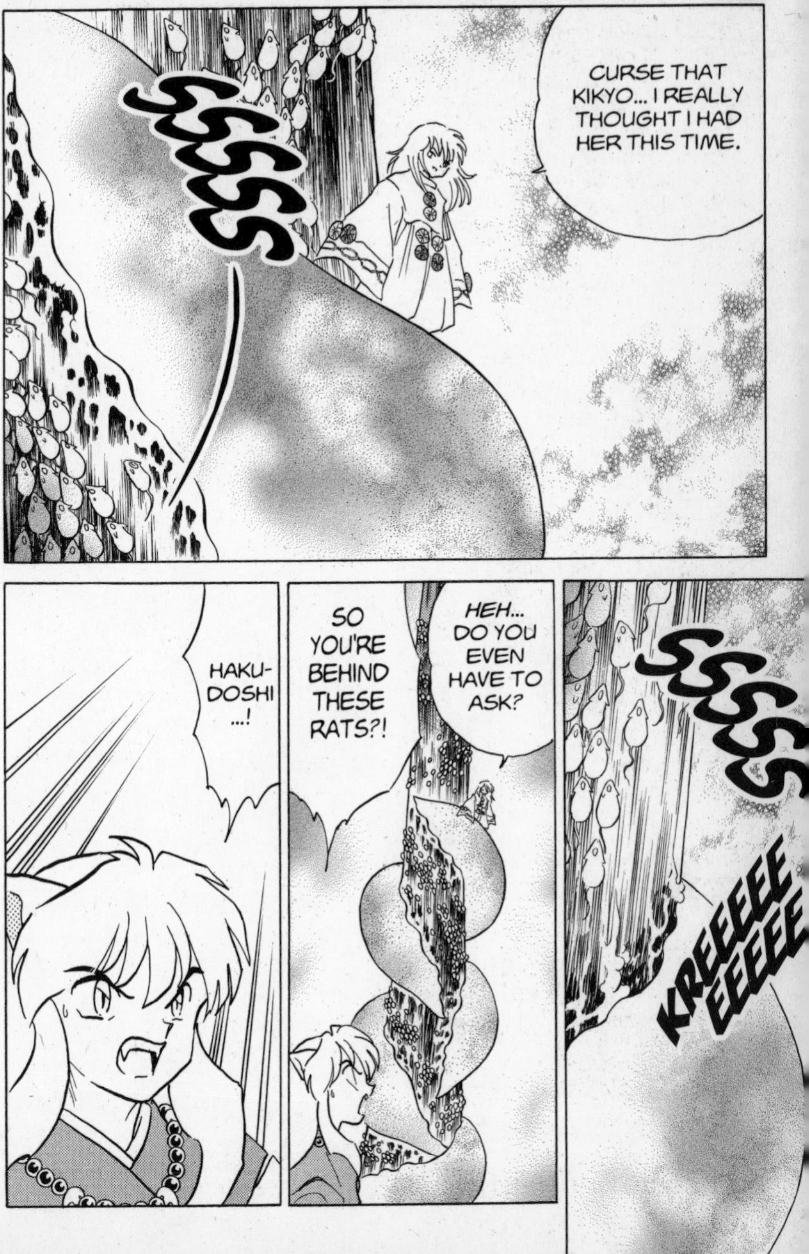
SSSSS
CURSE THAT KIKYO... I REALLY THOUGHT I HAD HER THIS TIME.
HAKU-DOSHI ...!
SO YOU'RE BEHIND THESE RATS?!
HEH... DO YOU EVEN HAVE TO ASK?
SSSSS
KREEEEE EEEEE

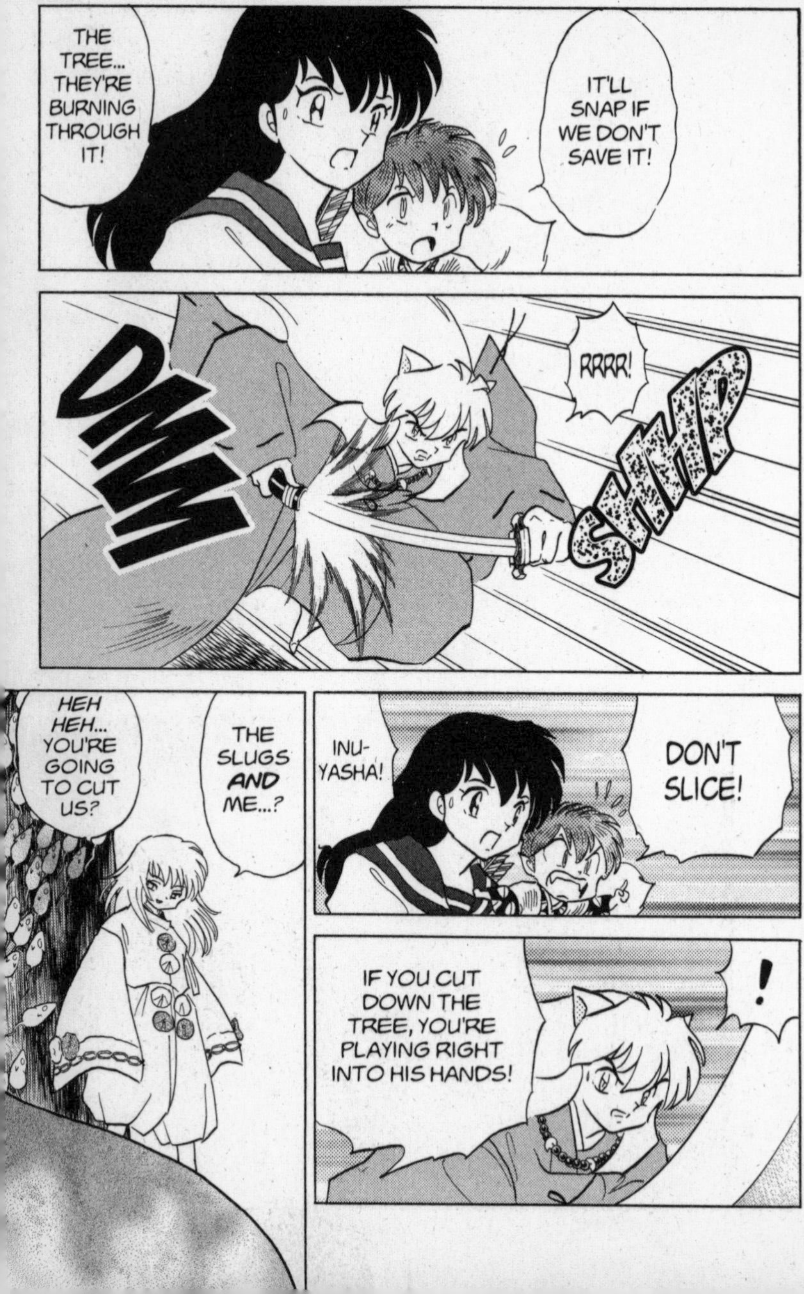
THE TREE... THEY'RE BURNING THROUGH IT!
IT'LL SNAP IF WE DON'T SAVE IT!
DMMM
RRRR!
SHHP
HEH HEH... YOU'RE GOING TO CUT US?
THE SLUGS AND ME...?
INU-YASHA!
DON'T SLICE!
IF YOU CUT DOWN THE TREE, YOU'RE PLAYING RIGHT INTO HIS HANDS!
!

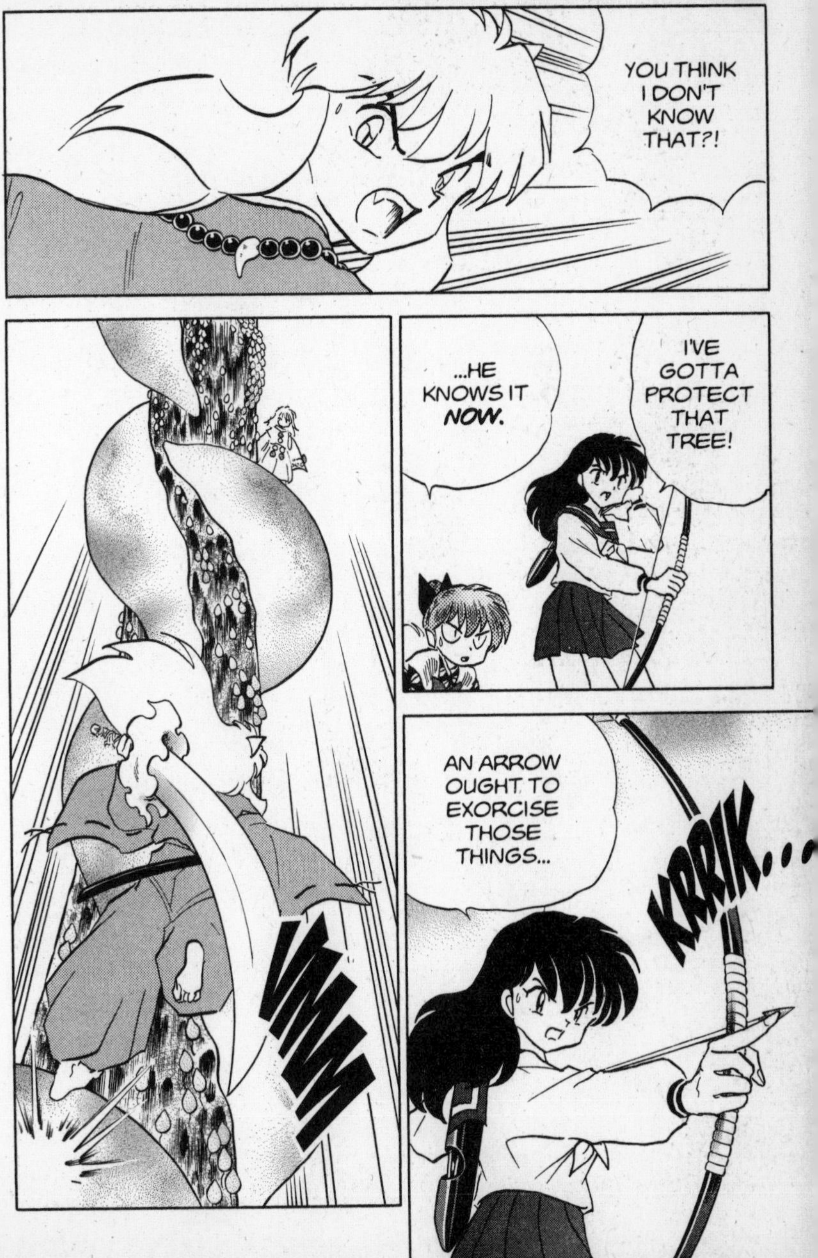
YOU THINK I DON'T KNOW THAT?!
VMM
...HE KNOWS IT *NOW.*
I'VE GOTTA PROTECT THAT TREE!
AN ARROW OUGHT TO EXORCISE THOSE THINGS...
KRRIK...

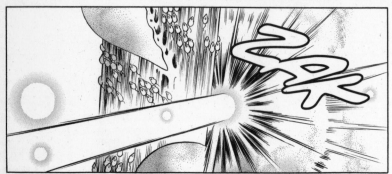

YOU HIT IT! YOU'RE AMAZING, KAGOME!

IT'S NOT EXACTLY A TINY TARGET!

KRRIK...

DM

STAY WHERE YOU ARE!

...

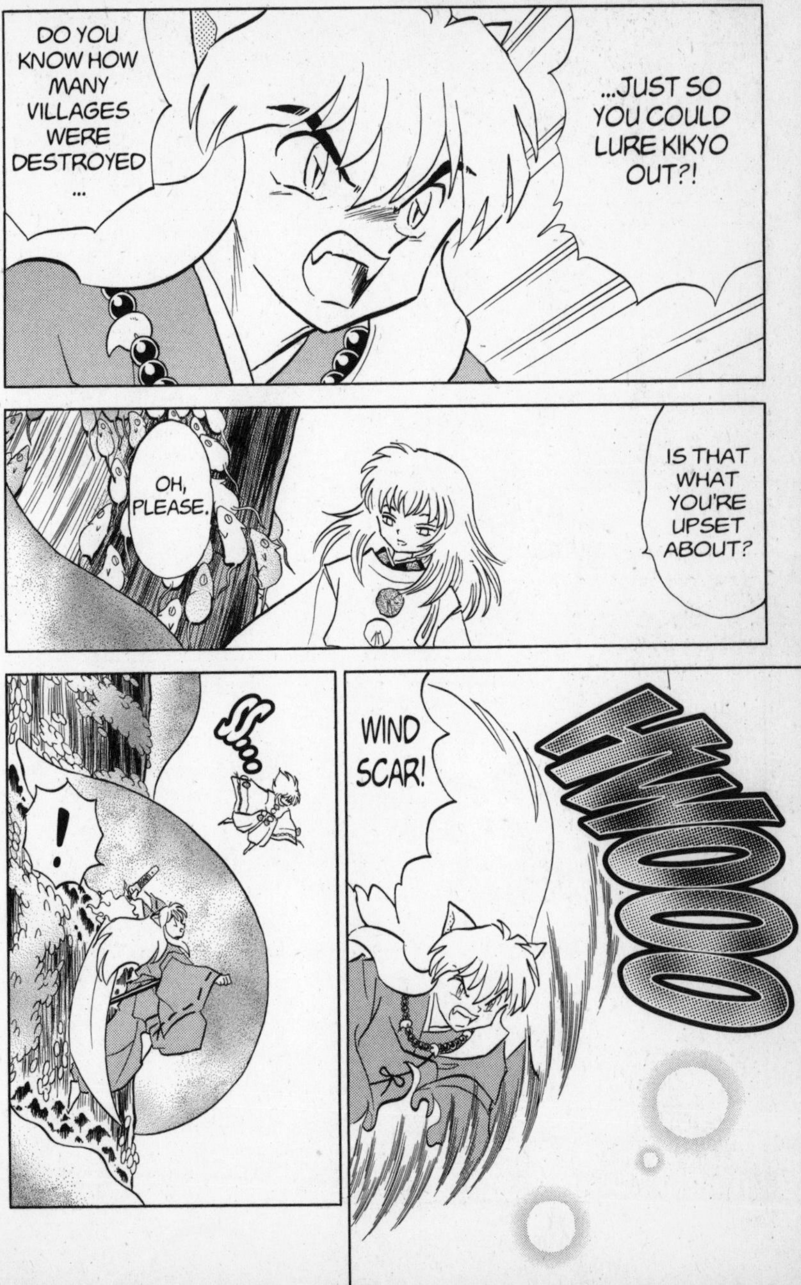
DO YOU KNOW HOW MANY VILLAGES WERE DESTROYED ...
...JUST SO YOU COULD LURE KIKYO OUT?!
OH, PLEASE.
IS THAT WHAT YOU'RE UPSET ABOUT?
Shooo
!
WIND SCAR!
WHOOOO

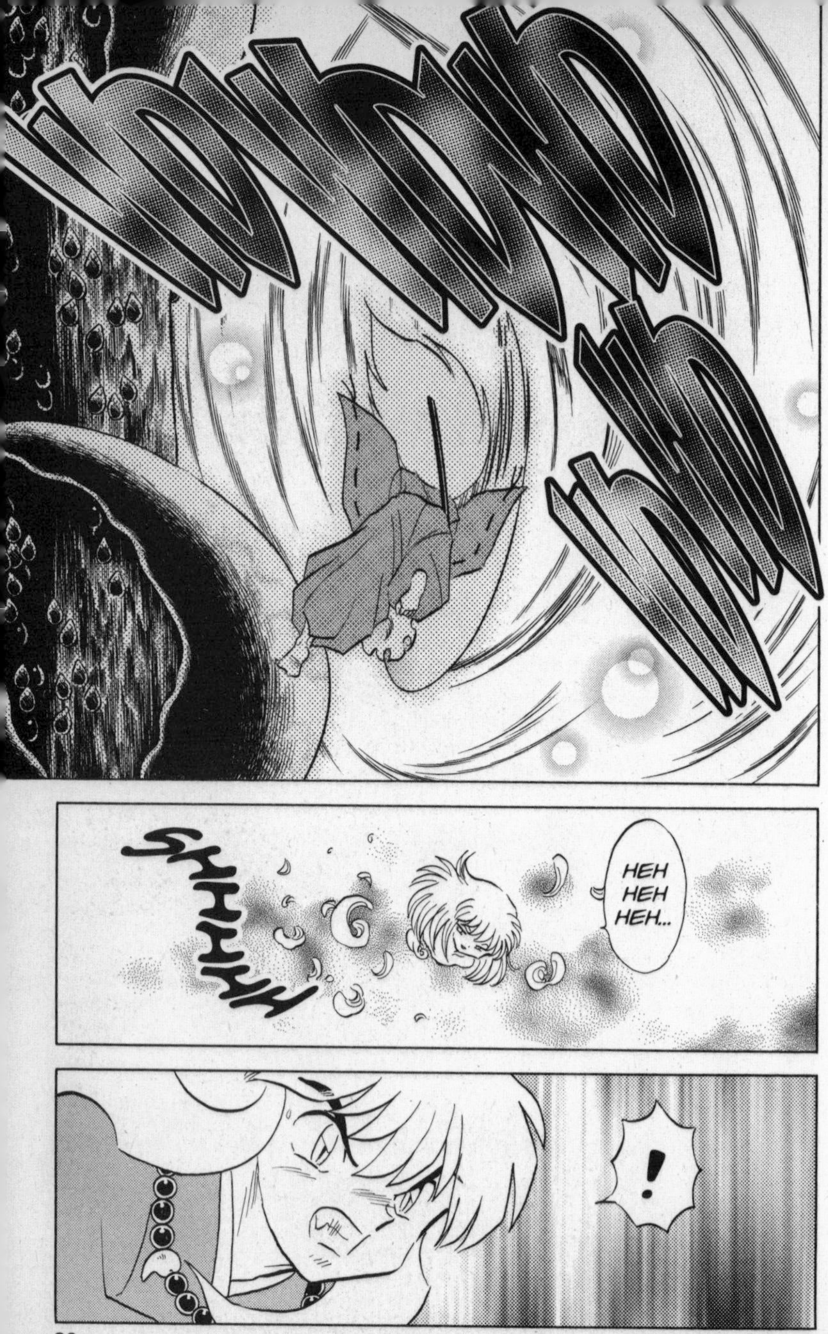
HEH HEH HEH...
!

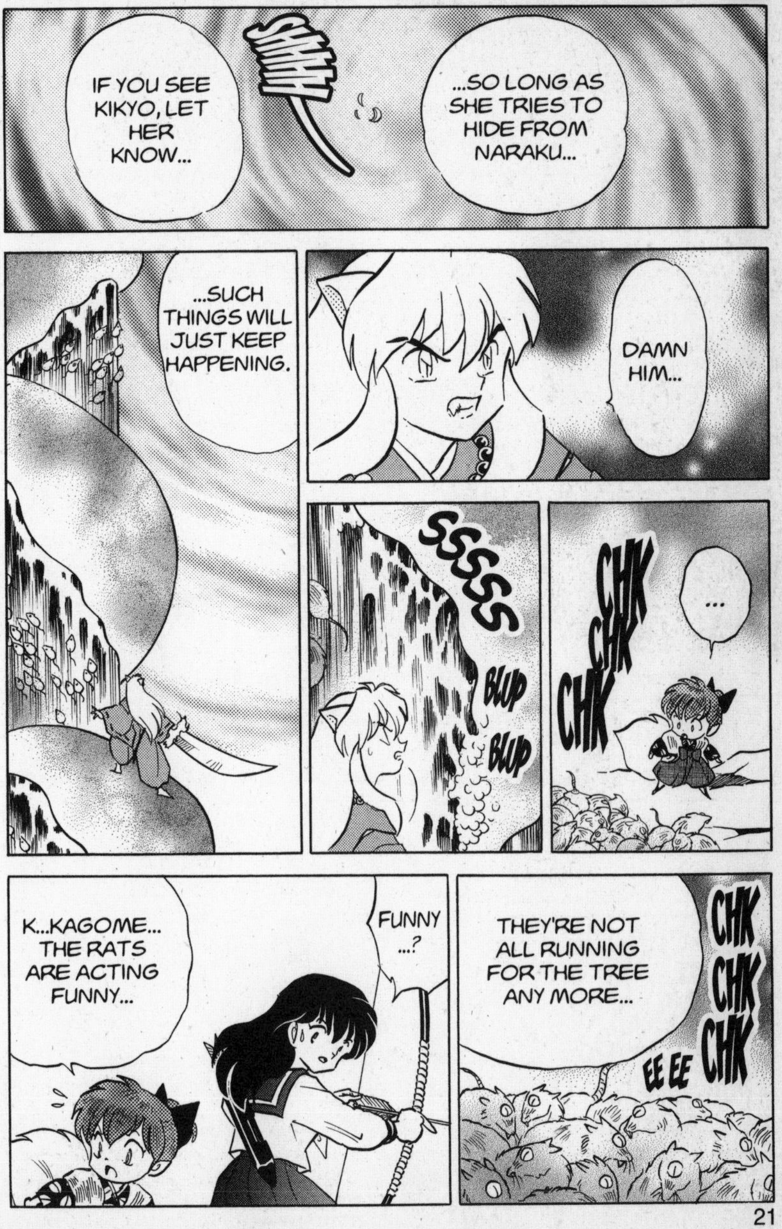
IF YOU SEE KIKYO, LET HER KNOW...
...SO LONG AS SHE TRIES TO HIDE FROM NARAKU...
...SUCH THINGS WILL JUST KEEP HAPPENING.
DAMN HIM...
SSSSS
BLUP
BLUP
CHK
CHK
CHK
...
K...KAGOME... THE RATS ARE ACTING FUNNY...
FUNNY ...?
THEY'RE NOT ALL RUNNING FOR THE TREE ANY MORE...
EE EE
CHK
CHK
CHK

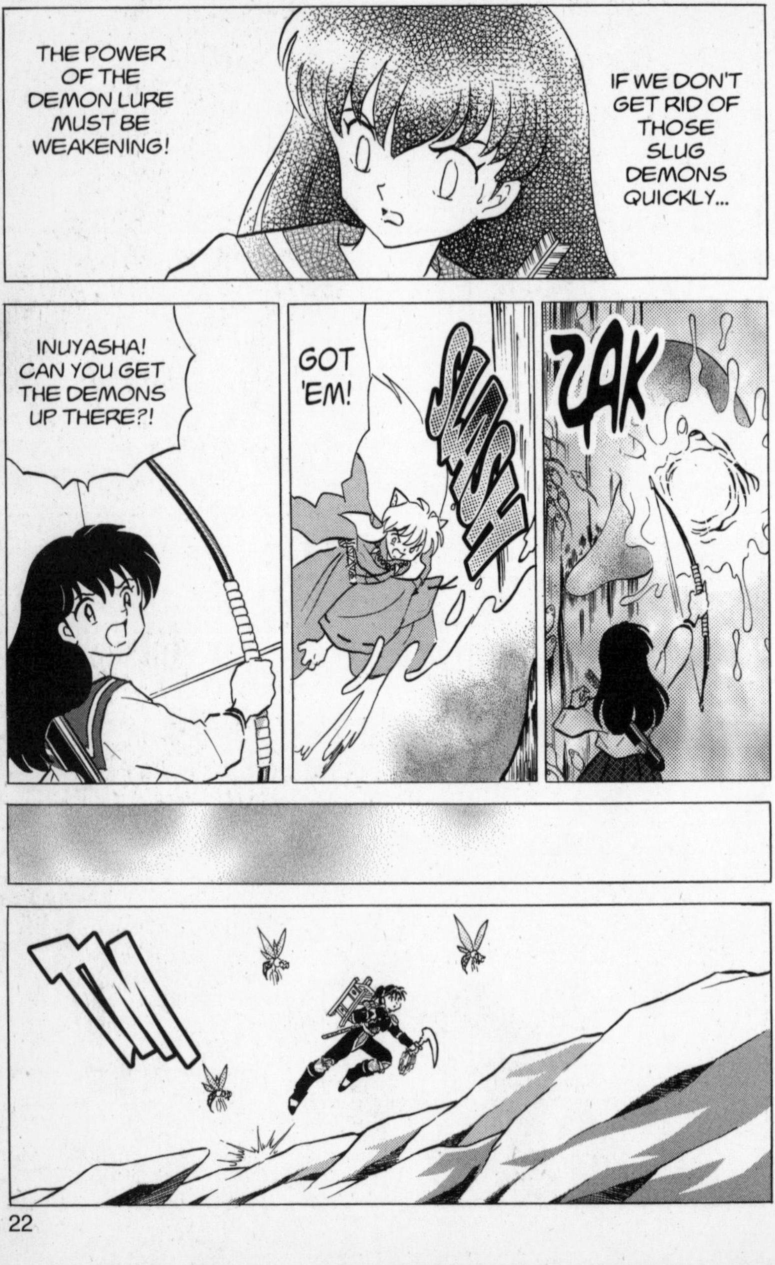
THE POWER OF THE DEMON LURE MUST BE WEAKENING!
IF WE DON'T GET RID OF THOSE SLUG DEMONS QUICKLY...
INUYASHA! CAN YOU GET THE DEMONS UP THERE?!
GOT 'EM!
SWOSH
ZAK
TM

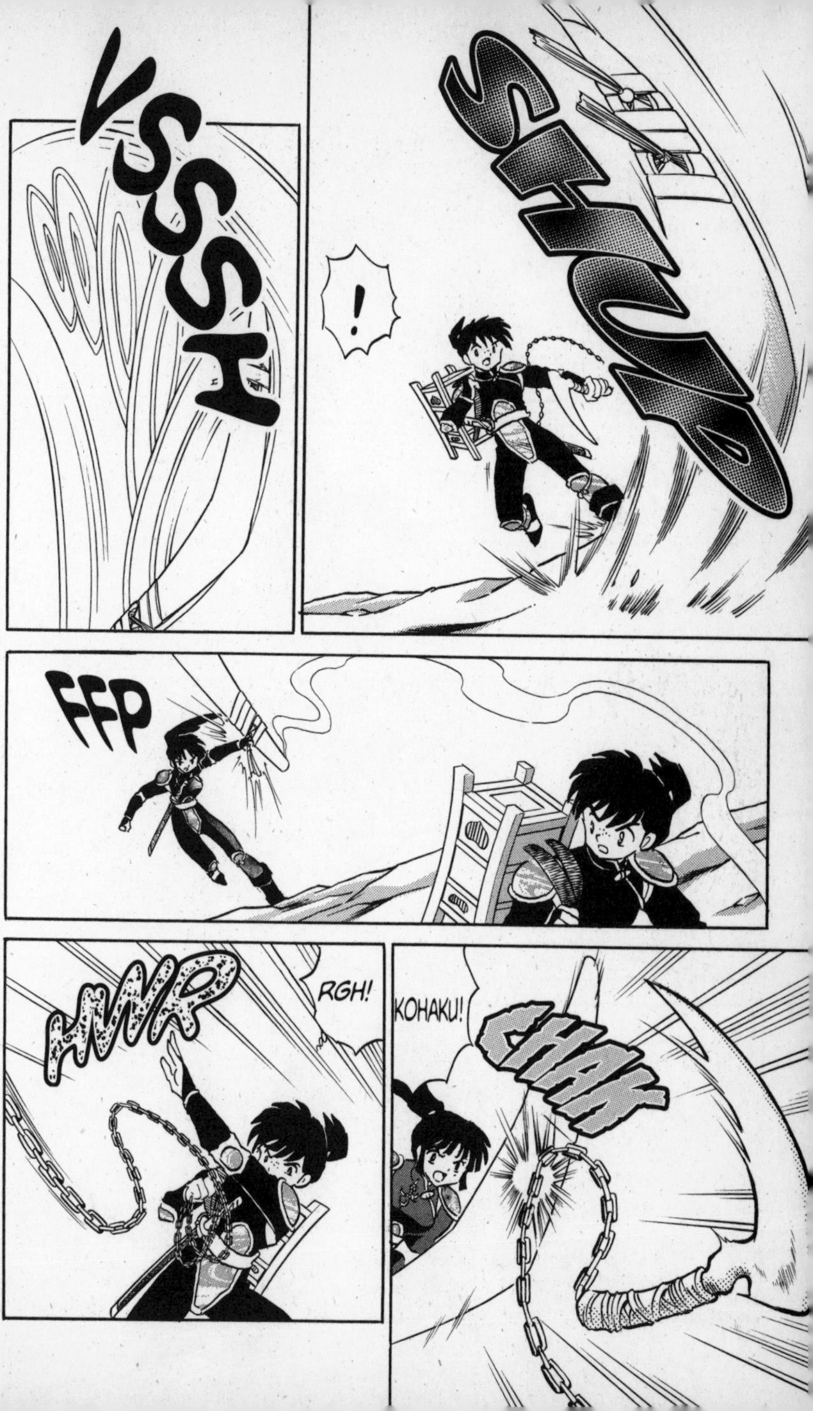
VSSSH
!
SHUNP
FFP
HWIP
RGH!
KOHAKU!
CHAK

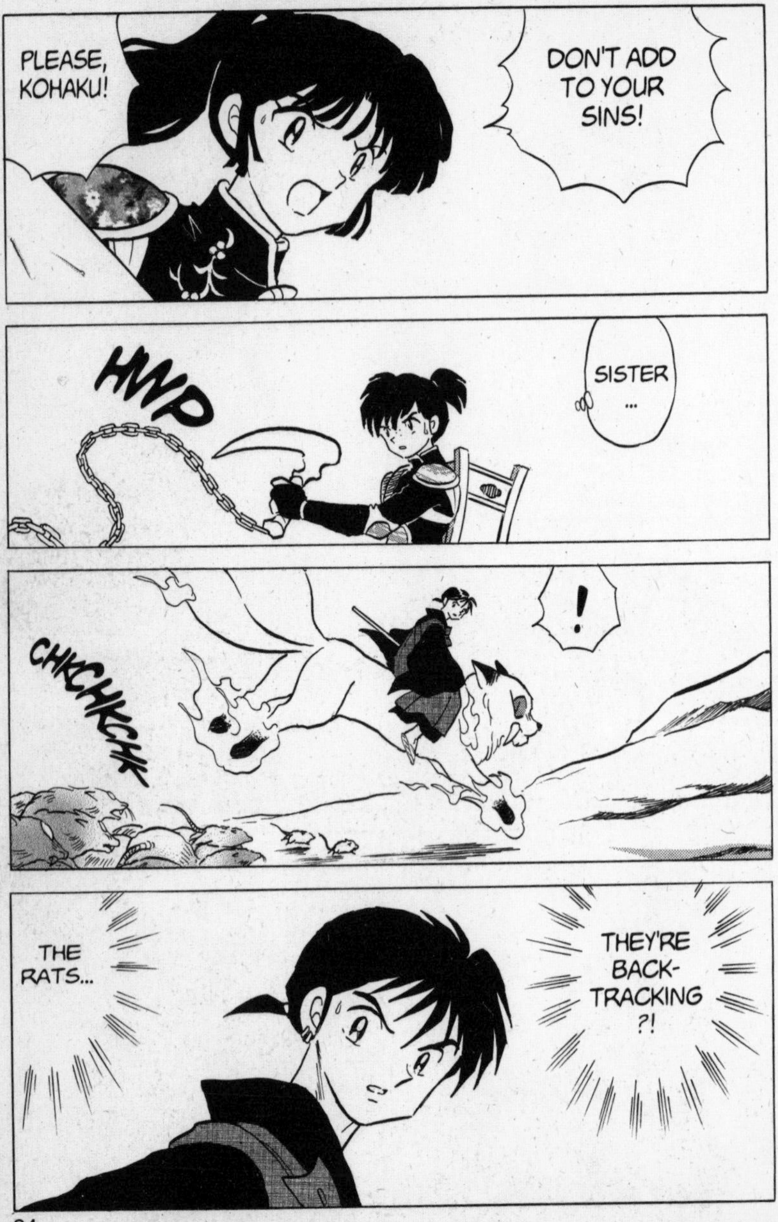

PLEASE, KOHAKU!
DON'T ADD TO YOUR SINS!
HNP
SISTER ...
CHKCHKCHK
!
THE RATS...
THEY'RE BACK-TRACKING ?!

SCROLL 2

RAMPAGE!

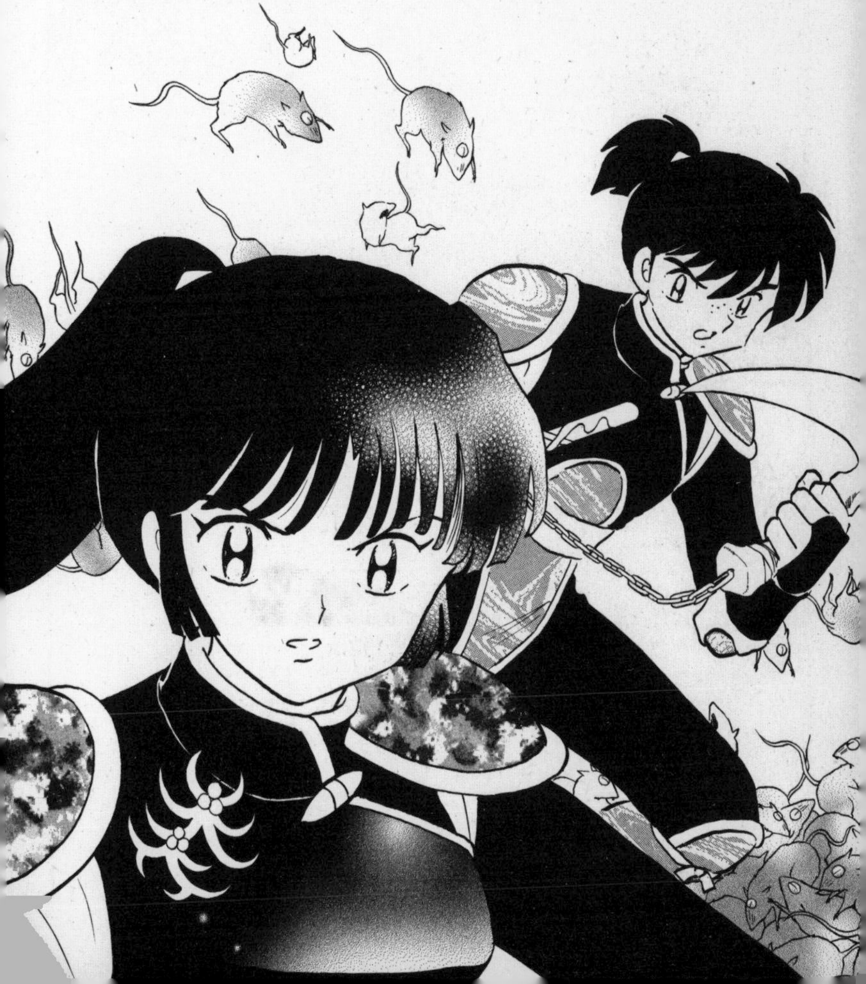

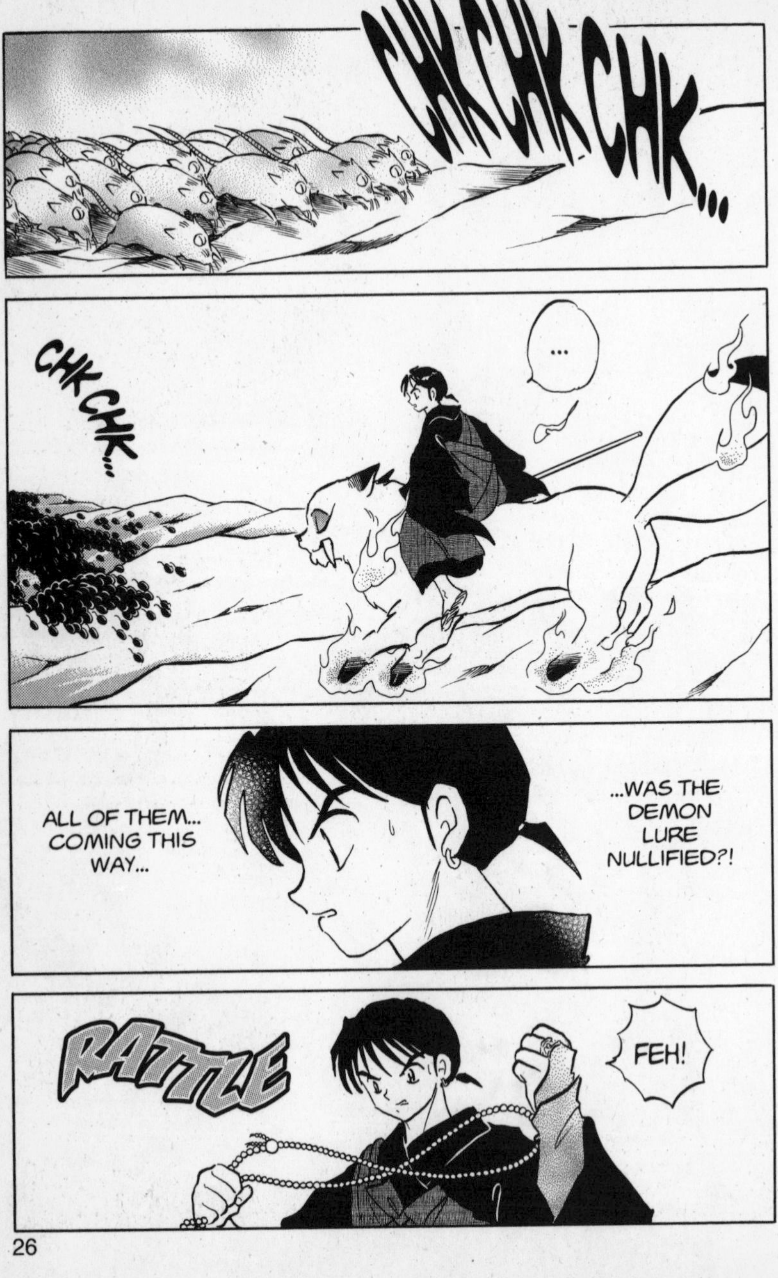
CHK CHK CHK CHK...
CHK CHK...
...
ALL OF THEM... COMING THIS WAY...
...WAS THE DEMON LURE NULLIFIED?!
RATTLE
FEH!

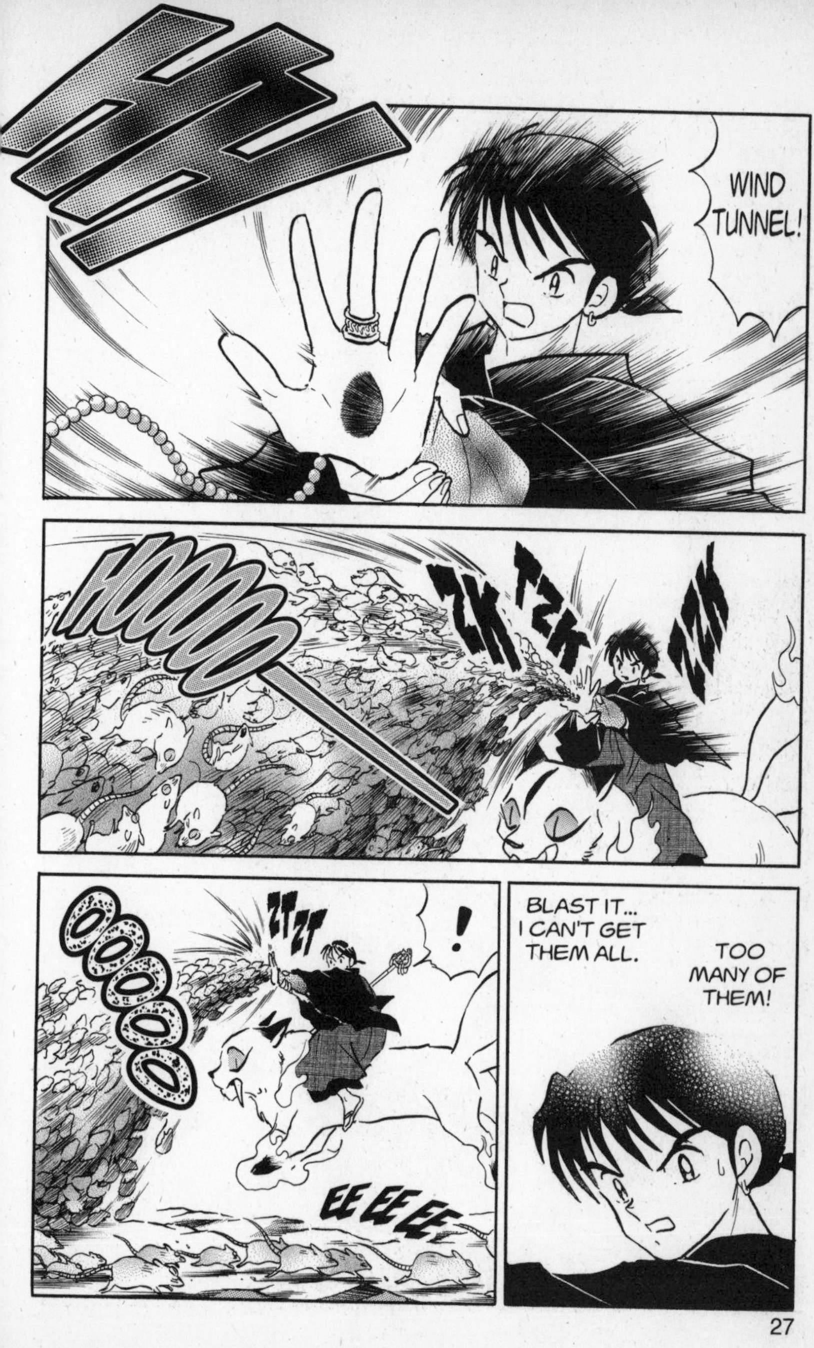

WIND TUNNEL!
HOOOO
ZK
TZK
ZT ZT
!
OOOOOO
EE EE EE
BLAST IT... I CAN'T GET THEM ALL.
TOO MANY OF THEM!

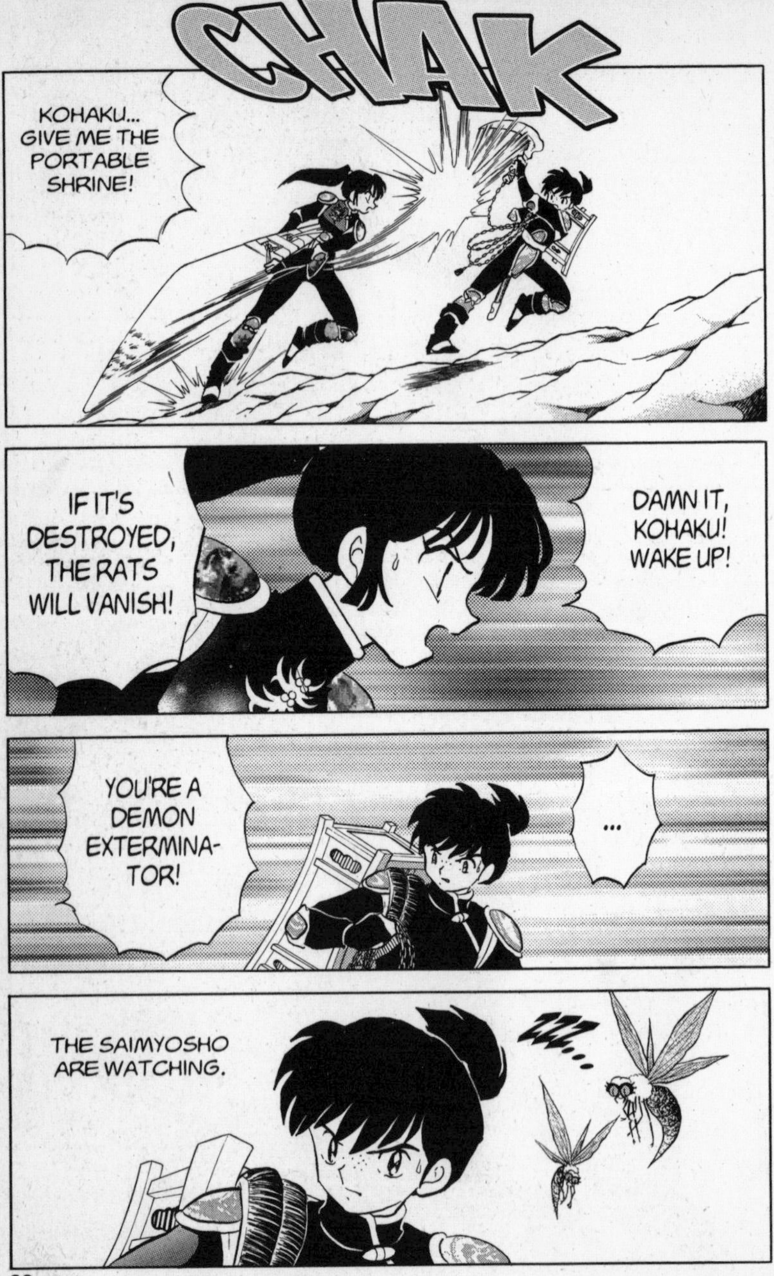
CHAK
KOHAKU... GIVE ME THE PORTABLE SHRINE!
IF IT'S DESTROYED, THE RATS WILL VANISH!
DAMN IT, KOHAKU! WAKE UP!
YOU'RE A DEMON EXTERMINA-TOR!
...
THE SAIMYOSHO ARE WATCHING.
ZZZ...

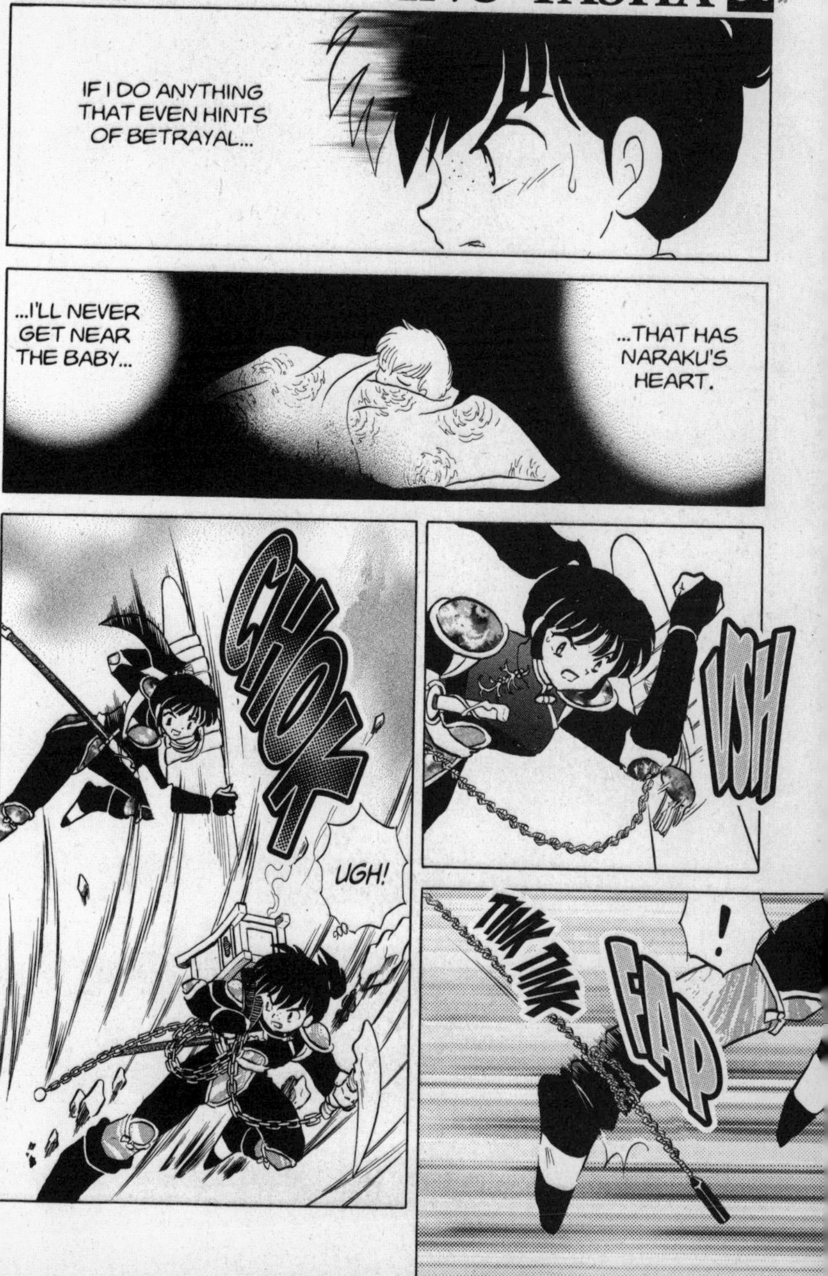
IF I DO ANYTHING THAT EVEN HINTS OF BETRAYAL...
...I'LL NEVER GET NEAR THE BABY...
...THAT HAS NARAKU'S HEART.
CHOK
UGH!
VSH
TINK TINK
FAP
!

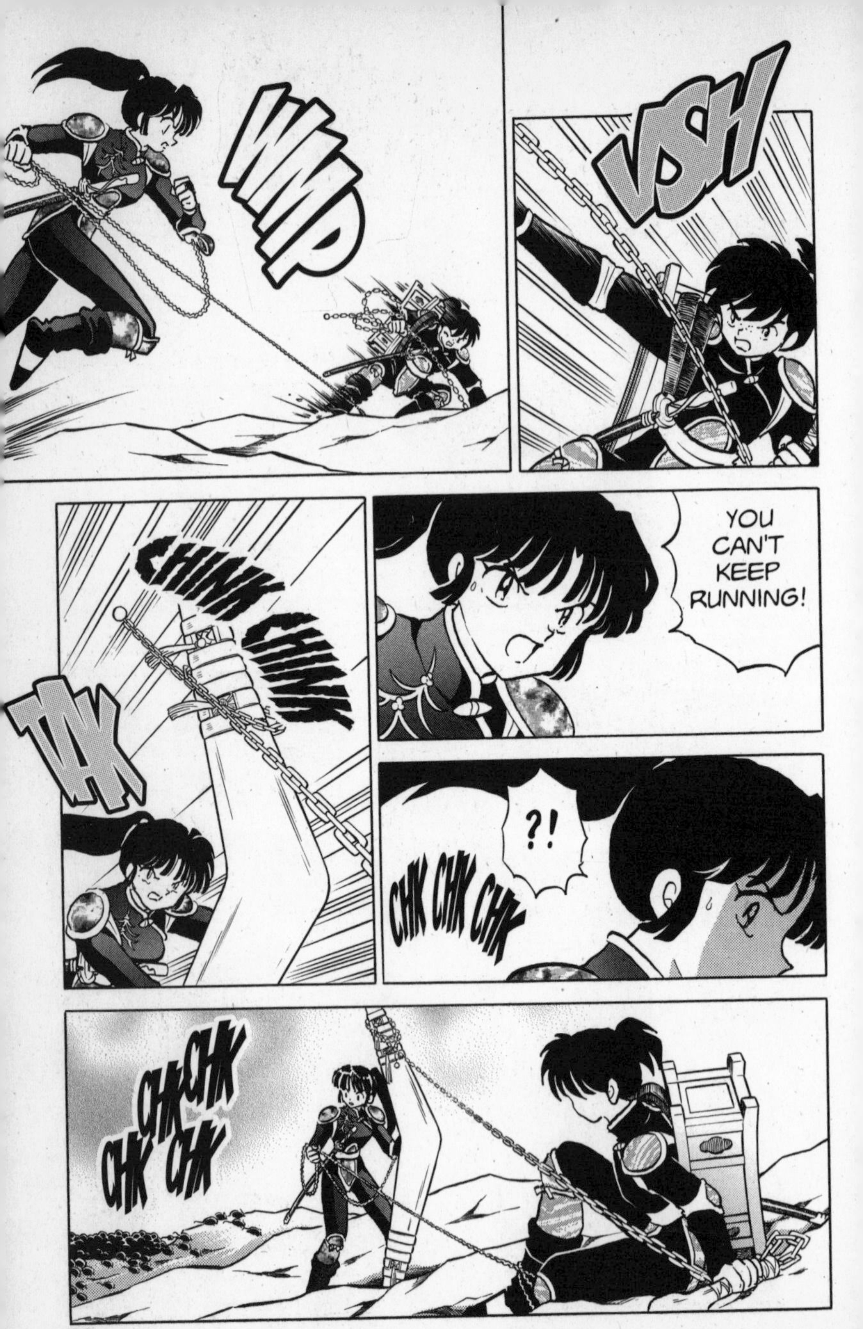
WMP
VSH
CHINK CHINK
TCHK
YOU CAN'T KEEP RUNNING!
?!
CHK CHK CHK
CHK CHK
CHK CHK

EE EE EE

CHK CHK CHK

THE RATS?!

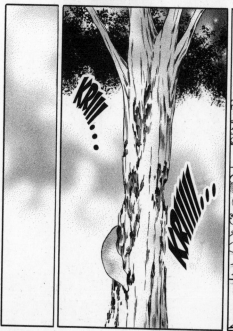

KRII!...

KRIIII!...

CHK CHK CHK

EE EE

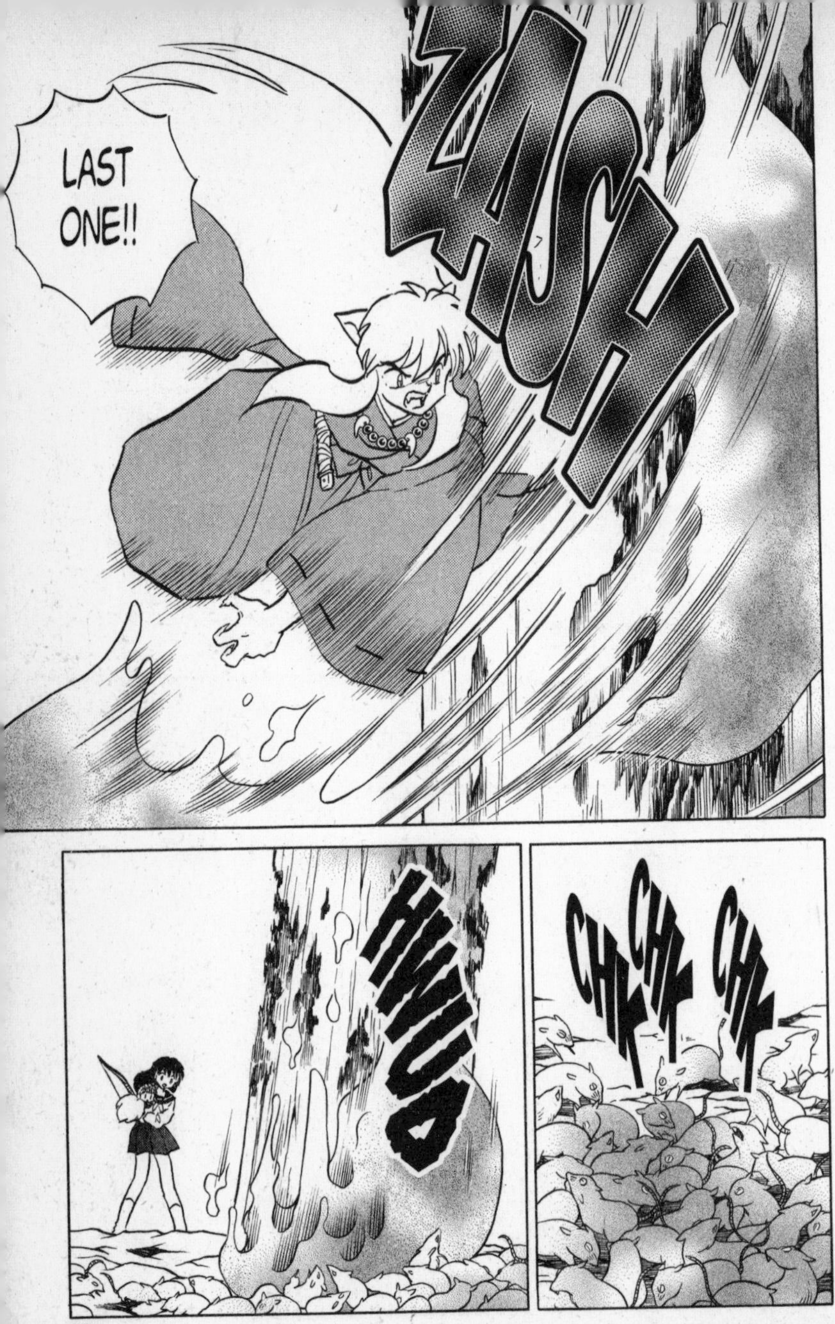
LAST ONE!!
ZASH
HWUD
CHK
CHK
CHK

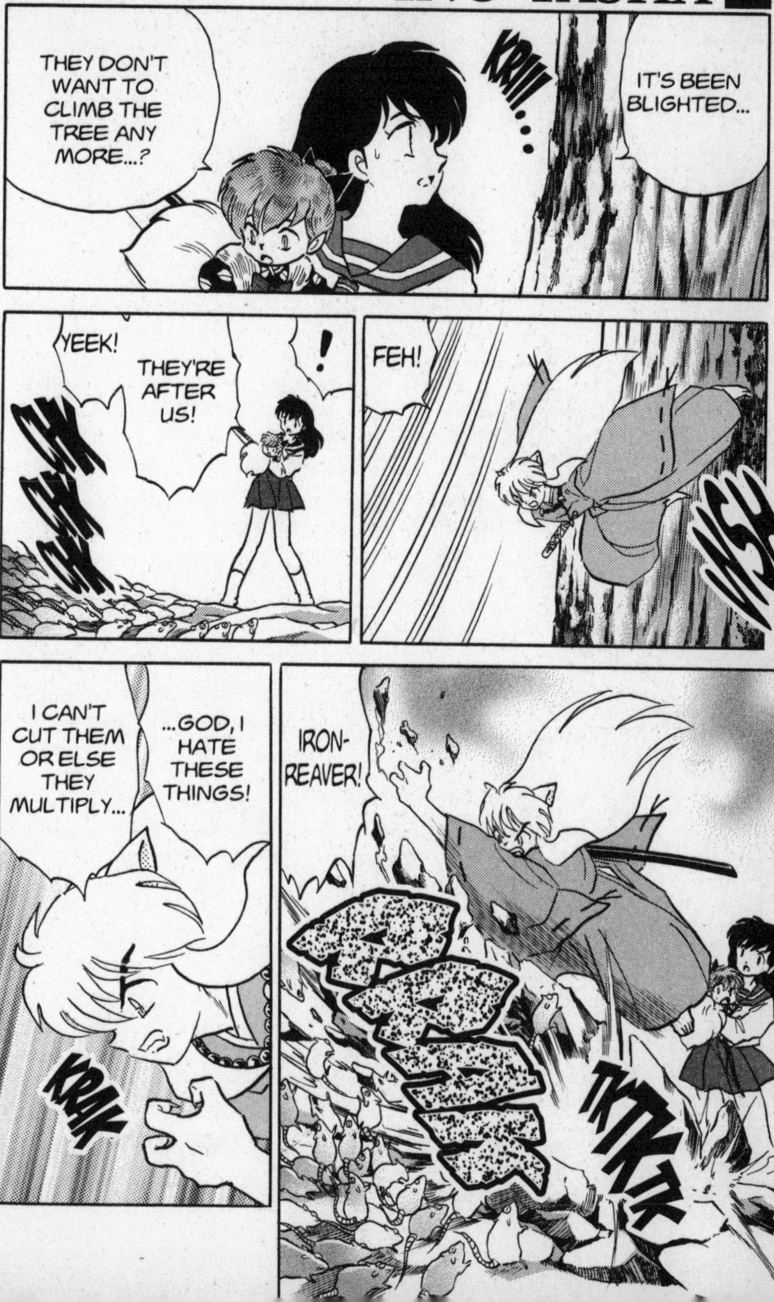
THEY DON'T WANT TO CLIMB THE TREE ANY MORE...?
KRIII...
IT'S BEEN BLIGHTED...
YEEK!
THEY'RE AFTER US!
!
FEH!
I CAN'T CUT THEM OR ELSE THEY MULTIPLY...
...GOD, I HATE THESE THINGS!
KRAK
IRON-REAVER!

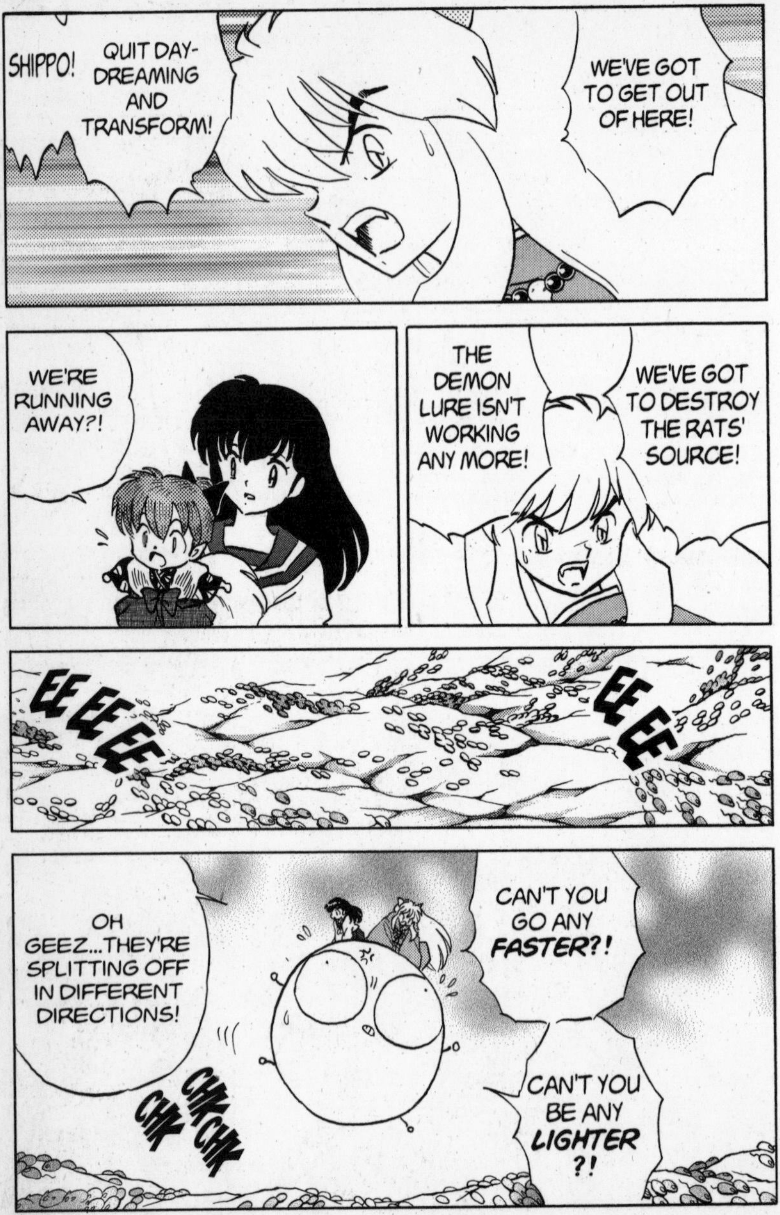
SHIPPO!
QUIT DAY-DREAMING AND TRANSFORM!
WE'VE GOT TO GET OUT OF HERE!
WE'RE RUNNING AWAY?!
THE DEMON LURE ISN'T WORKING ANY MORE!
WE'VE GOT TO DESTROY THE RATS' SOURCE!
EE EE EE
EE EE
OH GEEZ...THEY'RE SPLITTING OFF IN DIFFERENT DIRECTIONS!
CHK CHK CHK
CAN'T YOU GO ANY *FASTER*?!
CAN'T YOU BE ANY *LIGHTER*?!

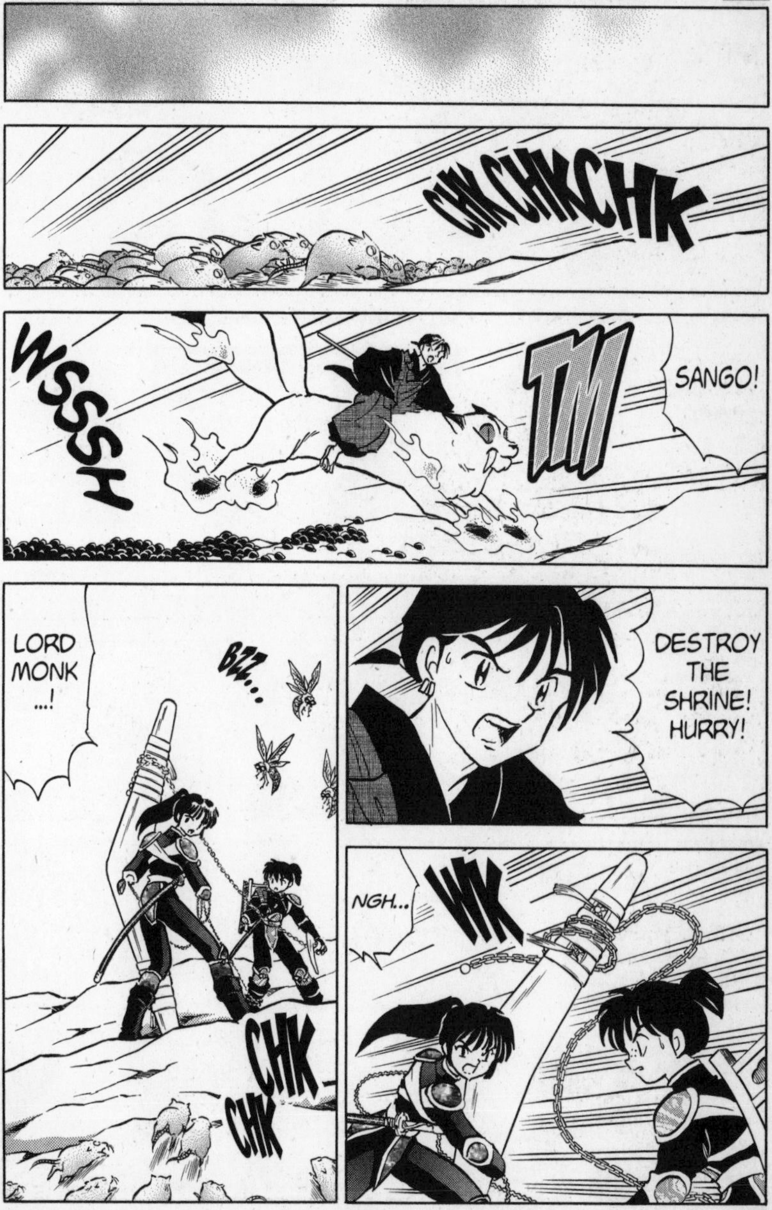
CHK CHKCHK
WSSSH
TM
SANGO!
LORD MONK ...!
BZZ...
CHK CHK
DESTROY THE SHRINE! HURRY!
NGH...
WK

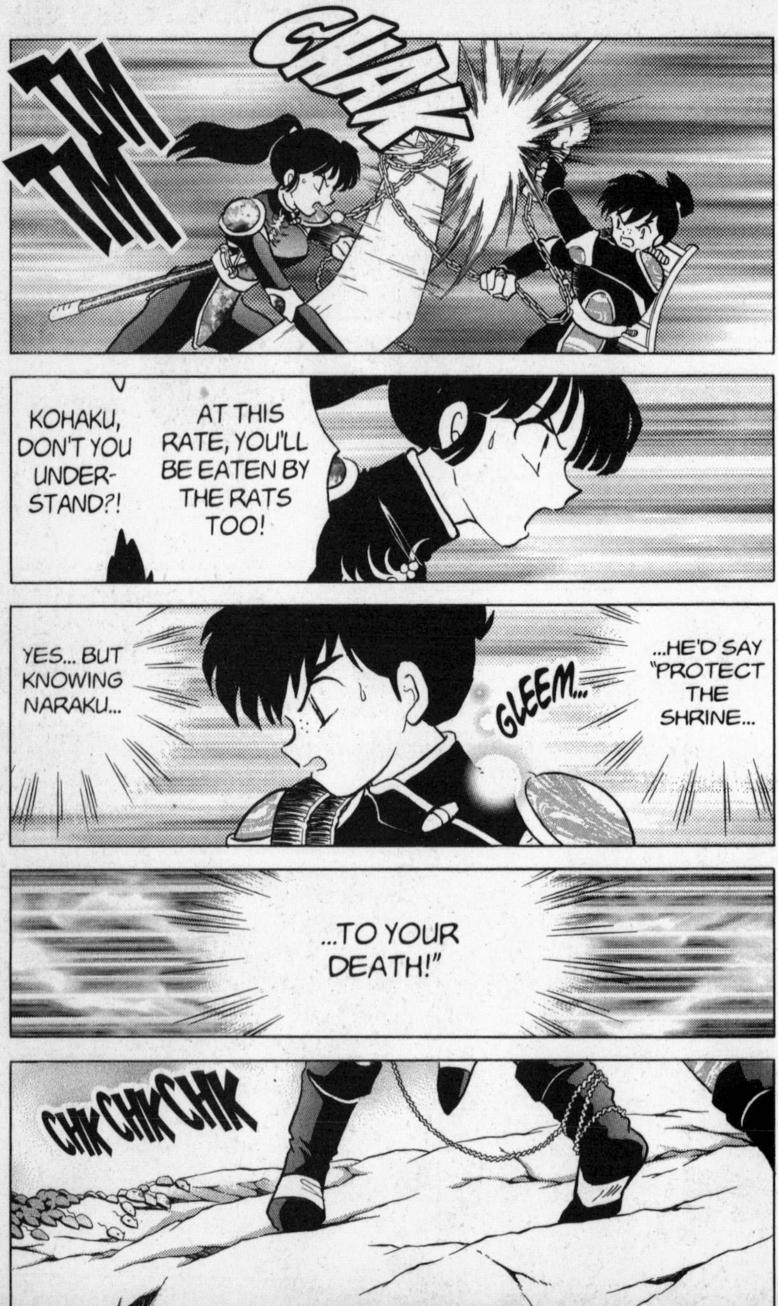
TWM TWM
CHAK
KOHAKU, DON'T YOU UNDER-STAND?!
AT THIS RATE, YOU'LL BE EATEN BY THE RATS TOO!
YES... BUT KNOWING NARAKU...
GLEEM...
...HE'D SAY "PROTECT THE SHRINE...
...TO YOUR DEATH!"
CHIK CHIK CHIK

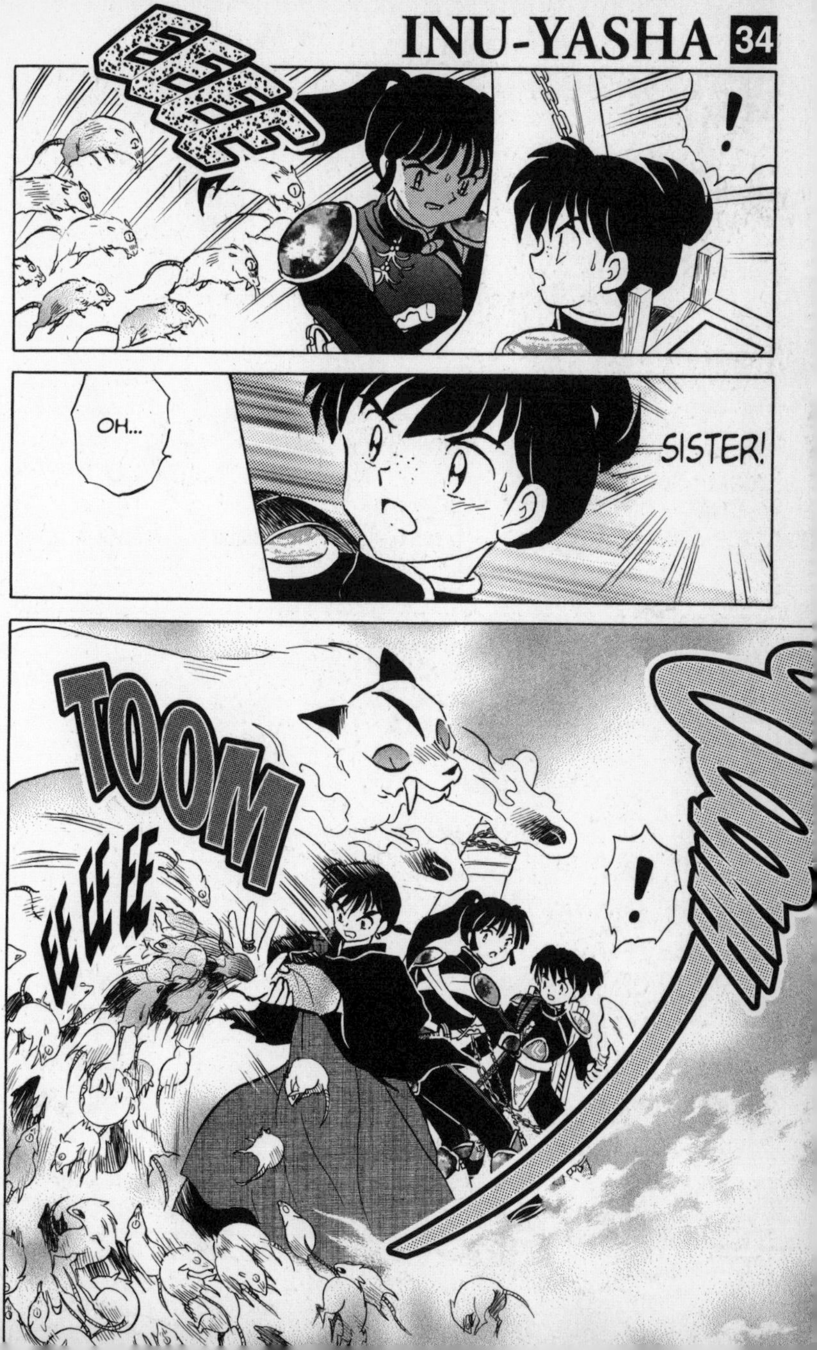
!
OH...
SISTER!
TOOM
EE EE EE
!

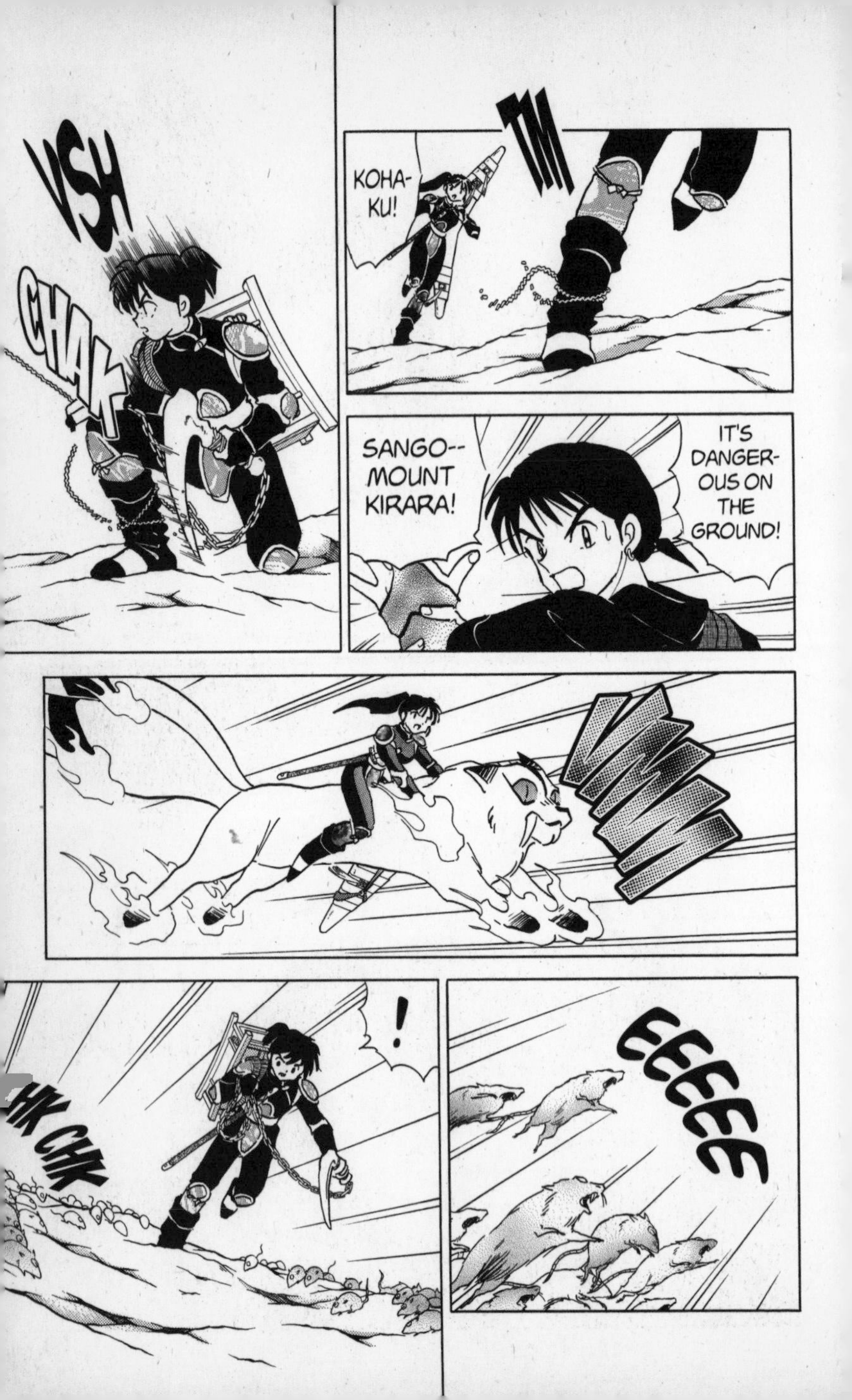
VSH
CHAK
KOHA-
KU!
TM
SANGO--
MOUNT
KIRARA!
IT'S
DANGER-
OUS ON
THE
GROUND!
!
HK CHK
EEEEE

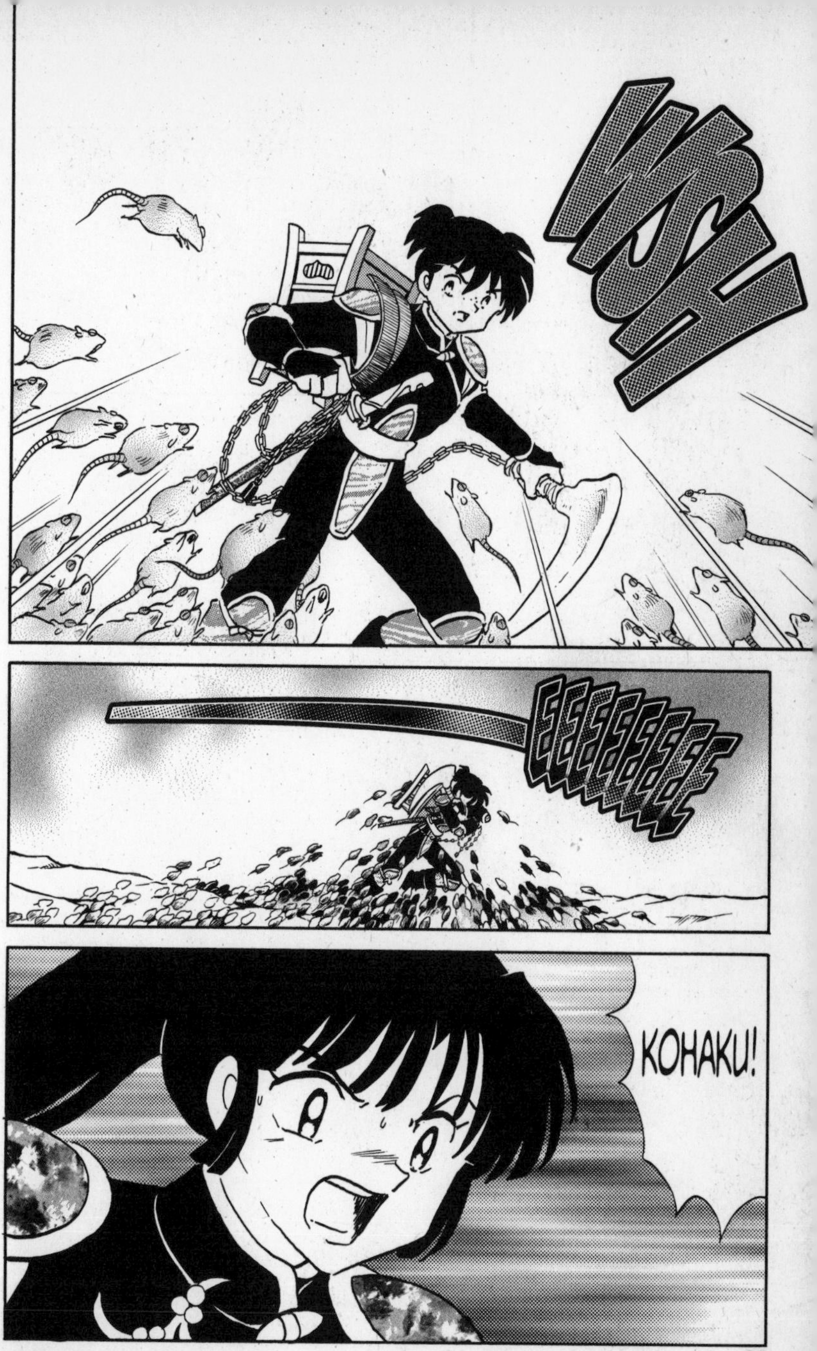
WSSH!
EEEEEEEEEE
KOHAKU!

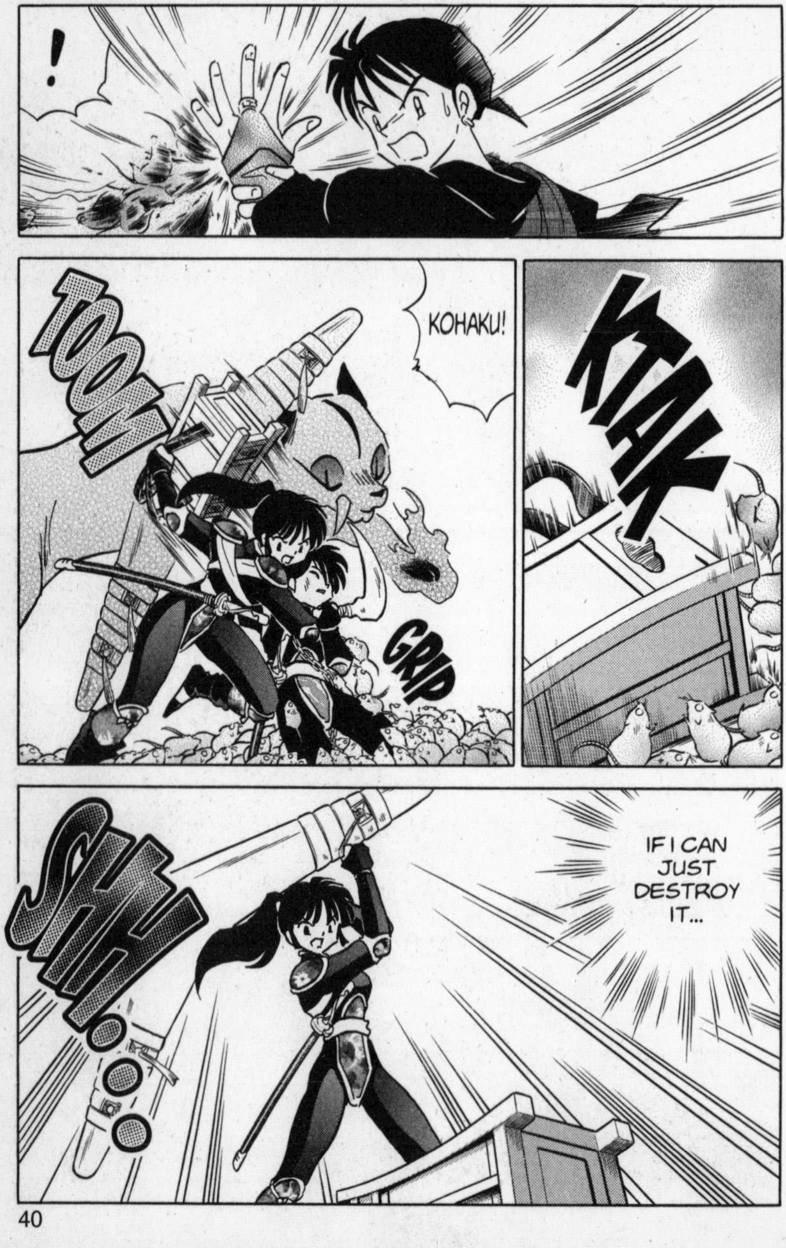
!
TOOM
KOHAKU!
GRIP
KTAK
SHH...
IF I CAN JUST DESTROY IT...

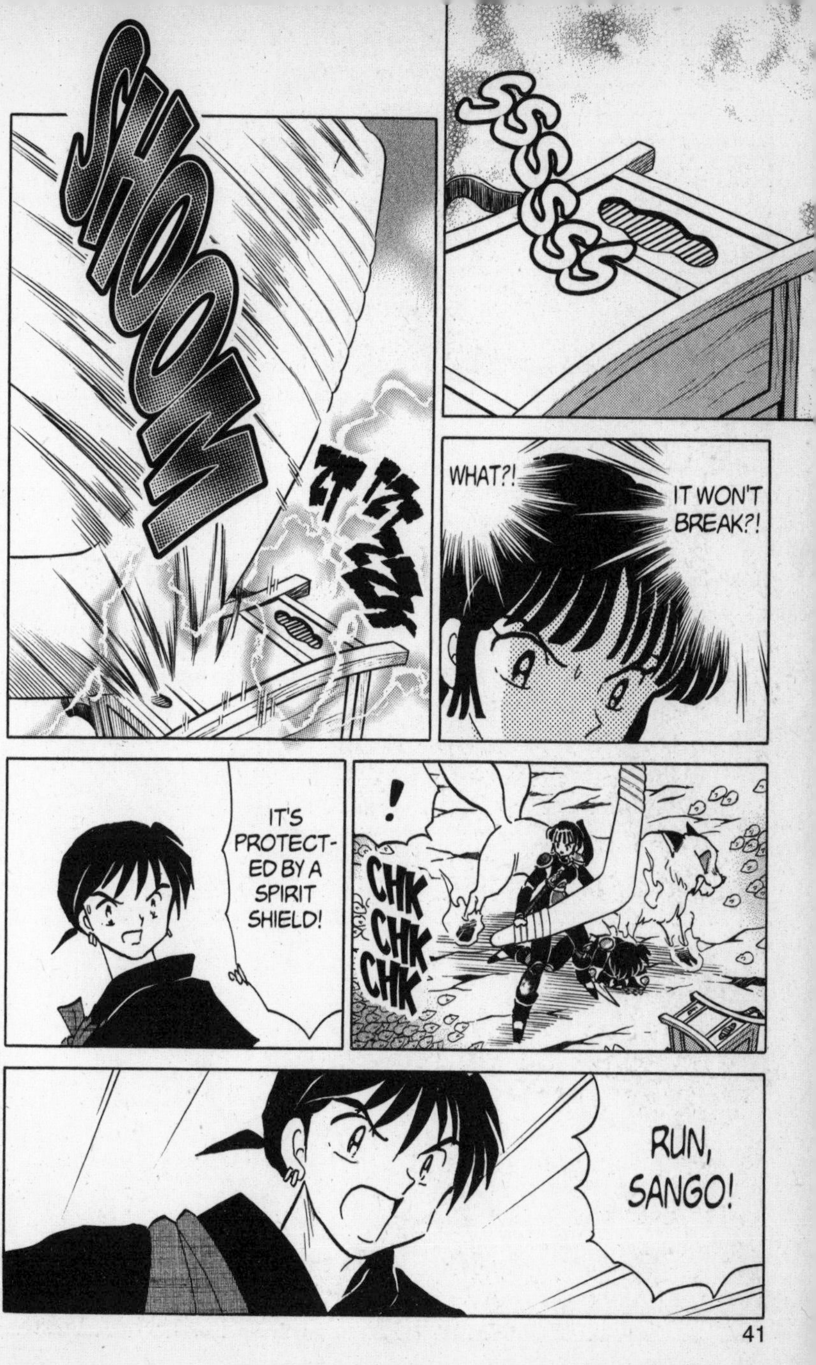
SHOOM
SSSSS
WHAT?!
IT WON'T BREAK?!
IT'S PROTECTED BY A SPIRIT SHIELD!
!
CHK CHK CHK
RUN, SANGO!

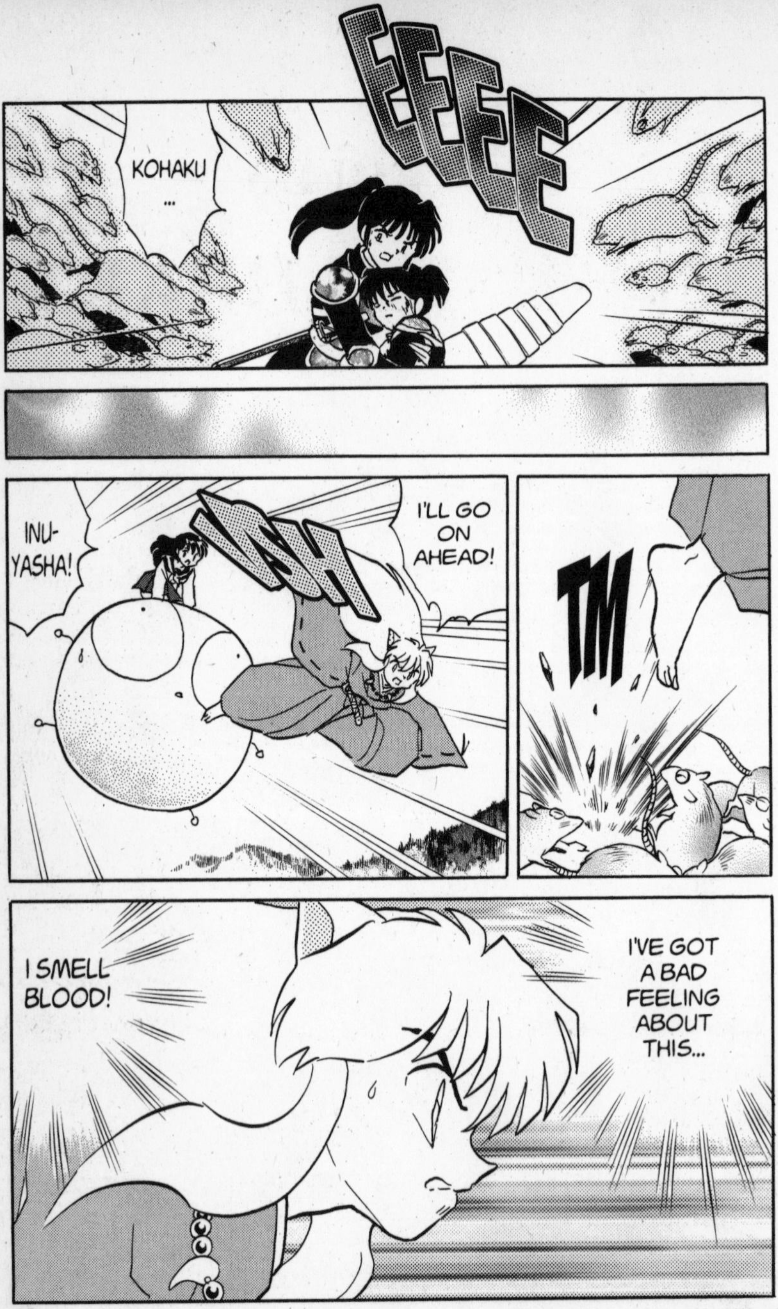
EEEEE
KOHAKU ...
INU-YASHA!
VSSH
I'LL GO ON AHEAD!
TM
I SMELL BLOOD!
I'VE GOT A BAD FEELING ABOUT THIS...

SCROLL 3

A HUMAN HEART

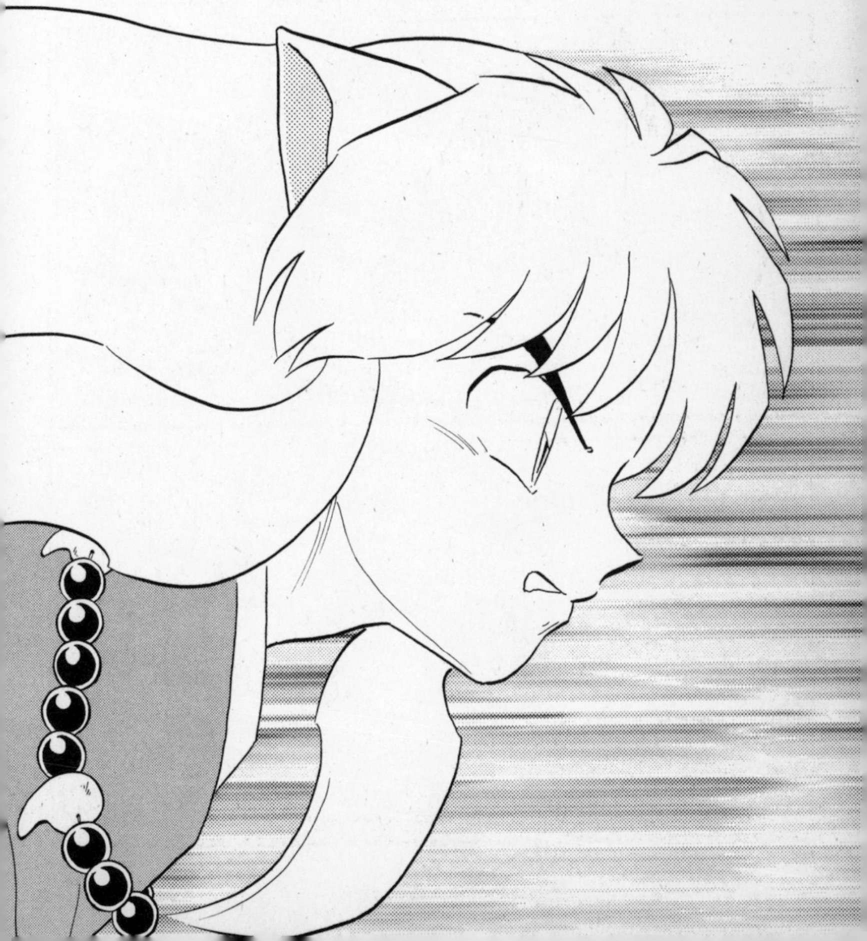

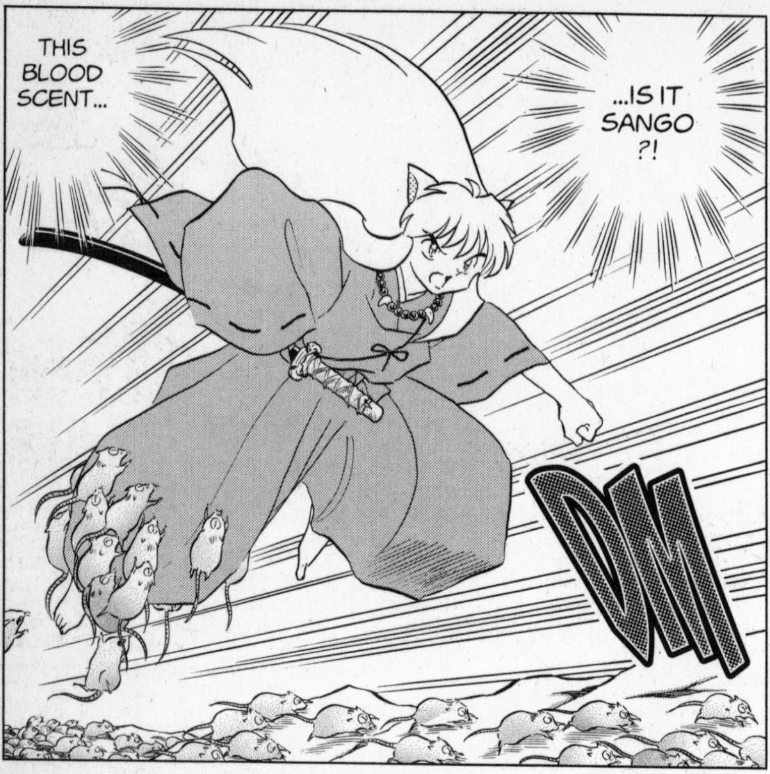
THIS BLOOD SCENT...
...IS IT SANGO ?!
DM
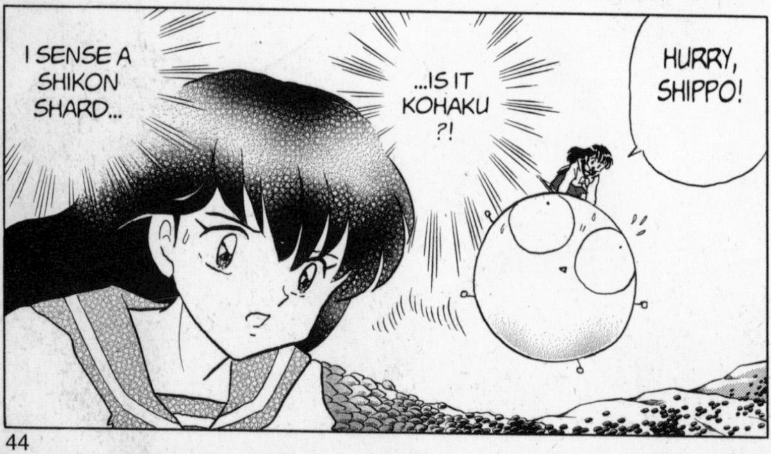
I SENSE A SHIKON SHARD...
...IS IT KOHAKU ?!
HURRY, SHIPPO!

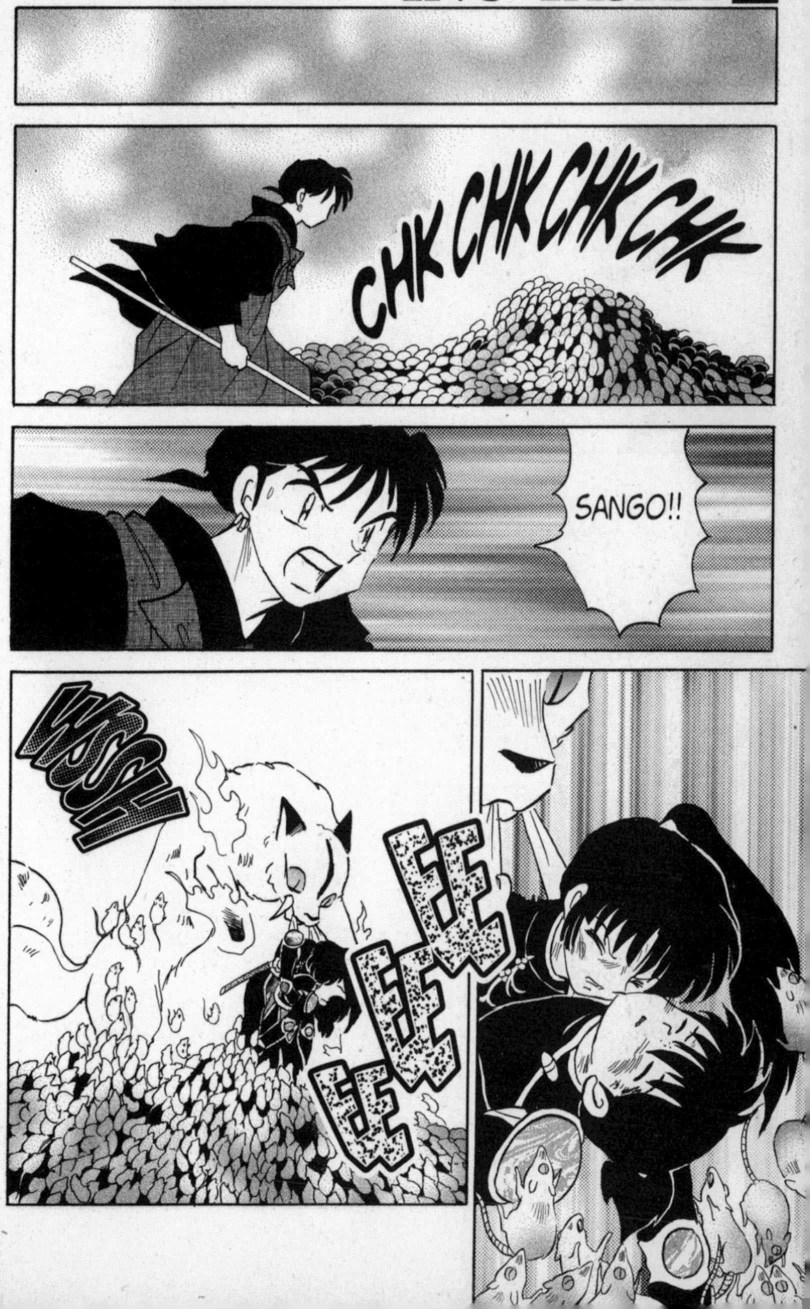
CHK CHK CHK CHK
SANGO!!
WSSH
EEW EEW EEW

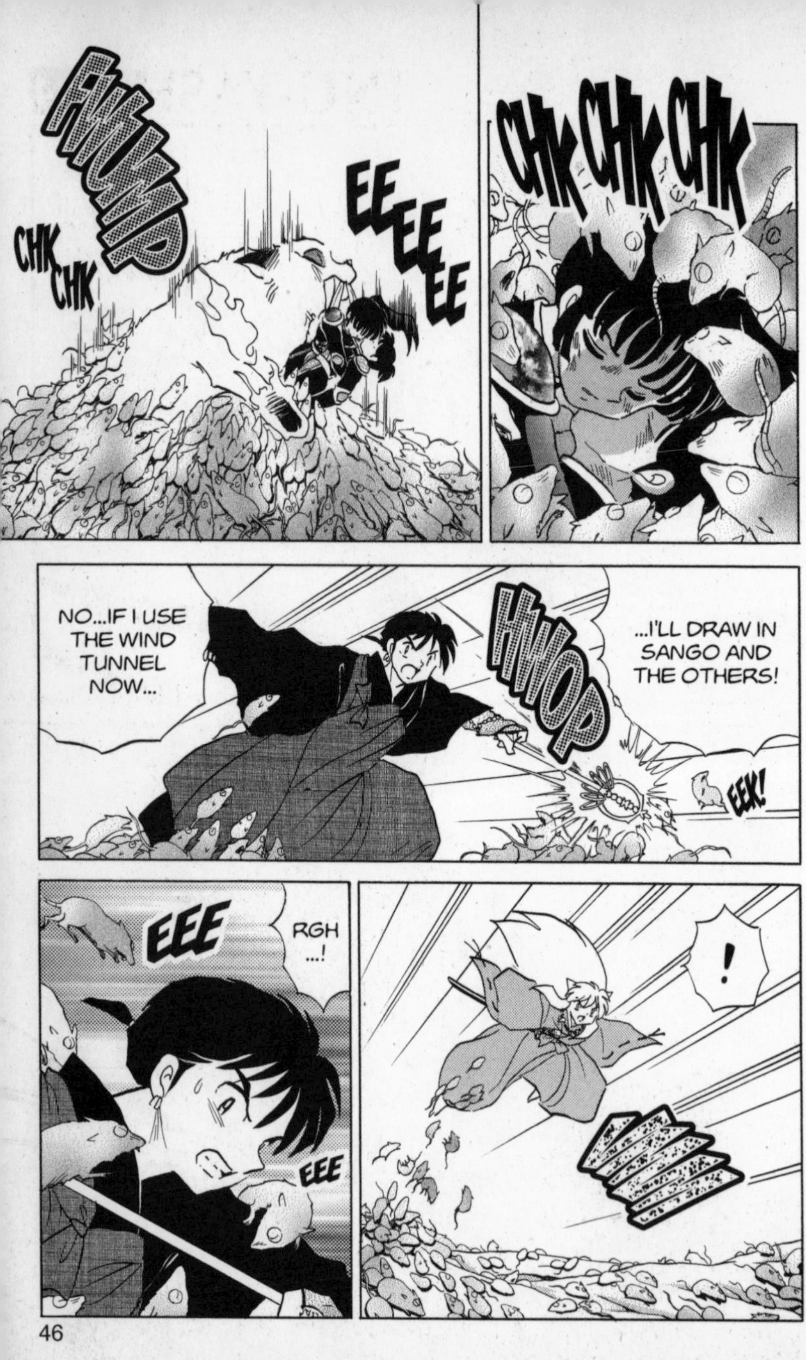
FWUMP
CHK CHK
EE EE EE
CHK CHK CHK
NO...IF I USE THE WIND TUNNEL NOW...
HWOP
...I'LL DRAW IN SANGO AND THE OTHERS!
EEK!
EEE
RGH ...!
EEE
!

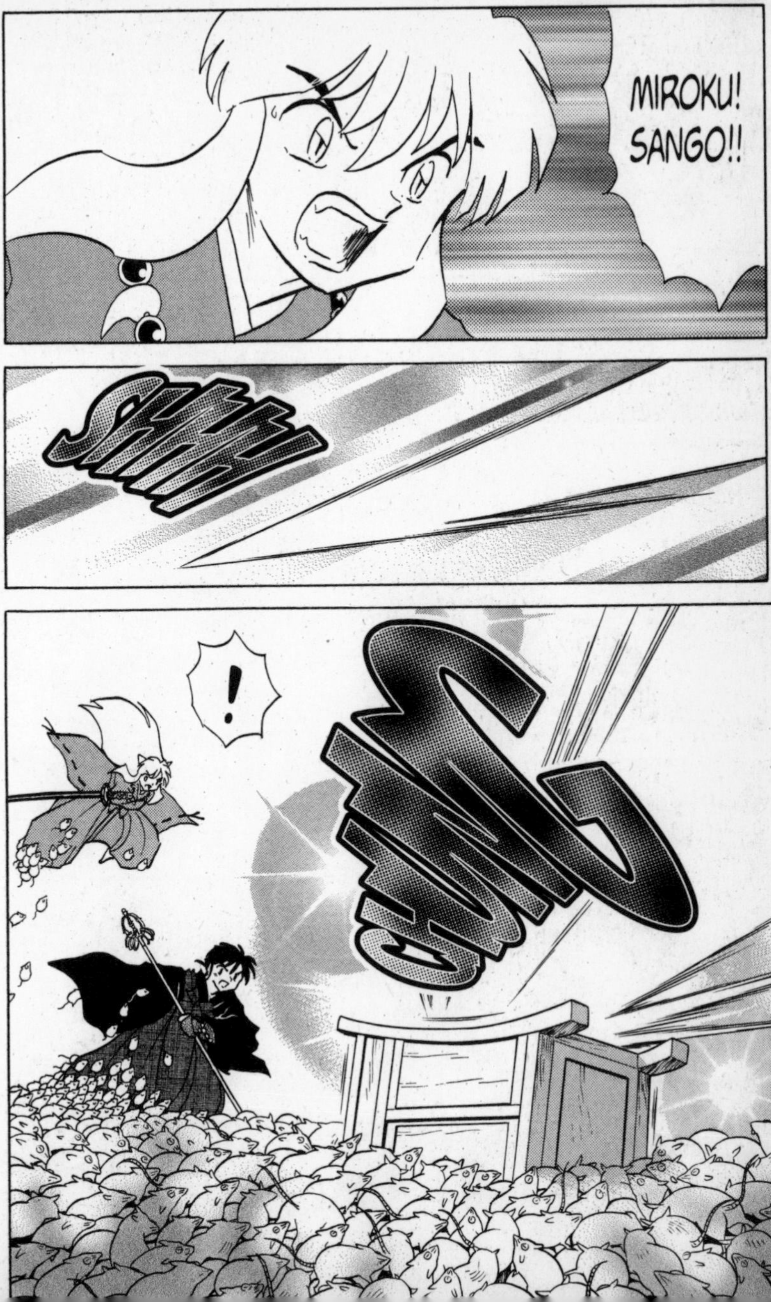
MIROKU!
SANGO!!
!

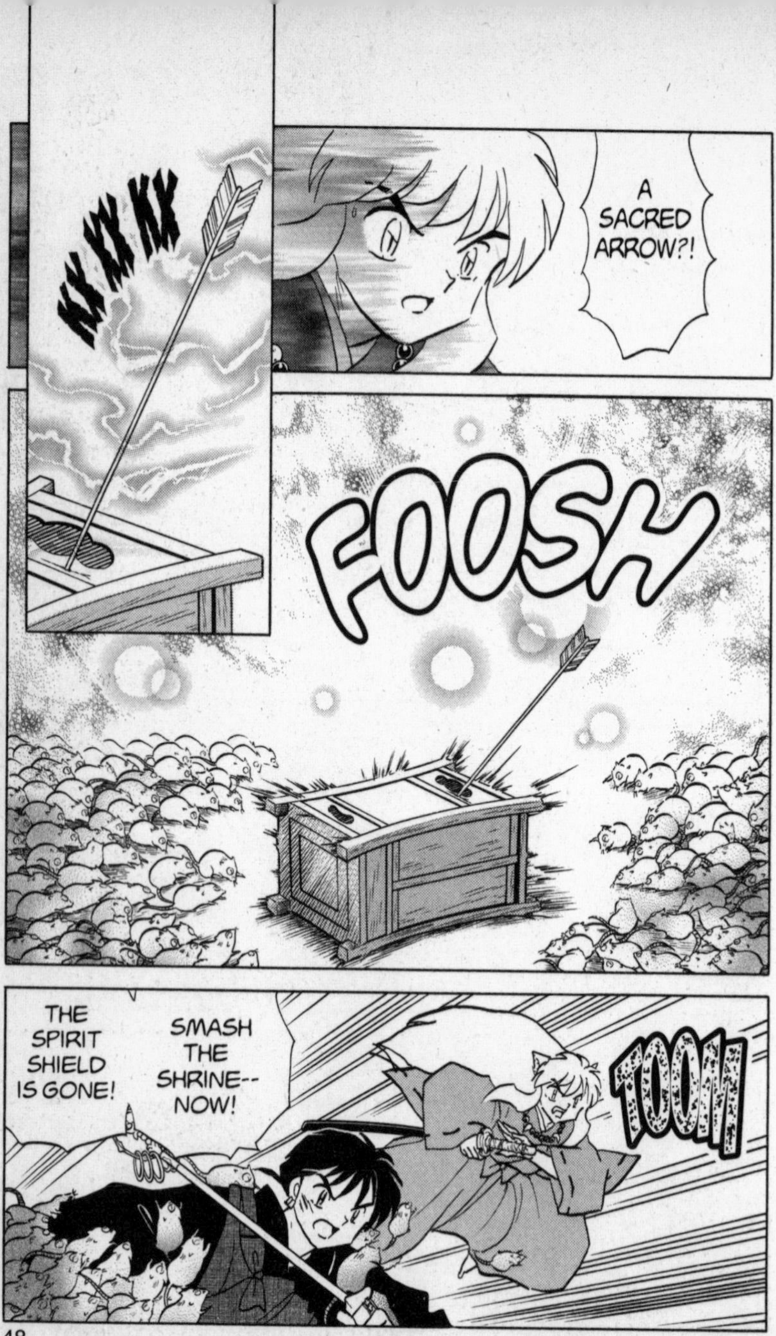
KX KX KX
A SACRED ARROW?!
FOOSH
THE SPIRIT SHIELD IS GONE!
SMASH THE SHRINE-- NOW!
TOOM

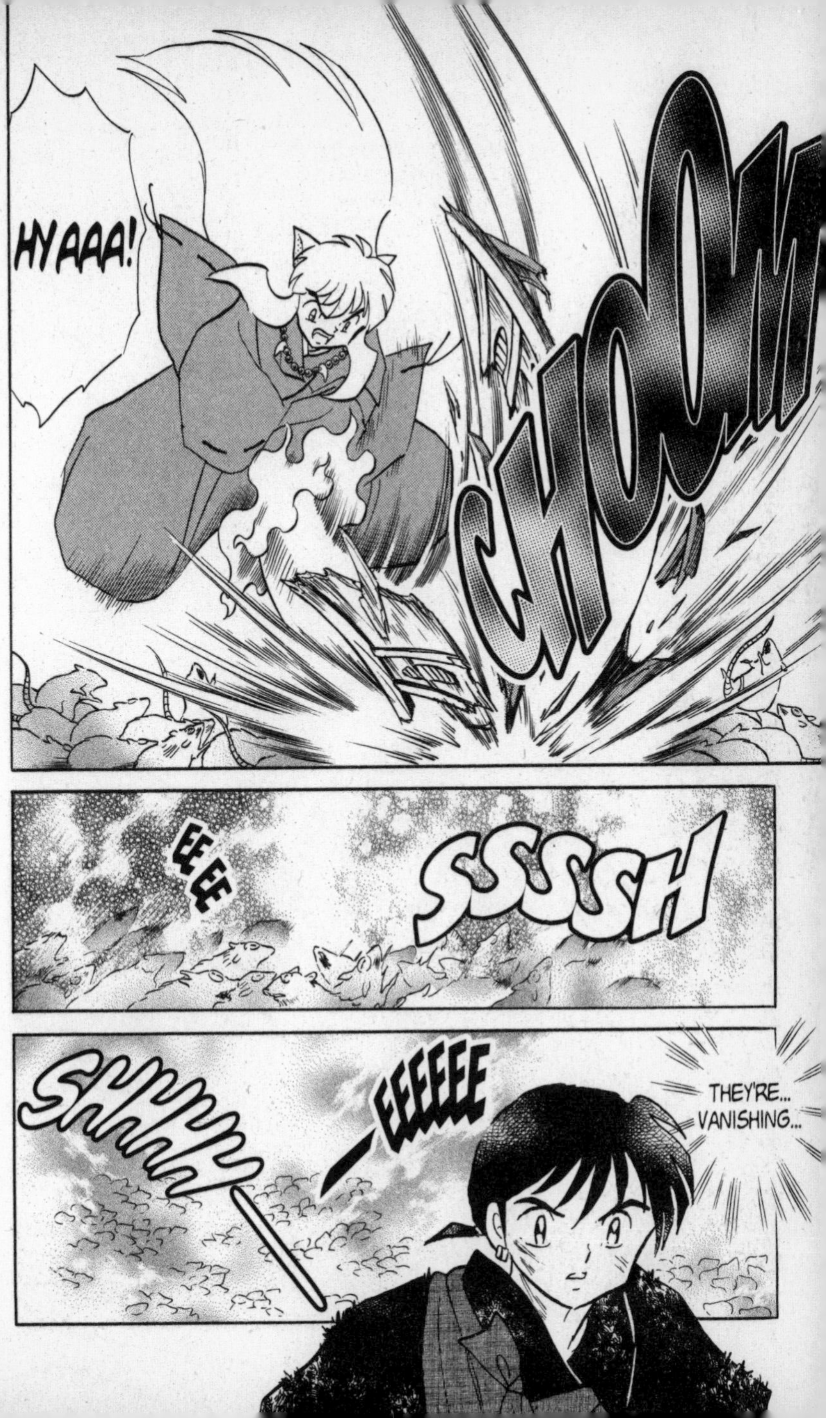
HYAAA!
CHOOM
EE EE
SSSSH
Shhhh
—EEEEEE
THEY'RE... VANISHING...

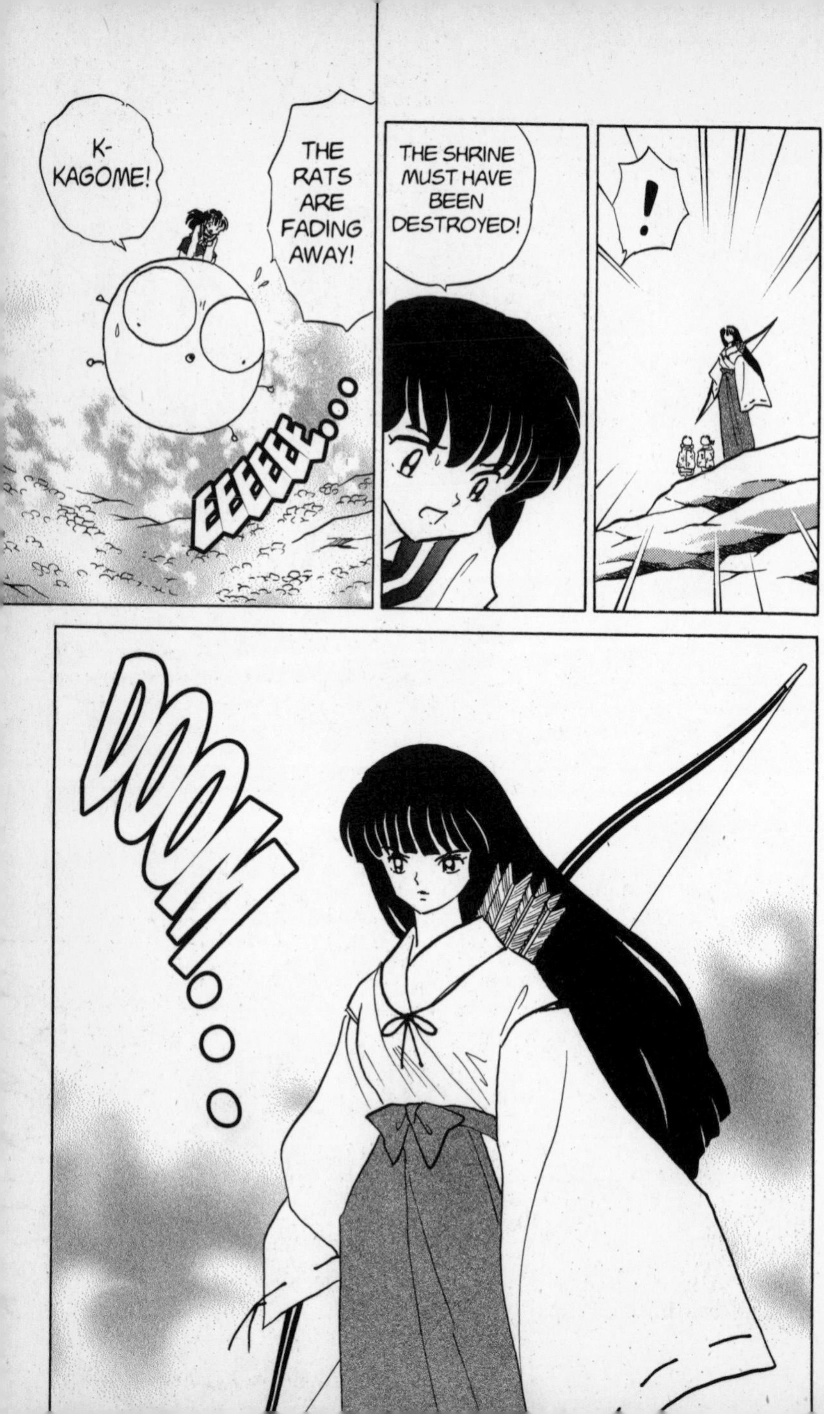
K-
KAGOME!
THE RATS ARE FADING AWAY!
EEEEEE...OOO
THE SHRINE MUST HAVE BEEN DESTROYED!
!
DOOM...

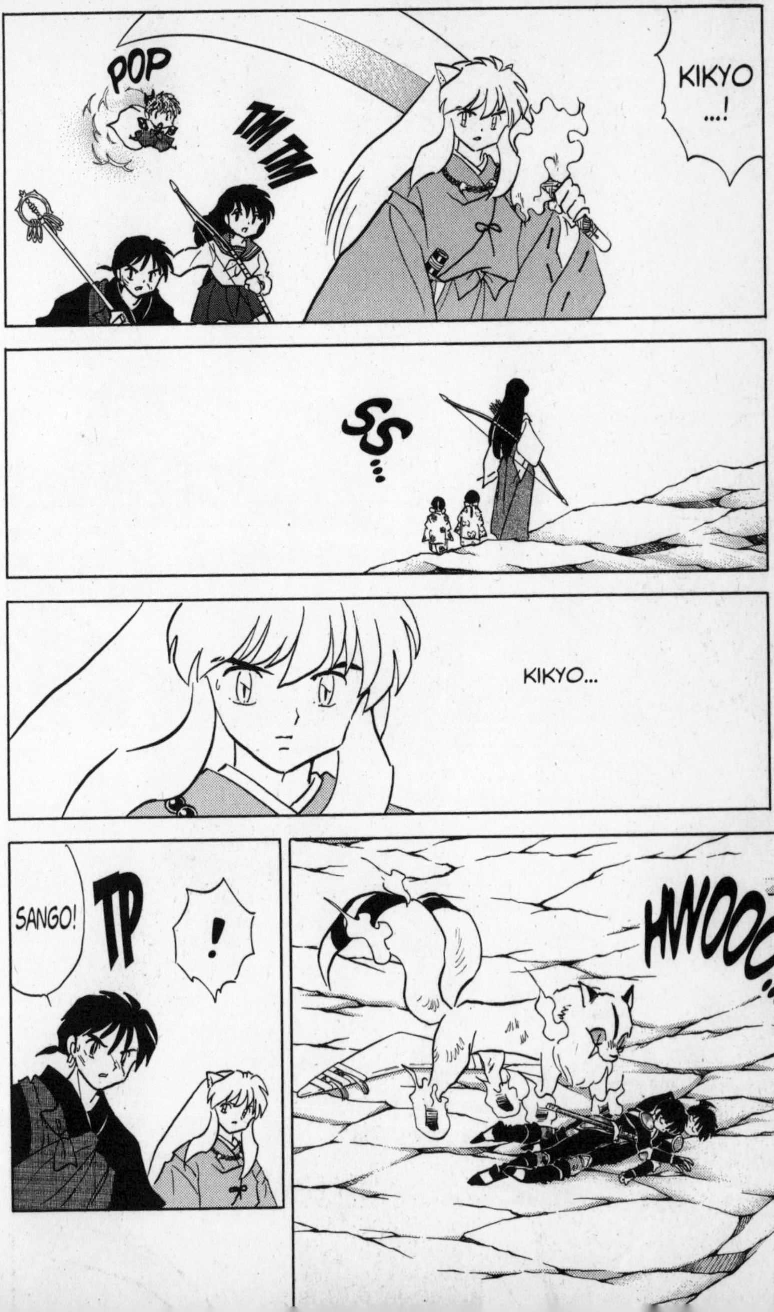
POP
TM TM
KIKYO ...!
SS...
KIKYO...
SANGO!
TP
!
HWOOO...

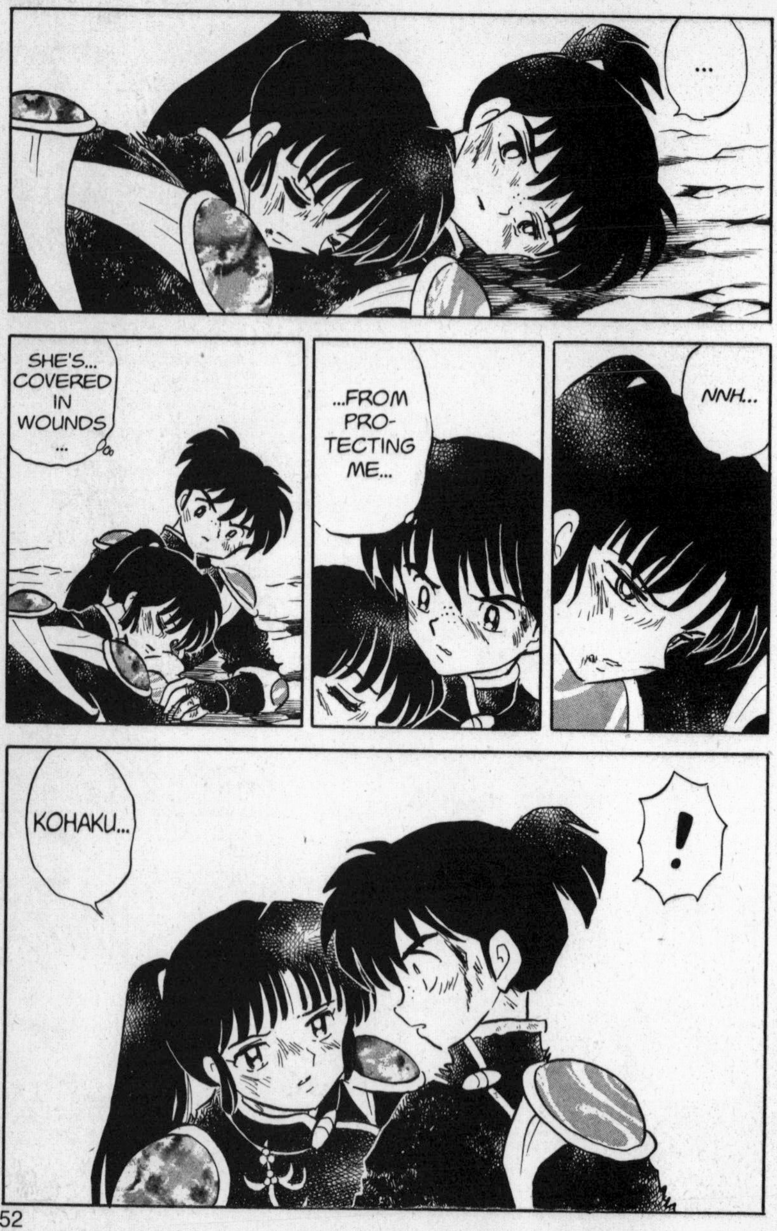
...
SHE'S... COVERED IN WOUNDS ...
...FROM PRO-TECTING ME...
NNH...
KOHAKU...
!

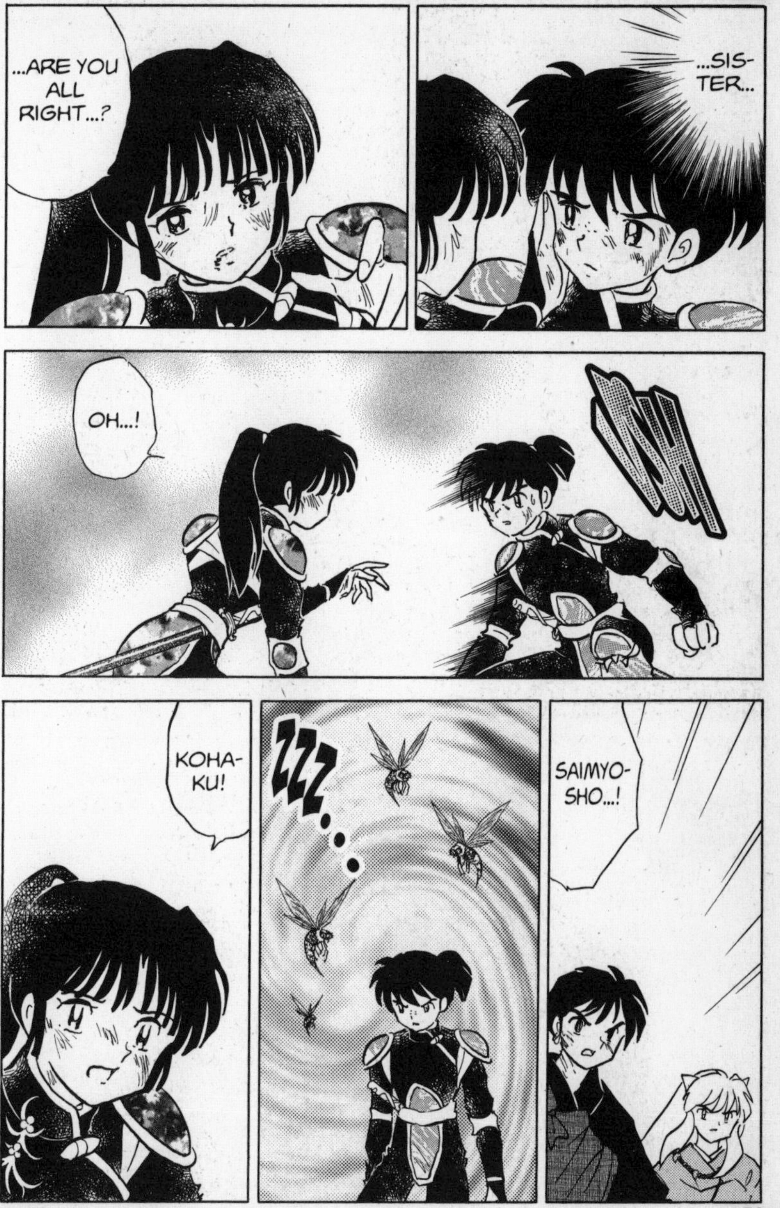
...ARE YOU ALL RIGHT...?
...SIS-TER...
OH...!
KOHA-KU!
ZZZ...
SAIMYO-SHO...!

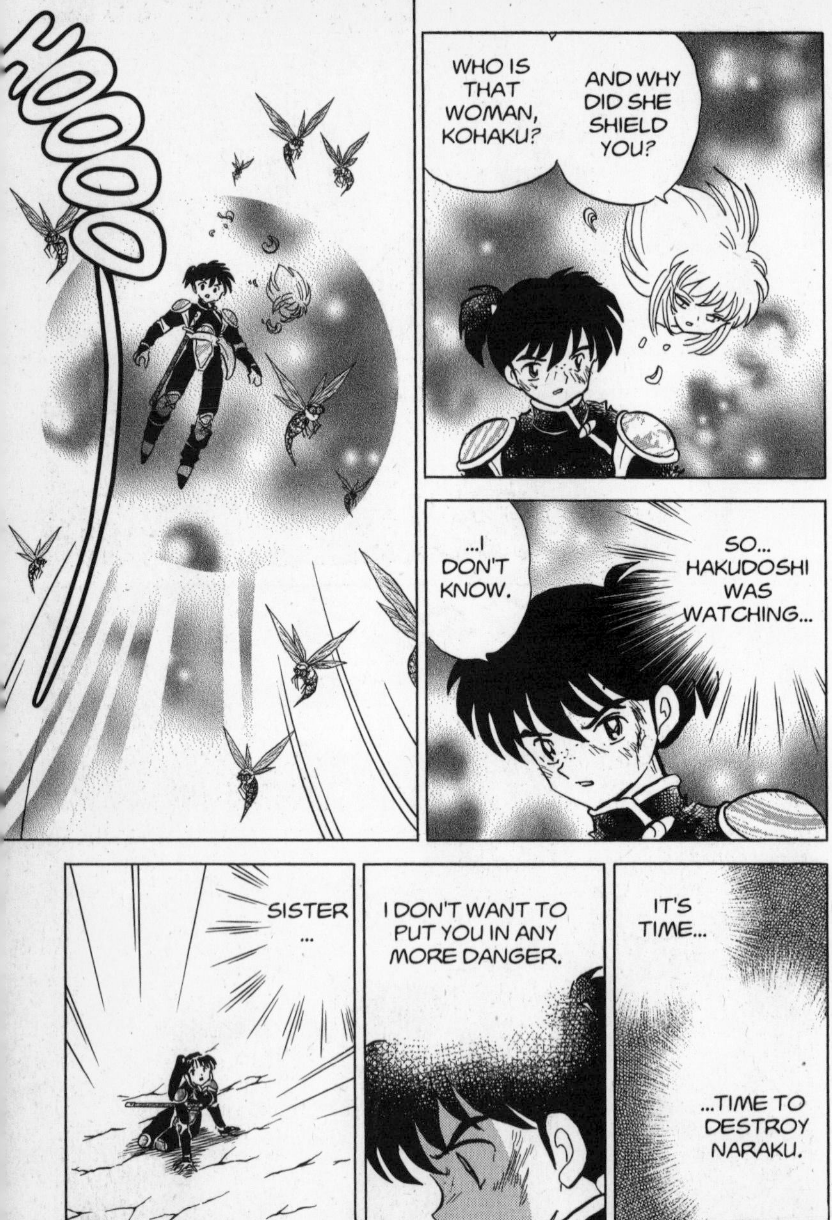
HOOOOO
WHO IS THAT WOMAN, KOHAKU?
AND WHY DID SHE SHIELD YOU?
...I DON'T KNOW.
SO... HAKUDOSHI WAS WATCHING...
SISTER ...
I DON'T WANT TO PUT YOU IN ANY MORE DANGER.
IT'S TIME...
...TIME TO DESTROY NARAKU.

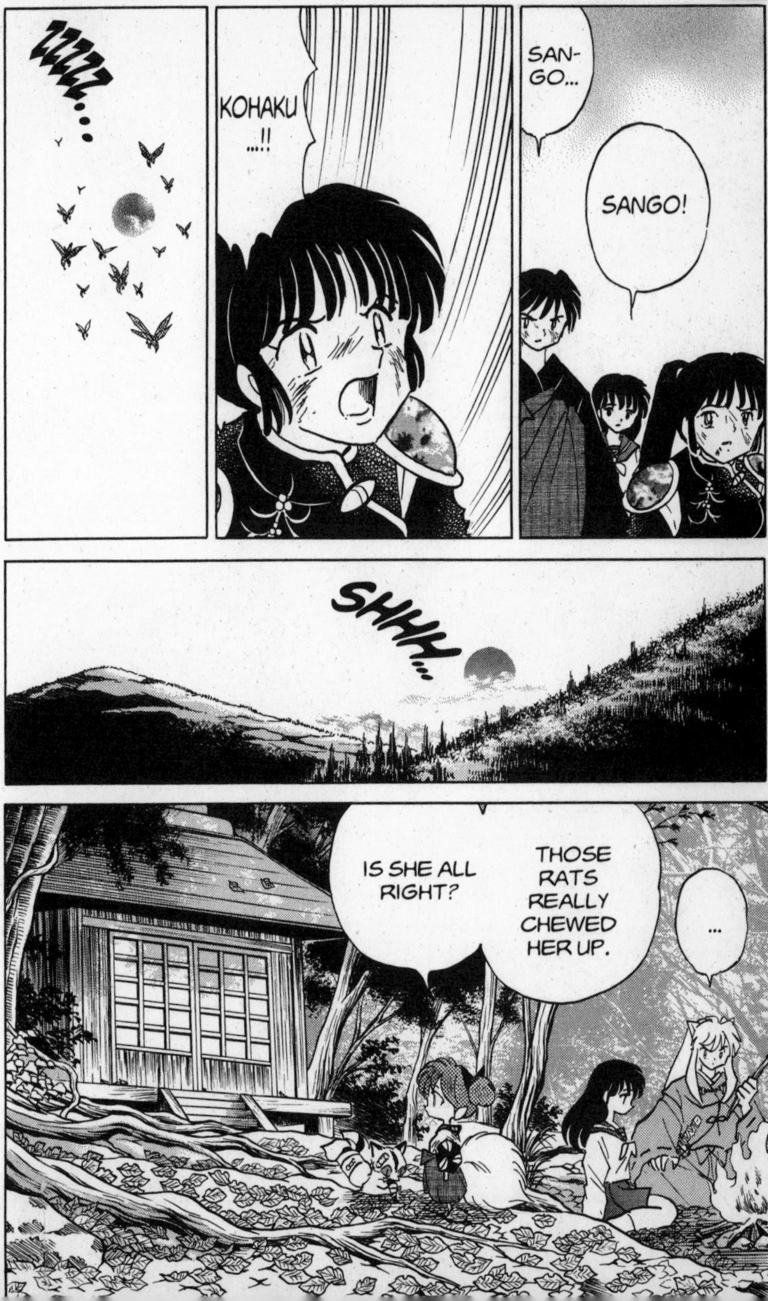
ZZZZZ...
KOHAKU ...!!
SAN-GO...
SANGO!
SHHH...
IS SHE ALL RIGHT?
THOSE RATS REALLY CHEWED HER UP.
...

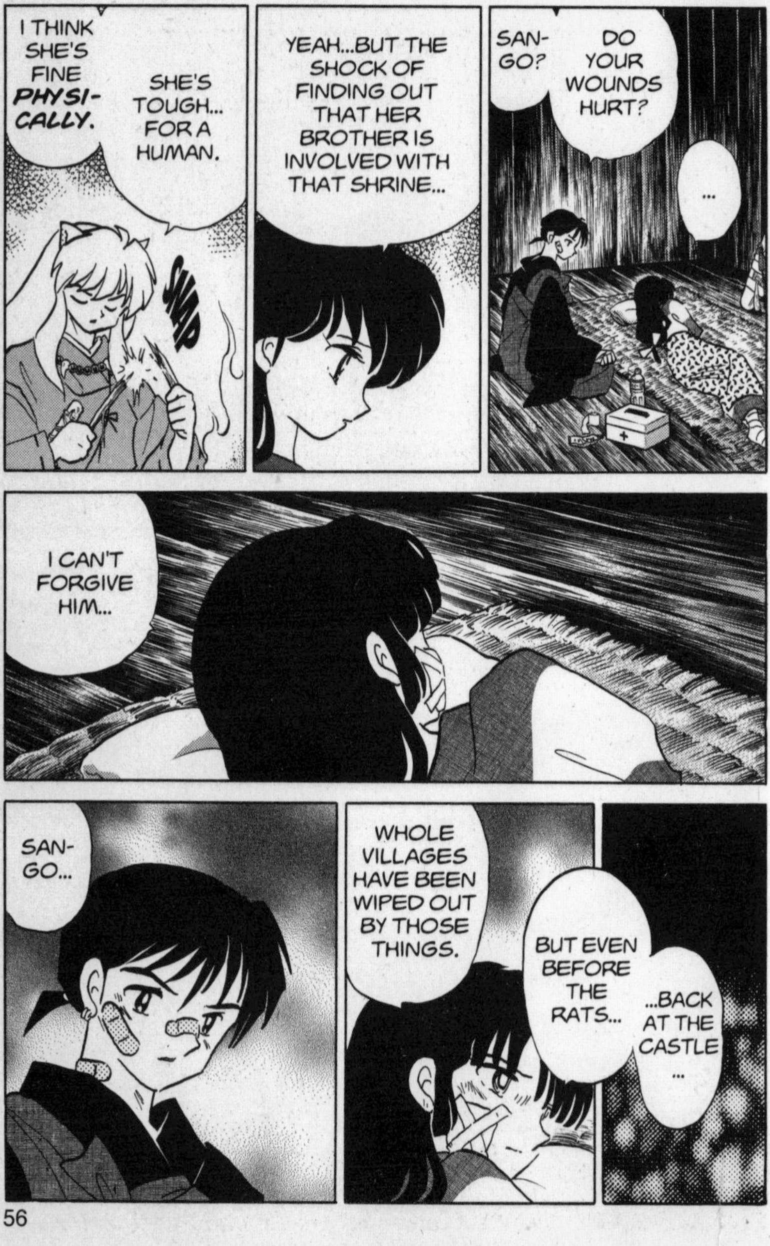
I THINK SHE'S FINE **PHYSICALLY.**
SHE'S TOUGH... FOR A HUMAN.
SNAP
YEAH...BUT THE SHOCK OF FINDING OUT THAT HER BROTHER IS INVOLVED WITH THAT SHRINE...
SAN-GO?
DO YOUR WOUNDS HURT?
...
I CAN'T FORGIVE HIM...
SAN-GO...
WHOLE VILLAGES HAVE BEEN WIPED OUT BY THOSE THINGS.
BUT EVEN BEFORE THE RATS...
...BACK AT THE CASTLE ...

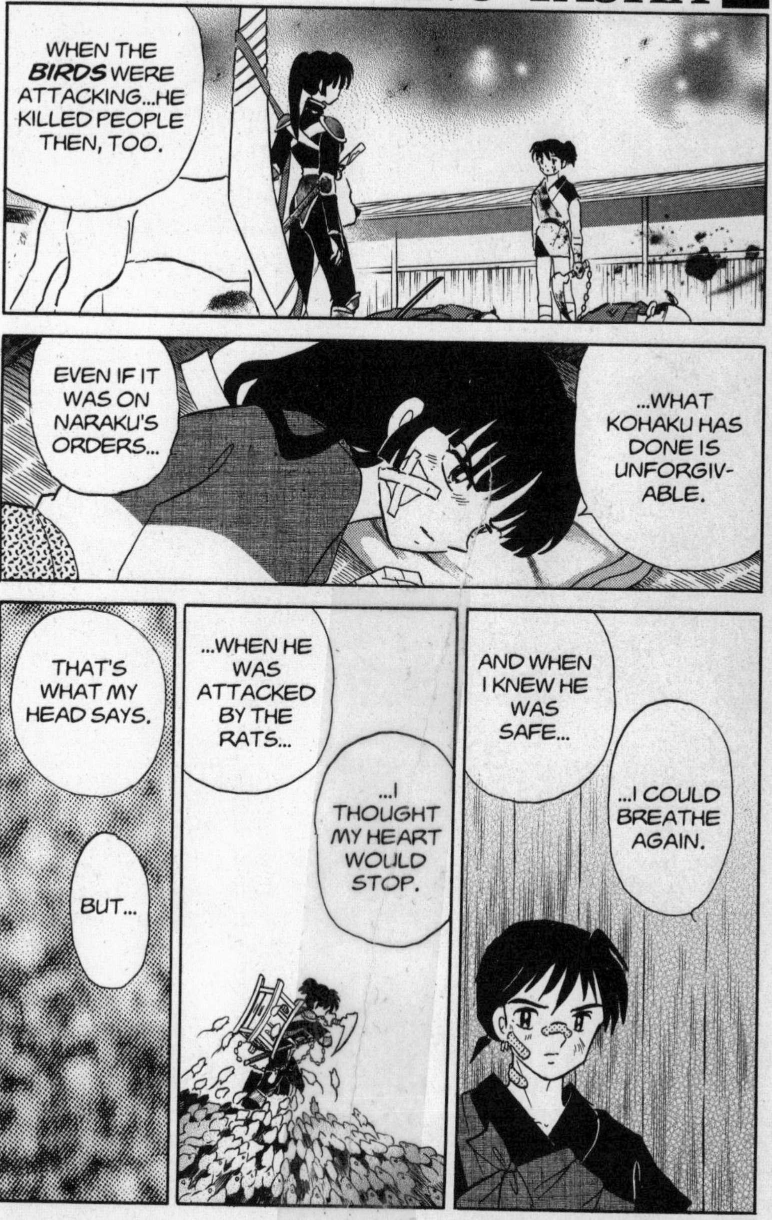
WHEN THE BIRDS WERE ATTACKING...HE KILLED PEOPLE THEN, TOO.
EVEN IF IT WAS ON NARAKU'S ORDERS...
...WHAT KOHAKU HAS DONE IS UNFORGIV-ABLE.
THAT'S WHAT MY HEAD SAYS.
BUT...
...WHEN HE WAS ATTACKED BY THE RATS...
...I THOUGHT MY HEART WOULD STOP.
AND WHEN I KNEW HE WAS SAFE...
...I COULD BREATHE AGAIN.

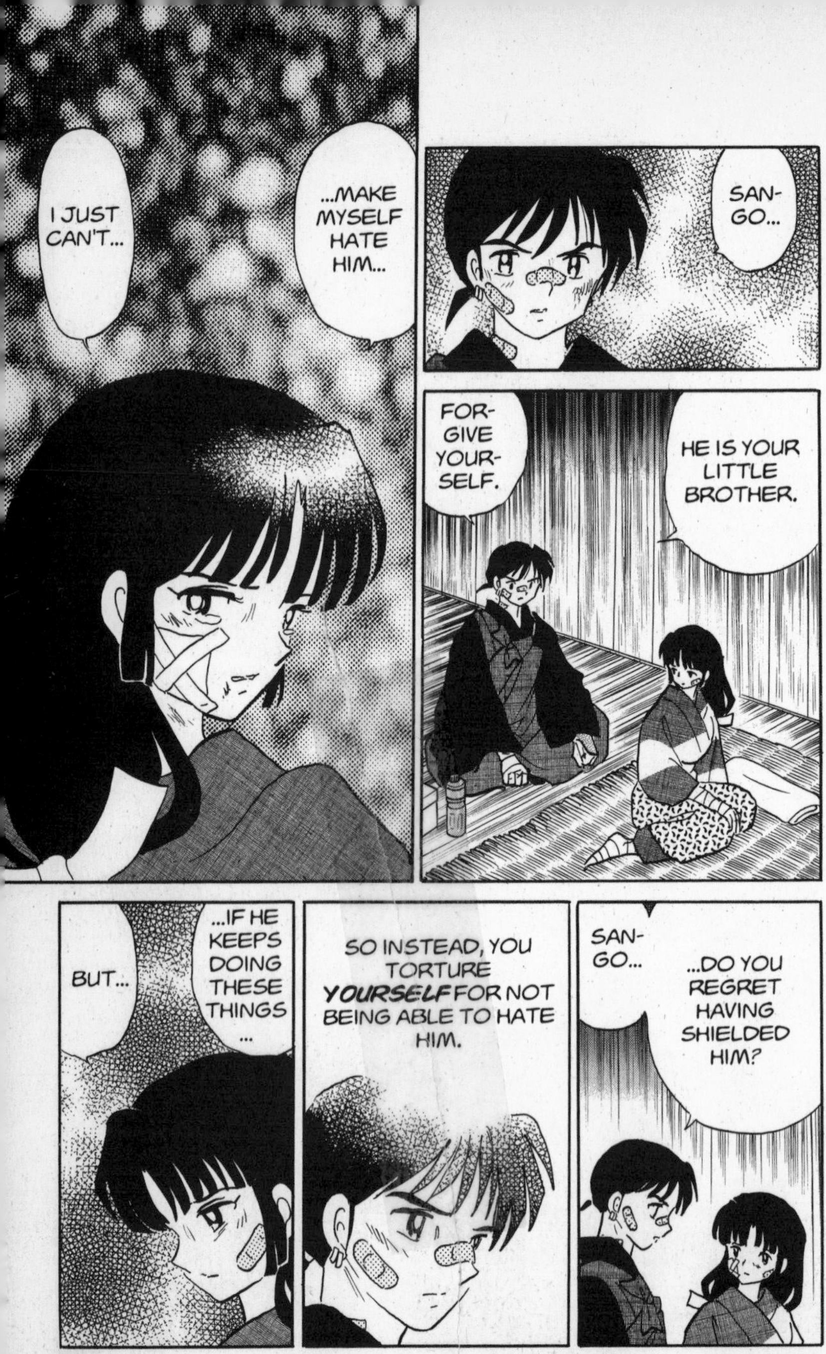
I JUST CAN'T...
...MAKE MYSELF HATE HIM...
SAN-GO...
FOR-GIVE YOUR-SELF.
HE IS YOUR LITTLE BROTHER.
BUT...
...IF HE KEEPS DOING THESE THINGS ...
SO INSTEAD, YOU TORTURE *YOURSELF* FOR NOT BEING ABLE TO HATE HIM.
SAN-GO...
...DO YOU REGRET HAVING SHIELDED HIM?

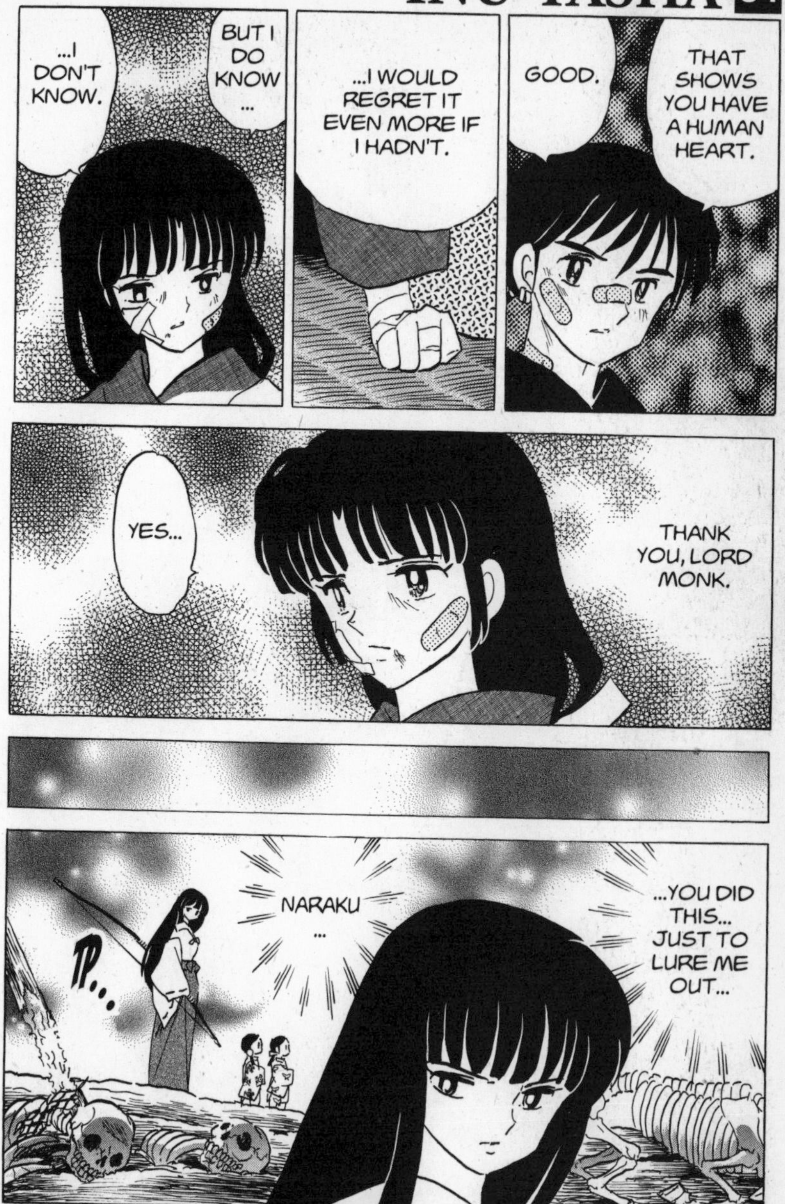
...I DON'T KNOW.
BUT I DO KNOW ...
...I WOULD REGRET IT EVEN MORE IF I HADN'T.
GOOD.
THAT SHOWS YOU HAVE A HUMAN HEART.
YES...
THANK YOU, LORD MONK.
TP...
NARAKU ...
...YOU DID THIS... JUST TO LURE ME OUT...

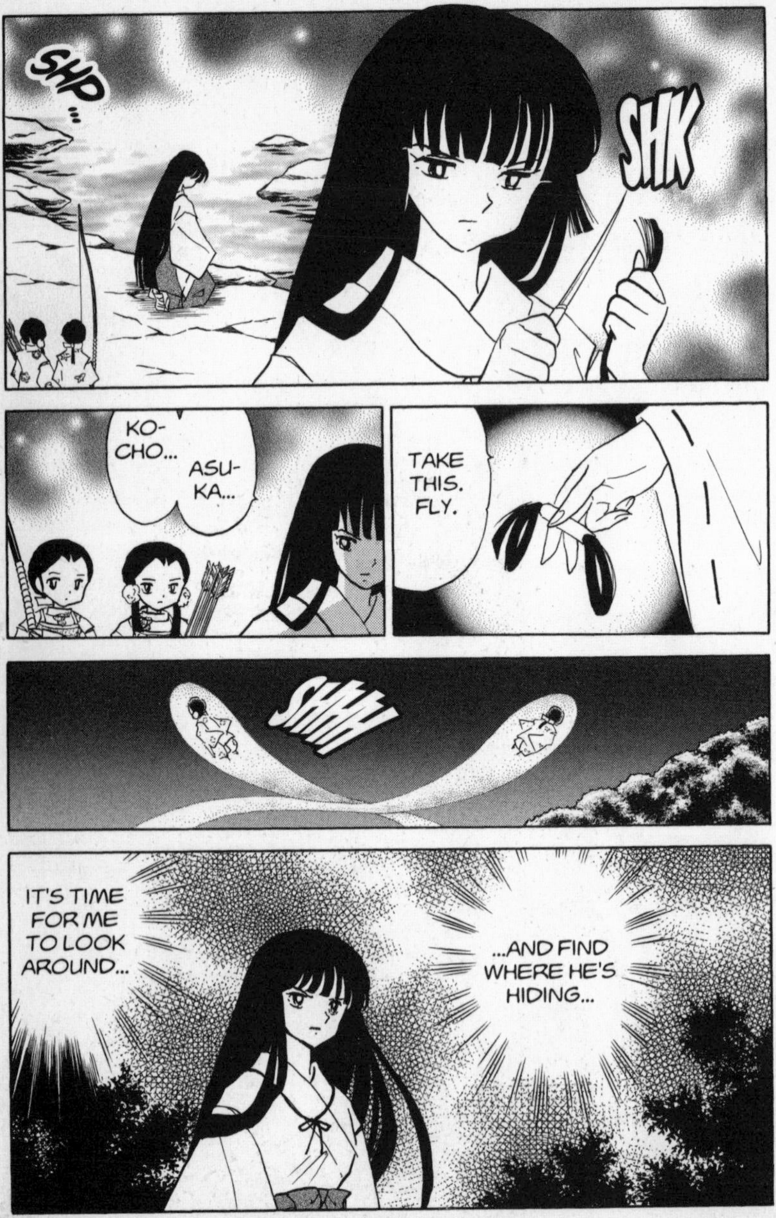
SHP...
SHK
KO-CHO... ASU-KA...
TAKE THIS. FLY.
SHHH
IT'S TIME FOR ME TO LOOK AROUND...
...AND FIND WHERE HE'S HIDING...

SCROLL 4

SMALL PLEASURES

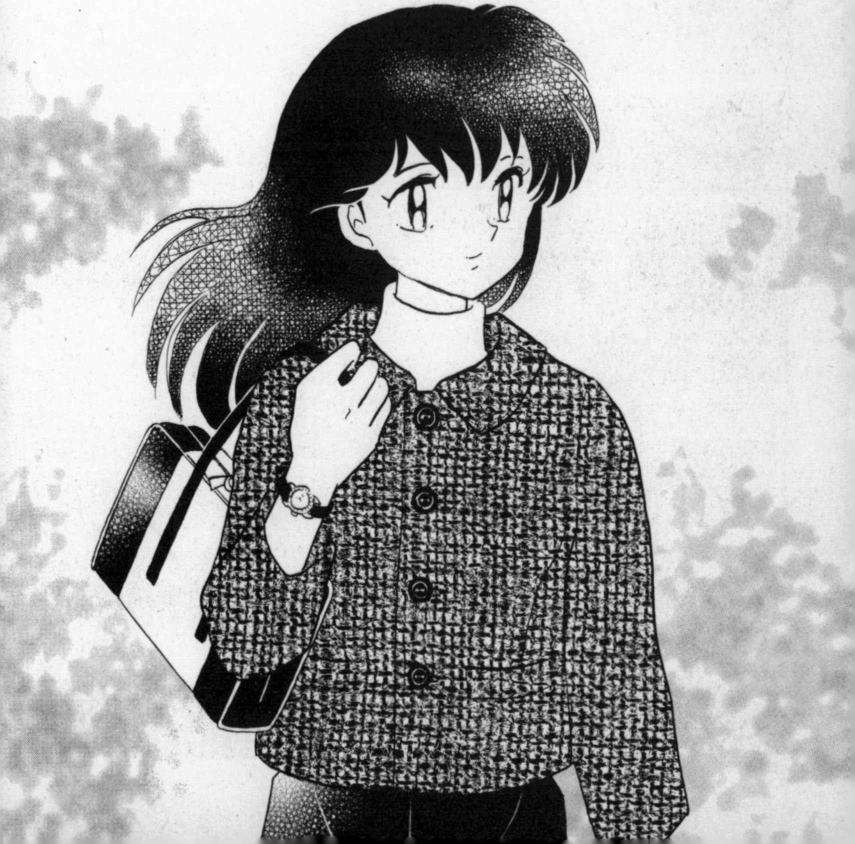

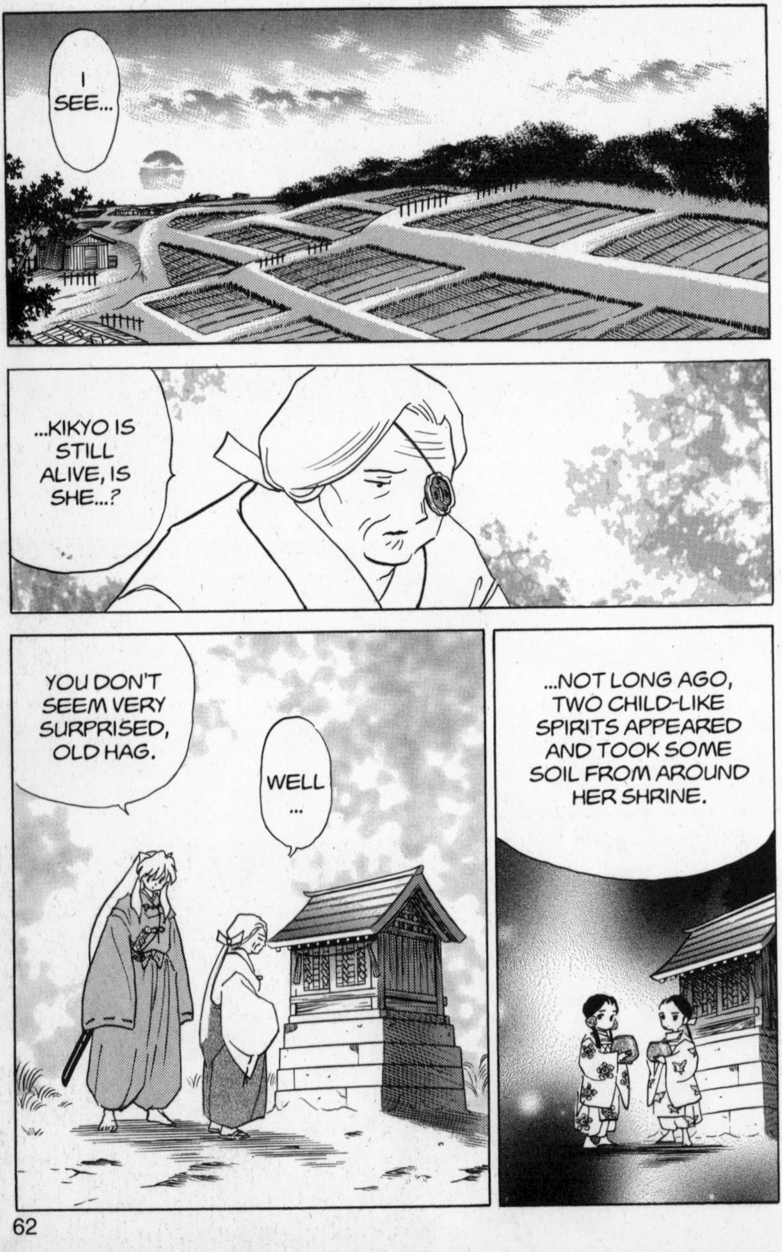
I SEE...
...KIKYO IS STILL ALIVE, IS SHE...?
YOU DON'T SEEM VERY SURPRISED, OLD HAG.
WELL ...
...NOT LONG AGO, TWO CHILD-LIKE SPIRITS APPEARED AND TOOK SOME SOIL FROM AROUND HER SHRINE.

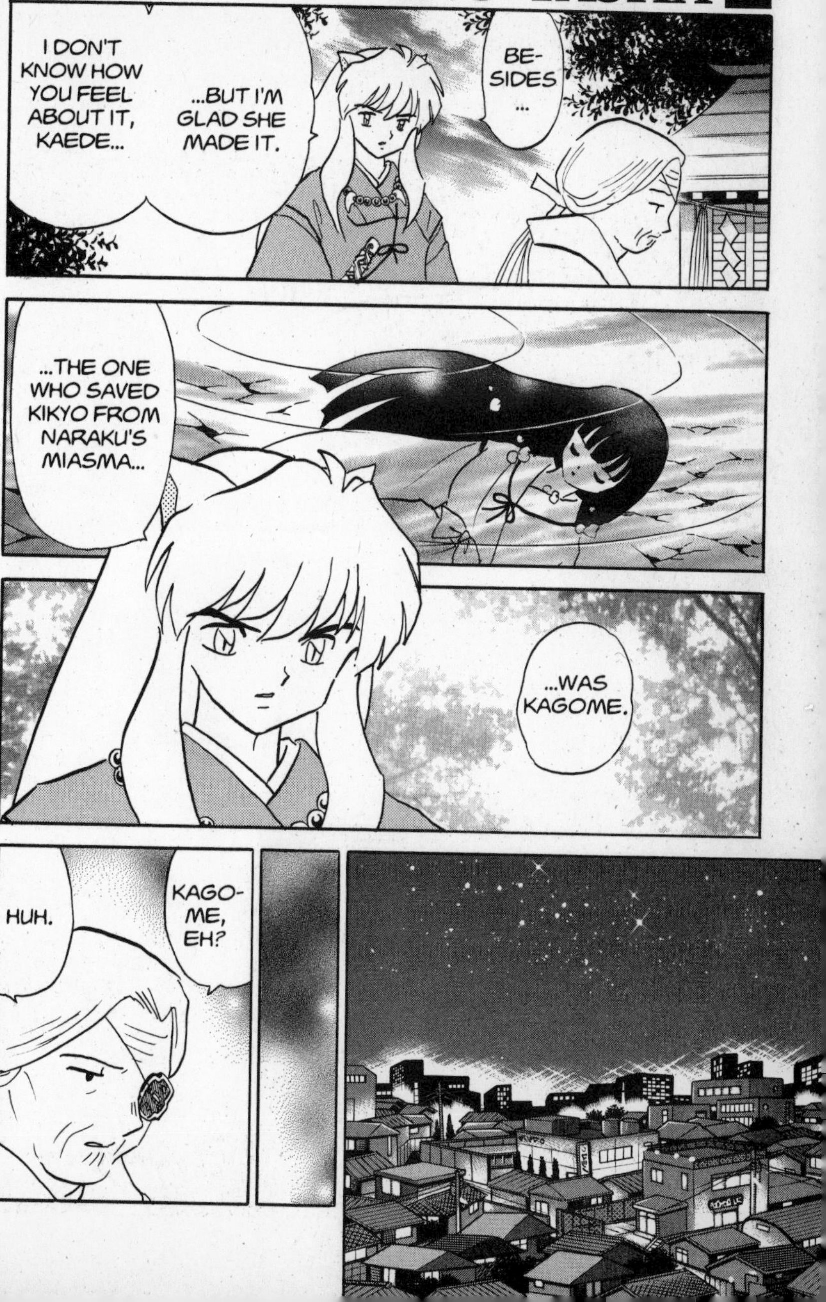
I DON'T KNOW HOW YOU FEEL ABOUT IT, KAEDE...
...BUT I'M GLAD SHE MADE IT.
BE-SIDES ...
...THE ONE WHO SAVED KIKYO FROM NARAKU'S MIASMA...
...WAS KAGOME.
HUH.
KAGO-ME, EH?

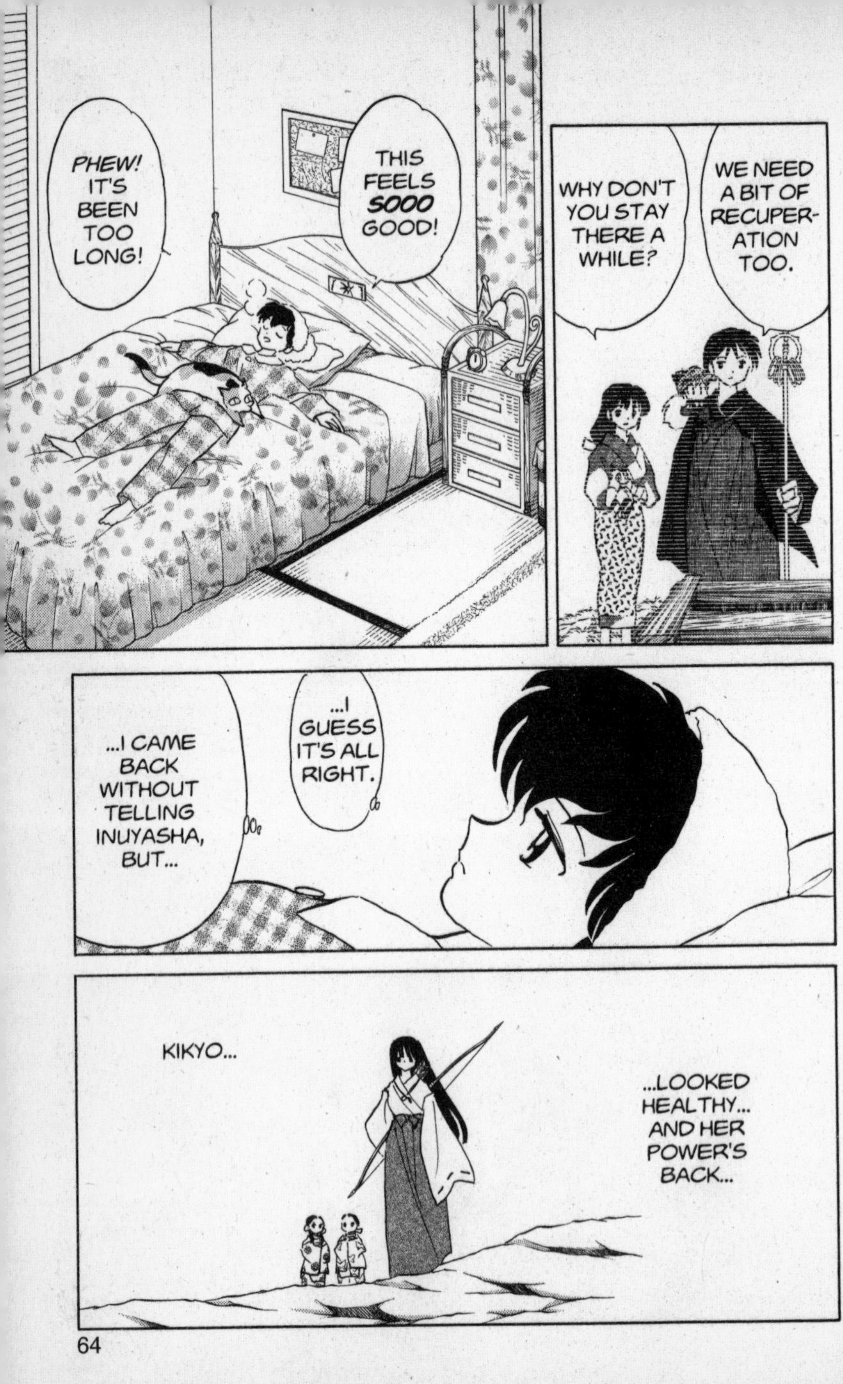
PHEW! IT'S BEEN TOO LONG!
THIS FEELS SOOO GOOD!
WHY DON'T YOU STAY THERE A WHILE?
WE NEED A BIT OF RECUPER-ATION TOO.
...I CAME BACK WITHOUT TELLING INUYASHA, BUT...
...I GUESS IT'S ALL RIGHT.
KIKYO...
...LOOKED HEALTHY... AND HER POWER'S BACK...

...SO WHY DID SHE JUST RUN OFF AGAIN?

I WONDER IF INUYASHA WANTED TO CHASE AFTER HER.

HE JUST SEEMED A LITTLE WEIRD...

...ON THE WAY BACK TO KAEDE'S VILLAGE...

...

I WONDER IF I'M...

...STILL JUST HIS BACK-UP CHOICE.

HOW COULD YOU JUST LET HER *LEAVE*?!

SHE DOESN'T NEED YOUR PERMISSION, DOES SHE?

GRRR

INUYASHA, YOU WERE TELLING LADY KAEDE ABOUT LADY KIKYO, YES?

YEAH. SO?

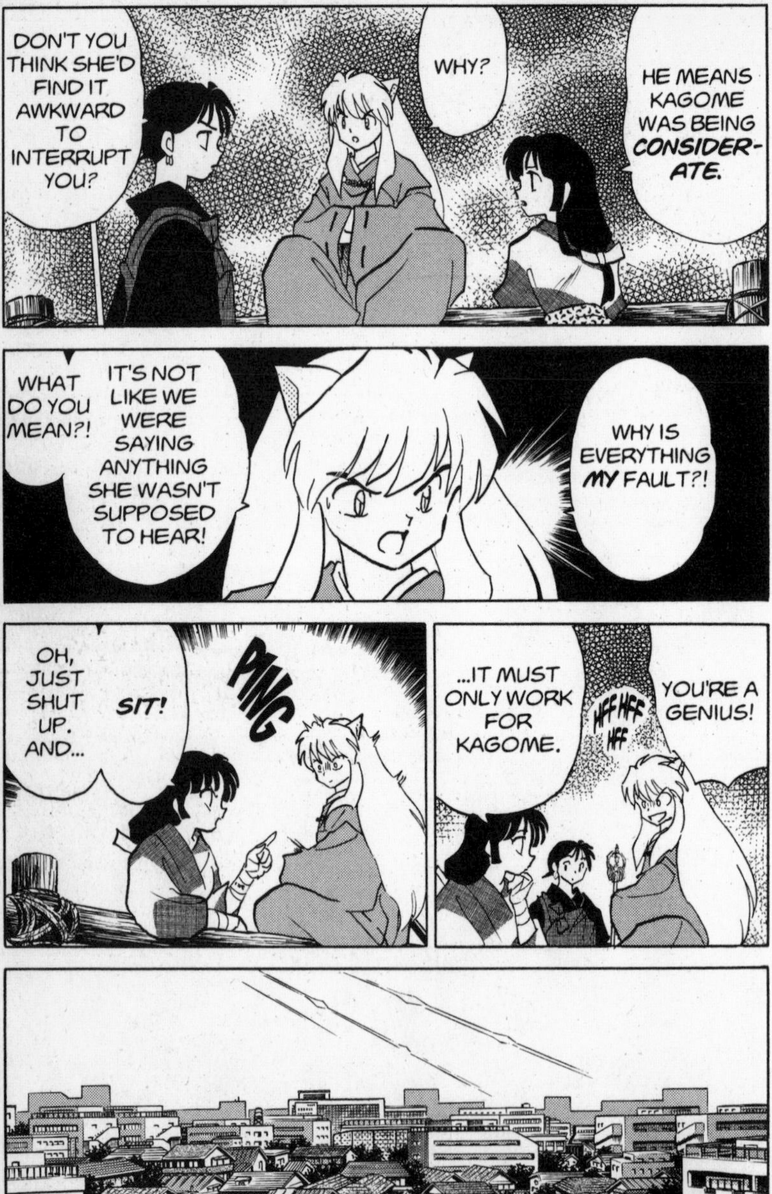
DON'T YOU THINK SHE'D FIND IT AWKWARD TO INTERRUPT YOU?
WHY?
HE MEANS KAGOME WAS BEING CONSIDER-ATE.
WHAT DO YOU MEAN?!
IT'S NOT LIKE WE WERE SAYING ANYTHING SHE WASN'T SUPPOSED TO HEAR!
WHY IS EVERYTHING MY FAULT?!
OH, JUST SHUT UP. AND...
SIT!
PING
...IT MUST ONLY WORK FOR KAGOME.
HFF HFF HFF
YOU'RE A GENIUS!

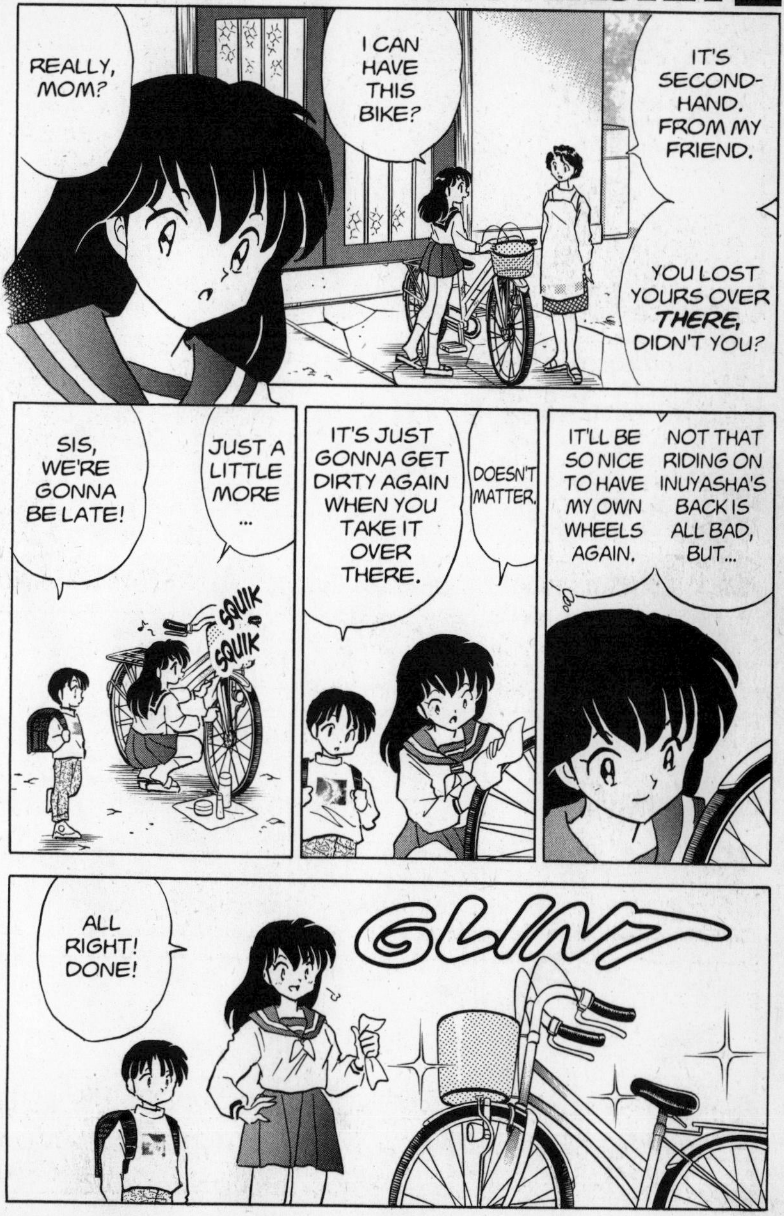
REALLY, MOM?
I CAN HAVE THIS BIKE?
IT'S SECOND-HAND. FROM MY FRIEND.
YOU LOST YOURS OVER ***THERE,*** DIDN'T YOU?
SIS, WE'RE GONNA BE LATE!
JUST A LITTLE MORE ...
SQUIK
SQUIK
IT'S JUST GONNA GET DIRTY AGAIN WHEN YOU TAKE IT OVER THERE.
DOESN'T MATTER.
IT'LL BE SO NICE TO HAVE MY OWN WHEELS AGAIN.
NOT THAT RIDING ON INUYASHA'S BACK IS ALL BAD, BUT...
ALL RIGHT! DONE!
GLINT

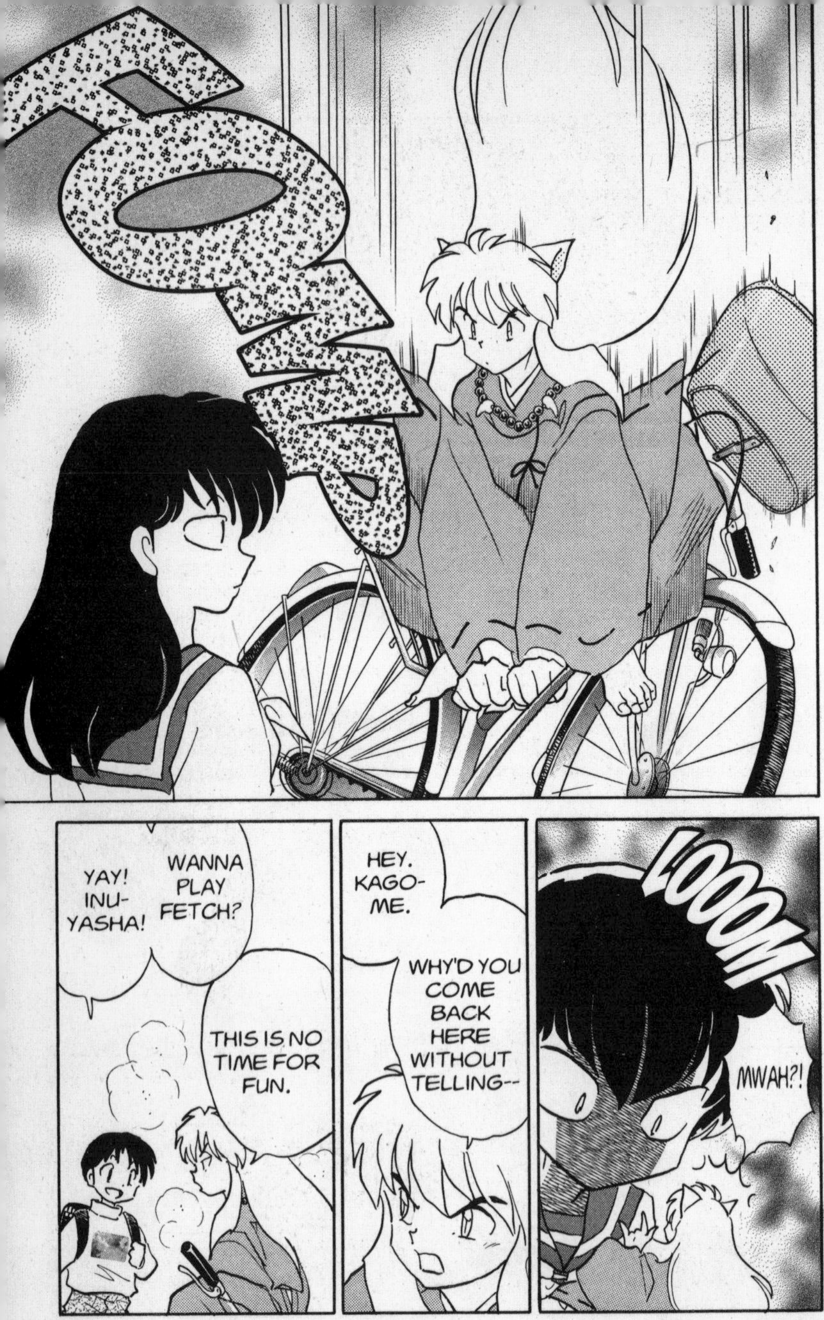
YAY! INU-YASHA!
WANNA PLAY FETCH?
THIS IS NO TIME FOR FUN.
HEY. KAGO-ME.
WHY'D YOU COME BACK HERE WITHOUT TELLING--
LOOOM
MWAH?!

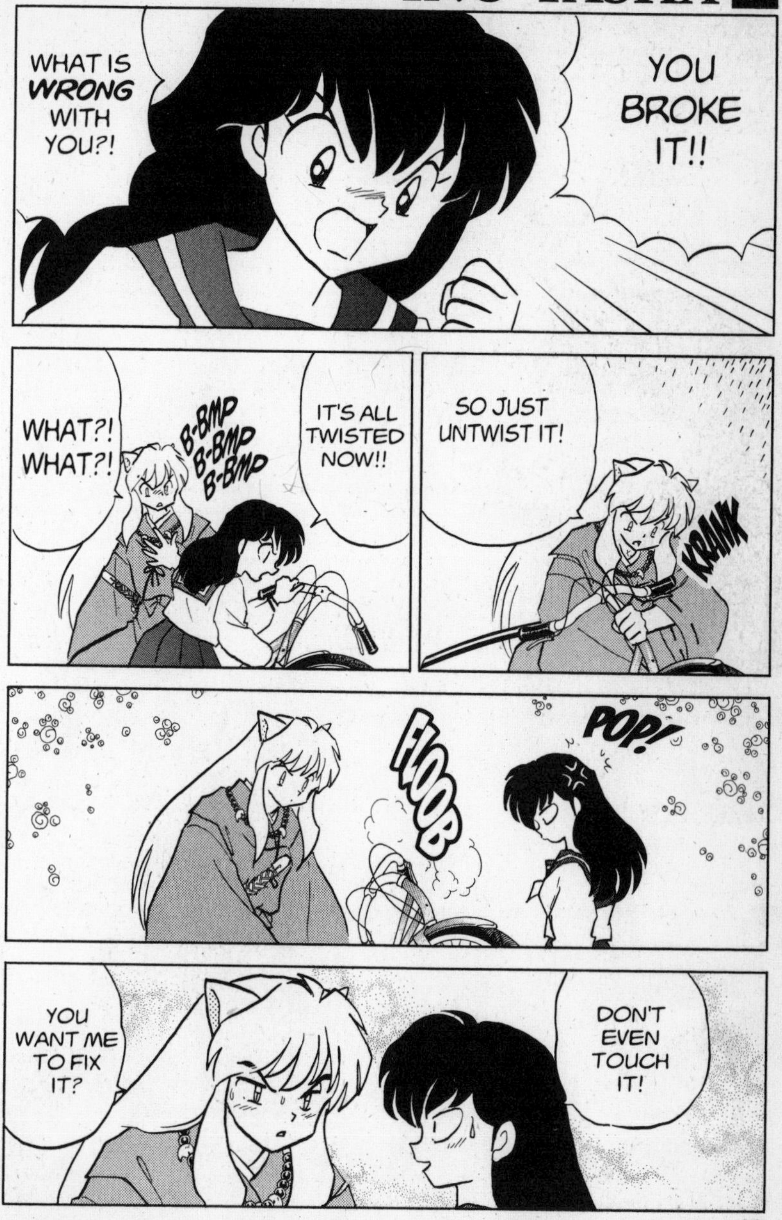
WHAT IS WRONG WITH YOU?!
YOU BROKE IT!!
WHAT?! WHAT?!
B-BMP B-BMP B-BMP
IT'S ALL TWISTED NOW!!
SO JUST UNTWIST IT!
KRANK
FLOOB
POP!
YOU WANT ME TO FIX IT?
DON'T EVEN TOUCH IT!

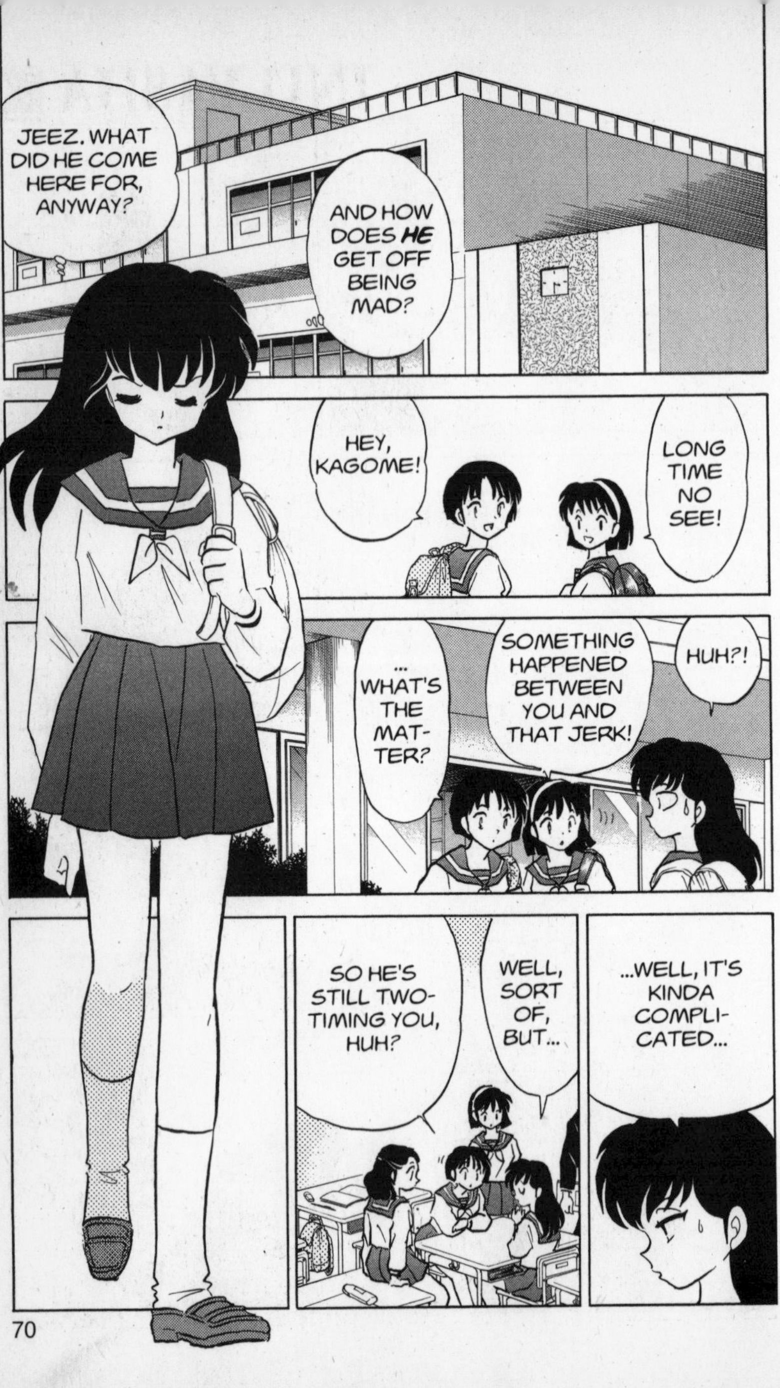
JEEZ. WHAT DID HE COME HERE FOR, ANYWAY?
AND HOW DOES **HE** GET OFF BEING MAD?
HEY, KAGOME!
LONG TIME NO SEE!
... WHAT'S THE MAT-TER?
SOMETHING HAPPENED BETWEEN YOU AND THAT JERK!
HUH?!
SO HE'S STILL TWO-TIMING YOU, HUH?
WELL, SORT OF, BUT...
...WELL, IT'S KINDA COMPLICATED...

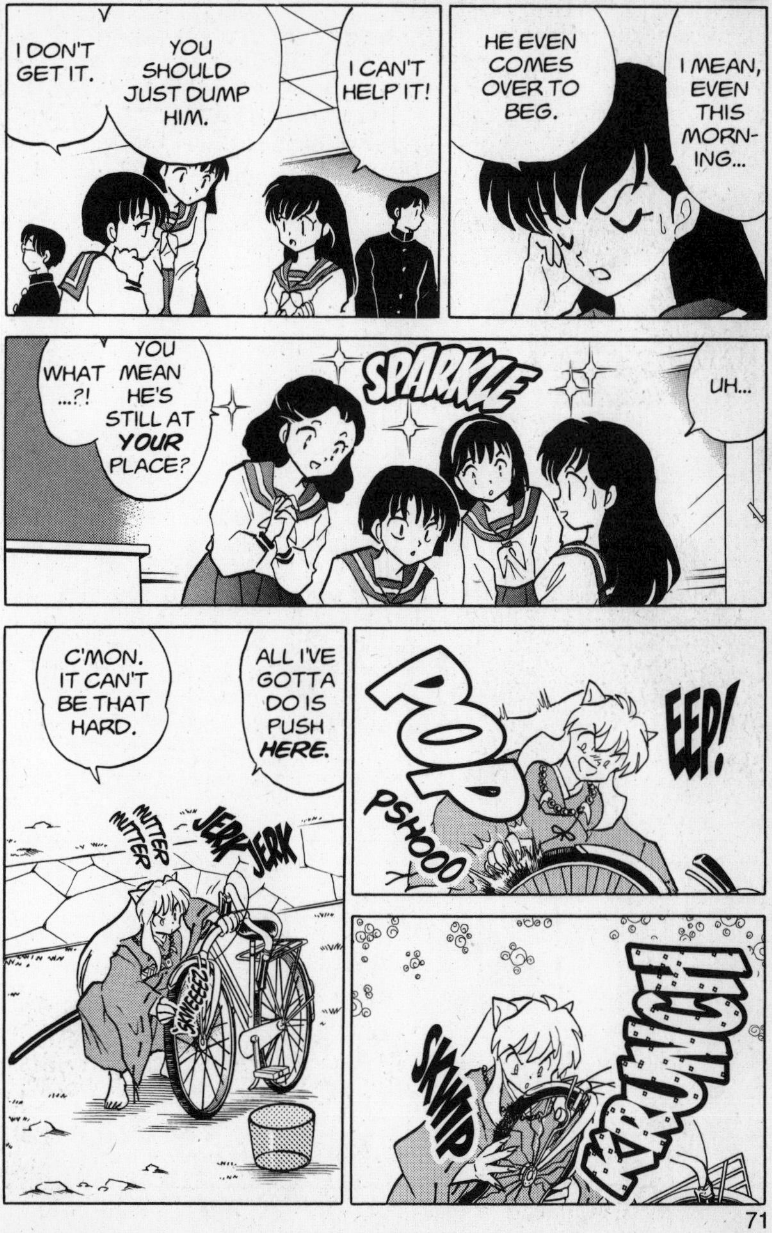
I DON'T GET IT.
YOU SHOULD JUST DUMP HIM.
I CAN'T HELP IT!
HE EVEN COMES OVER TO BEG.
I MEAN, EVEN THIS MORNING...
WHAT ...?!
YOU MEAN HE'S STILL AT ***YOUR*** PLACE?
SPARKLE
UH...
C'MON. IT CAN'T BE THAT HARD.
ALL I'VE GOTTA DO IS PUSH ***HERE.***
MUTTER MUTTER
JERK JERK
SKWEEEEZ
POP
PSHOOO
EEP!
SKWIP
KRUNCH!!

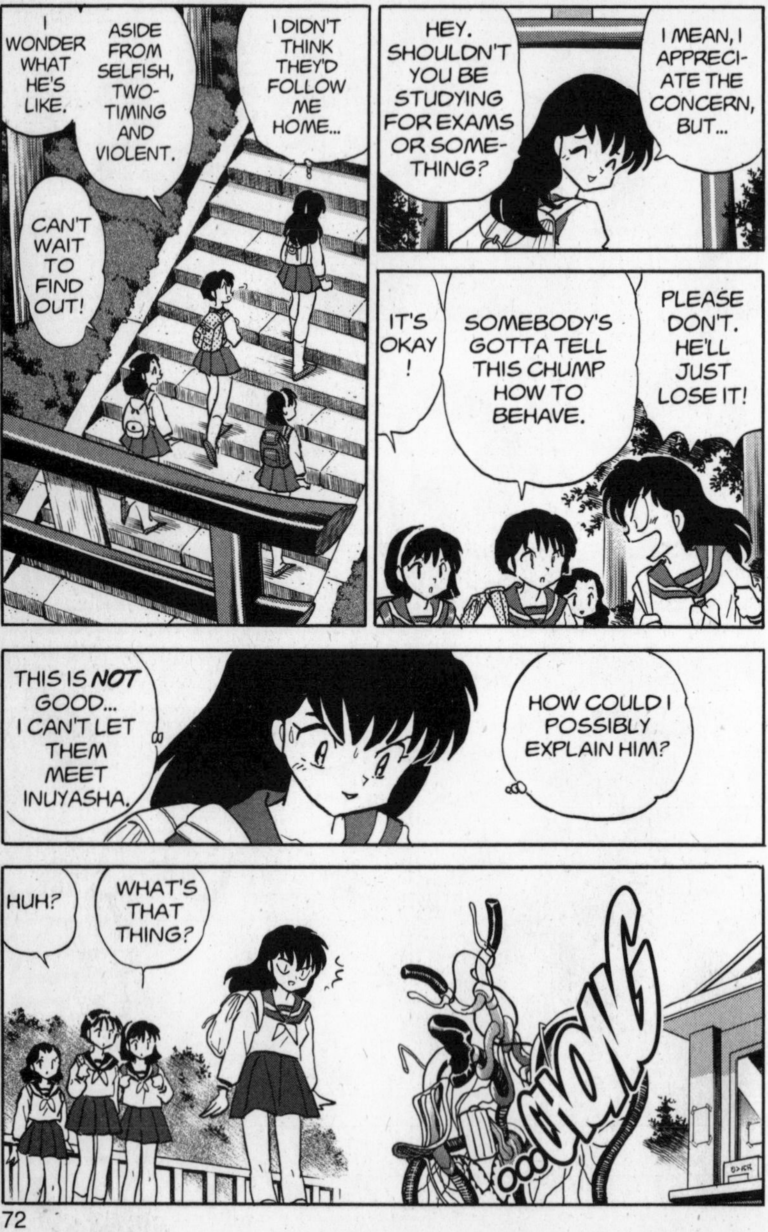
I WONDER WHAT HE'S LIKE.
ASIDE FROM SELFISH, TWO-TIMING AND VIOLENT.
I DIDN'T THINK THEY'D FOLLOW ME HOME...
CAN'T WAIT TO FIND OUT!
HEY. SHOULDN'T YOU BE STUDYING FOR EXAMS OR SOMETHING?
I MEAN, I APPRECIATE THE CONCERN, BUT...
IT'S OKAY!
SOMEBODY'S GOTTA TELL THIS CHUMP HOW TO BEHAVE.
PLEASE DON'T. HE'LL JUST LOSE IT!
THIS IS ***NOT*** GOOD... I CAN'T LET THEM MEET INUYASHA.
HOW COULD I POSSIBLY EXPLAIN HIM?
HUH?
WHAT'S THAT THING?
...CHONG

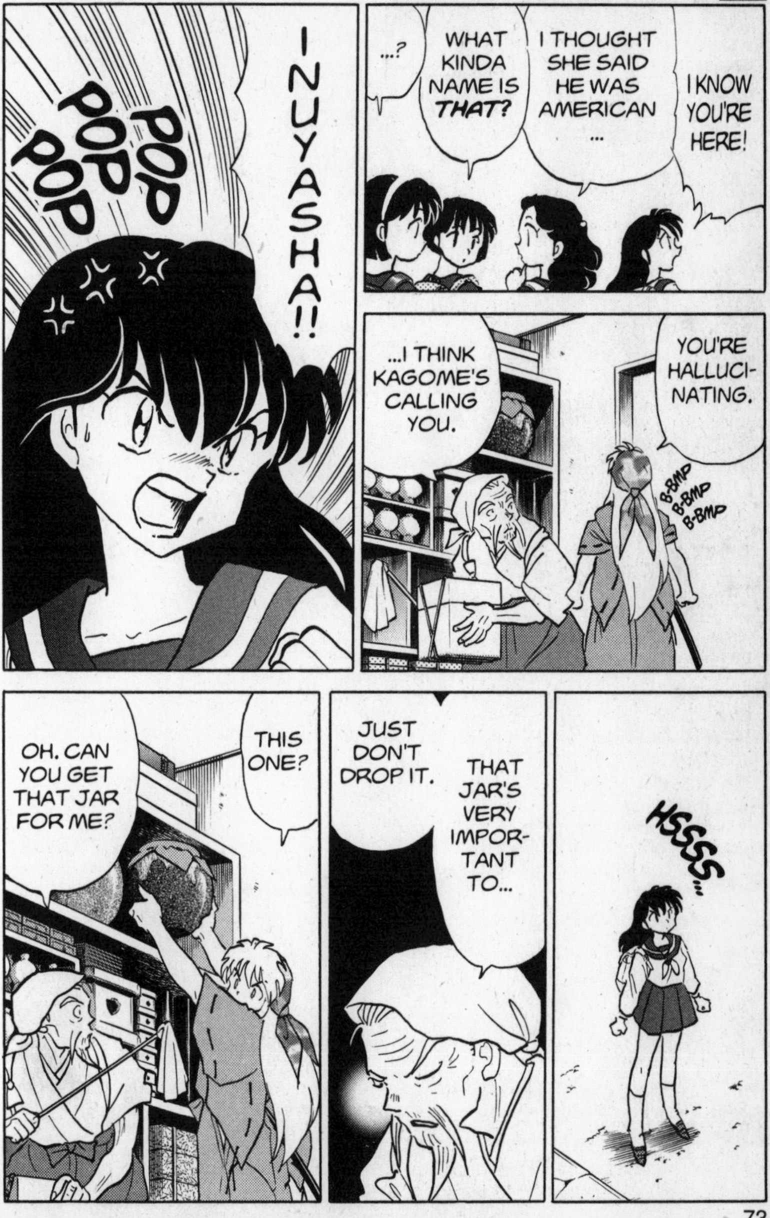
POP POP POP
INUYASHA!!
...?
WHAT KINDA NAME IS *THAT?*
I THOUGHT SHE SAID HE WAS AMERICAN ...
I KNOW YOU'RE HERE!
...I THINK KAGOME'S CALLING YOU.
YOU'RE HALLUCINATING.
B-BMP B-BMP B-BMP
OH. CAN YOU GET THAT JAR FOR ME?
THIS ONE?
JUST DON'T DROP IT.
THAT JAR'S VERY IMPORTANT TO...
HSSSS...

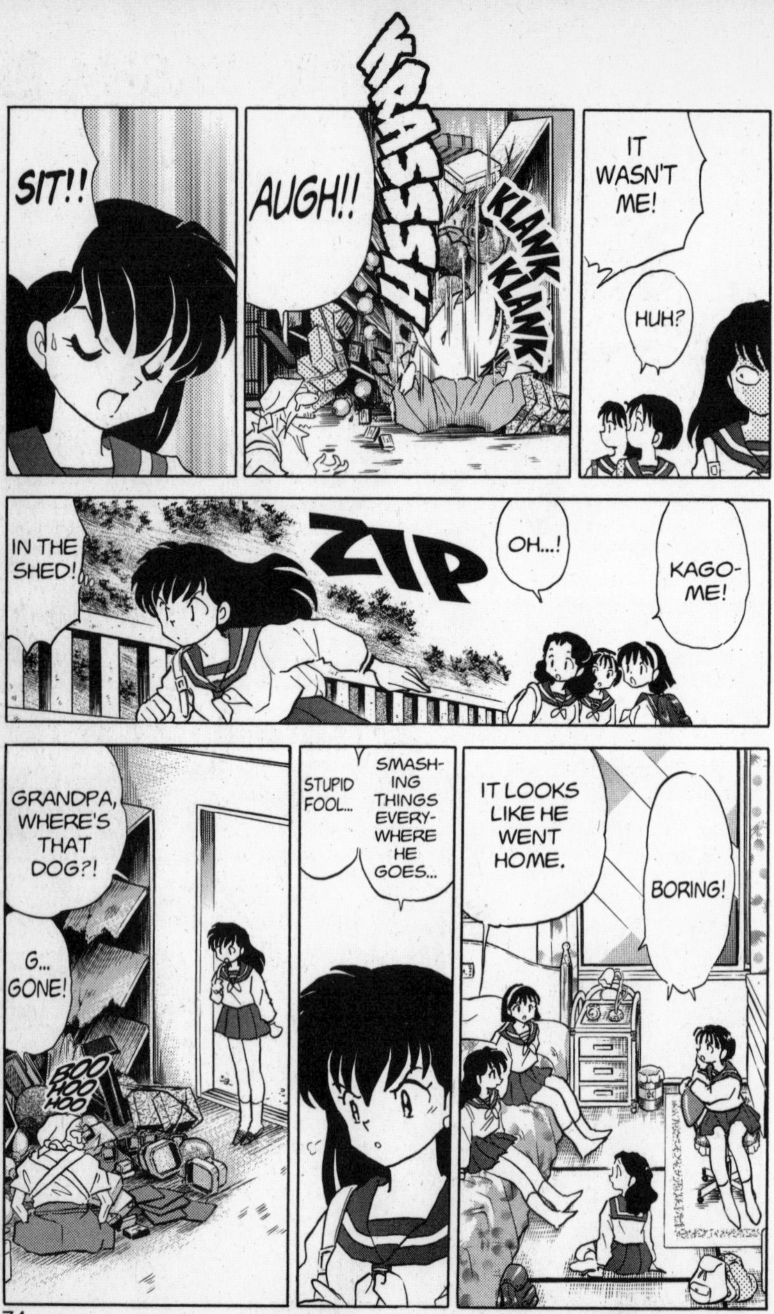
SIT!!
KRASSH
AUGH!!
KLANK KLANK KLANK
IT WASN'T ME!
HUH?
IN THE SHED!
ZIP
OH...!
KAGO-ME!
GRANDPA, WHERE'S THAT DOG?!
G... GONE!
BOO HOO HOO
STUPID FOOL...
SMASHING THINGS EVERYWHERE HE GOES...
IT LOOKS LIKE HE WENT HOME.
BORING!

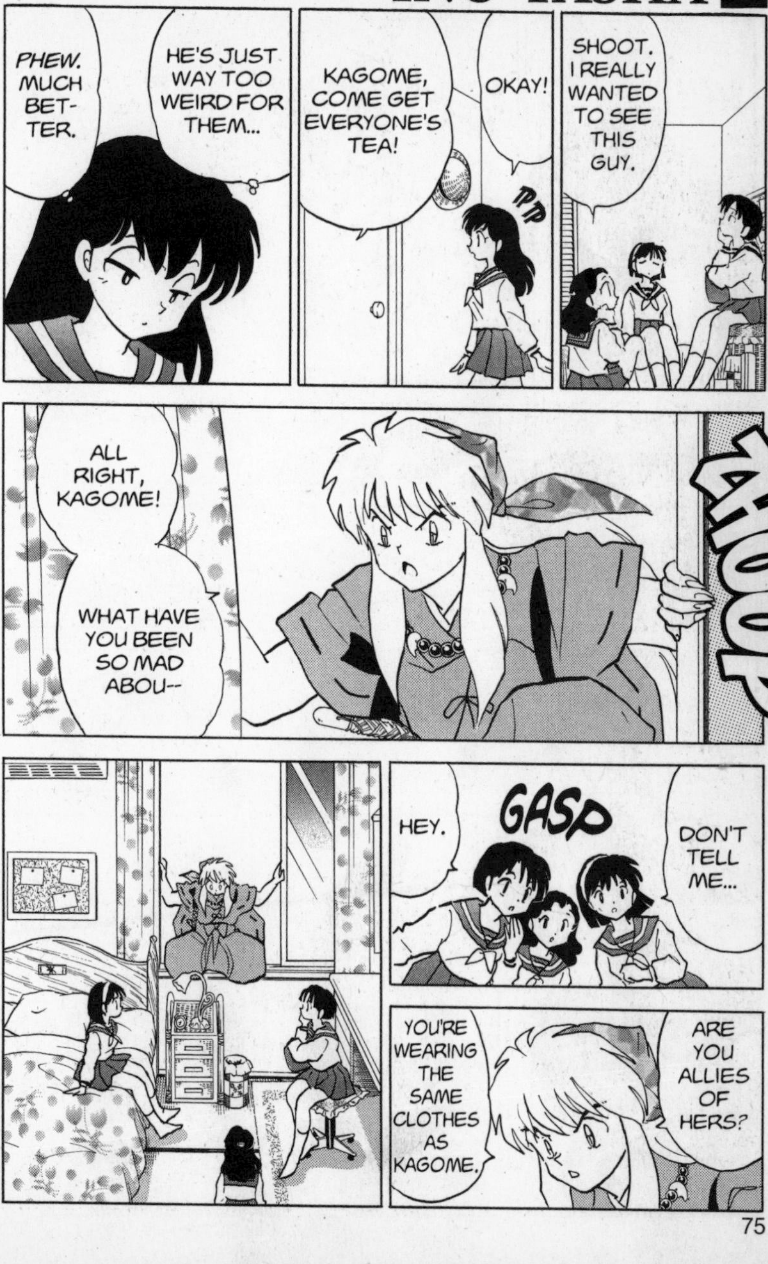
HE'S JUST WAY TOO WEIRD FOR THEM...
PHEW. MUCH BET-TER.
KAGOME, COME GET EVERYONE'S TEA!
OKAY!
SHOOT. I REALLY WANTED TO SEE THIS GUY.
ALL RIGHT, KAGOME!
WHAT HAVE YOU BEEN SO MAD ABOU--
ZHOOP
HEY.
GASP
DON'T TELL ME...
YOU'RE WEARING THE SAME CLOTHES AS KAGOME.
ARE YOU ALLIES OF HERS?

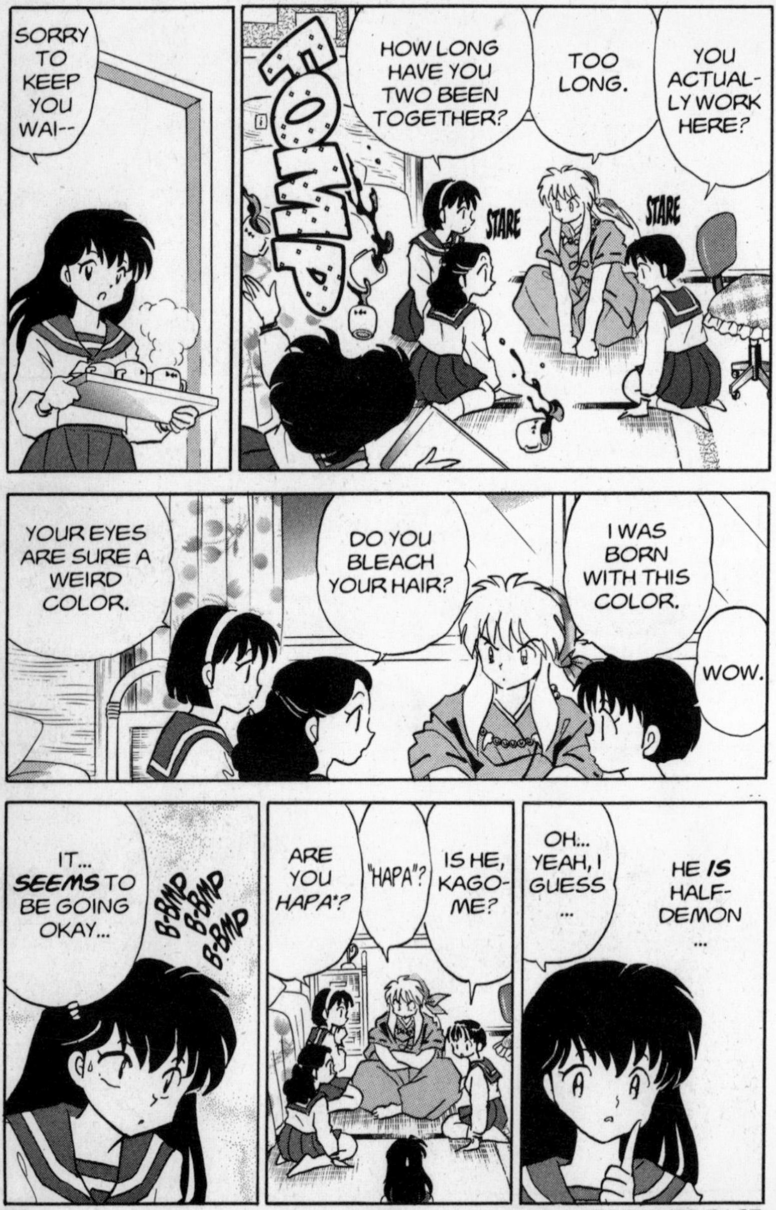
SORRY TO KEEP YOU WAI--
FOMP
HOW LONG HAVE YOU TWO BEEN TOGETHER?
TOO LONG.
YOU ACTUAL-LY WORK HERE?
STARE
STARE
YOUR EYES ARE SURE A WEIRD COLOR.
DO YOU BLEACH YOUR HAIR?
I WAS BORN WITH THIS COLOR.
WOW.
IT... *SEEMS* TO BE GOING OKAY...
B-BMP B-BMP B-BMP
ARE YOU HAPA*?
"HAPA"?
IS HE, KAGO-ME?
OH... YEAH, I GUESS ...
HE *IS* HALF-DEMON ...

*HAPA: HAWAIIAN TERM FOR MIXED RACE.

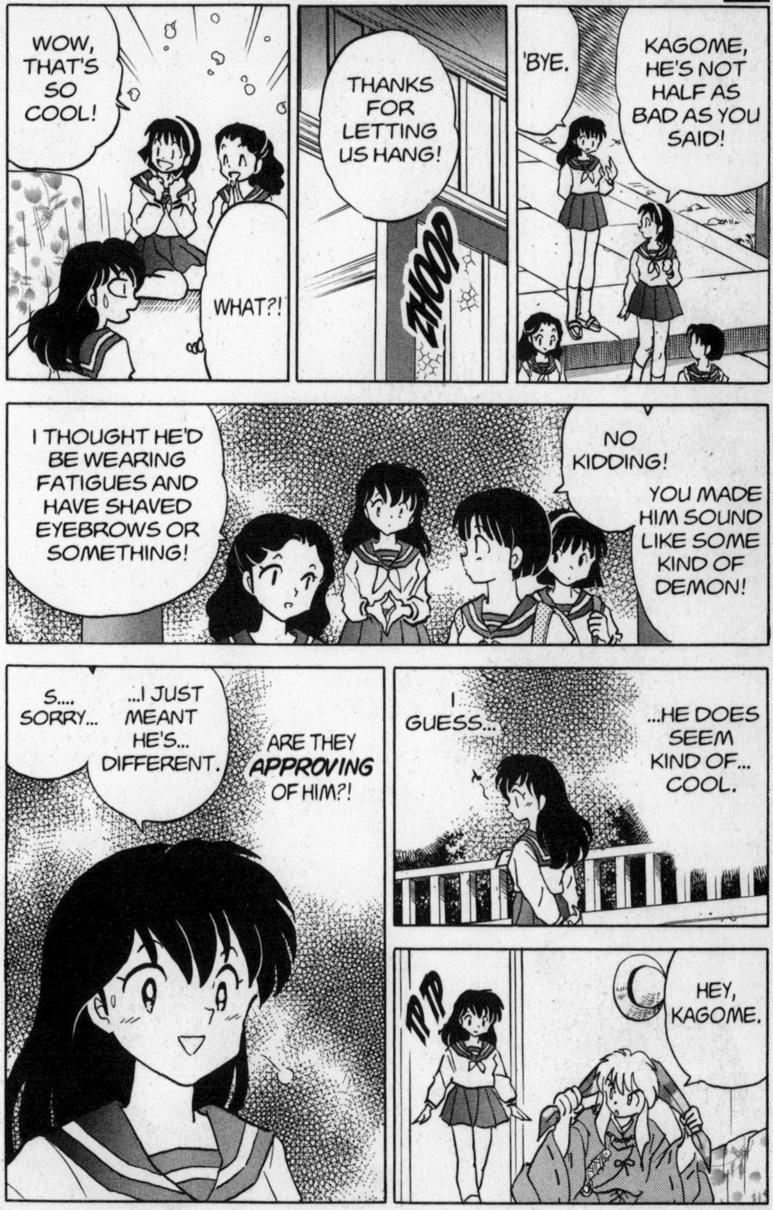
WOW, THAT'S SO COOL!
WHAT?!
THANKS FOR LETTING US HANG!
ZHOOP
'BYE.
KAGOME, HE'S NOT HALF AS BAD AS YOU SAID!
I THOUGHT HE'D BE WEARING FATIGUES AND HAVE SHAVED EYEBROWS OR SOMETHING!
NO KIDDING!
YOU MADE HIM SOUND LIKE SOME KIND OF DEMON!
S.... SORRY...
...I JUST MEANT HE'S... DIFFERENT.
ARE THEY APPROVING OF HIM?!
I GUESS...
...HE DOES SEEM KIND OF... COOL.
TP TP
HEY, KAGOME.

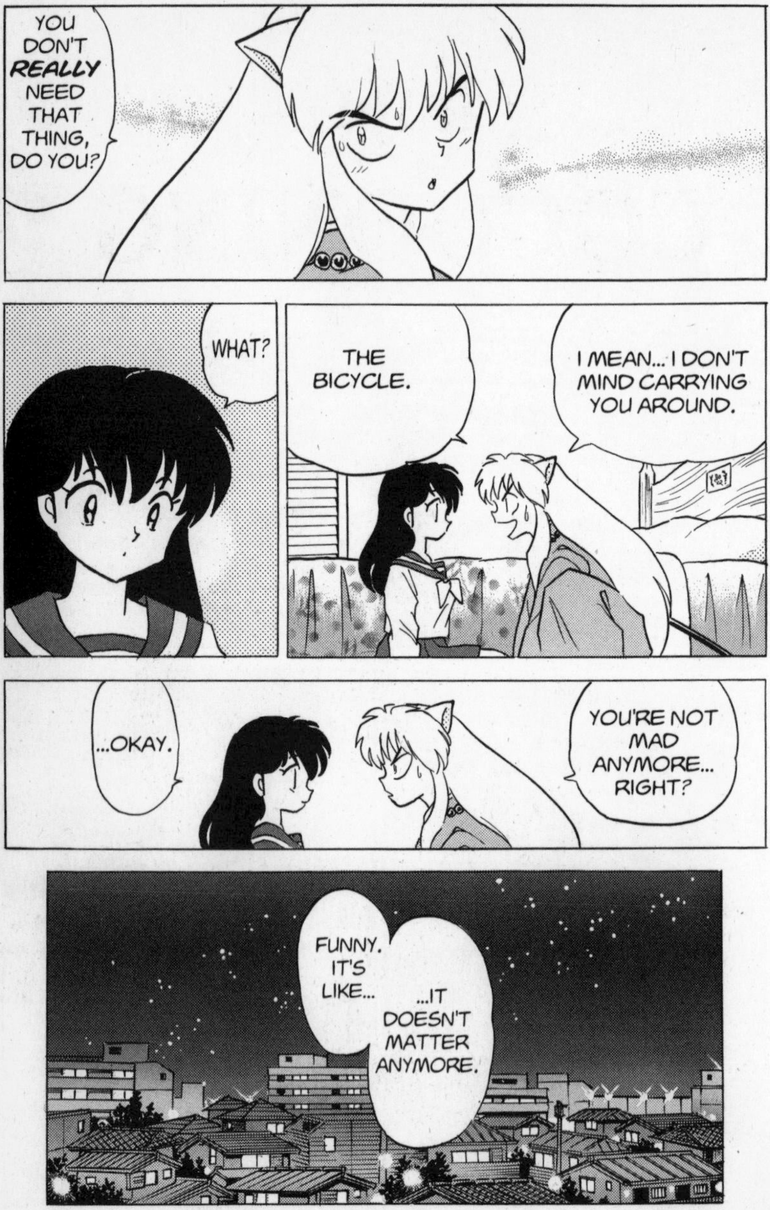
YOU DON'T **REALLY** NEED THAT THING, DO YOU?
WHAT?
THE BICYCLE.
I MEAN... I DON'T MIND CARRYING YOU AROUND.
...OKAY.
YOU'RE NOT MAD ANYMORE... RIGHT?
FUNNY. IT'S LIKE...
...IT DOESN'T MATTER ANYMORE.

SCROLL 5

COCOONING

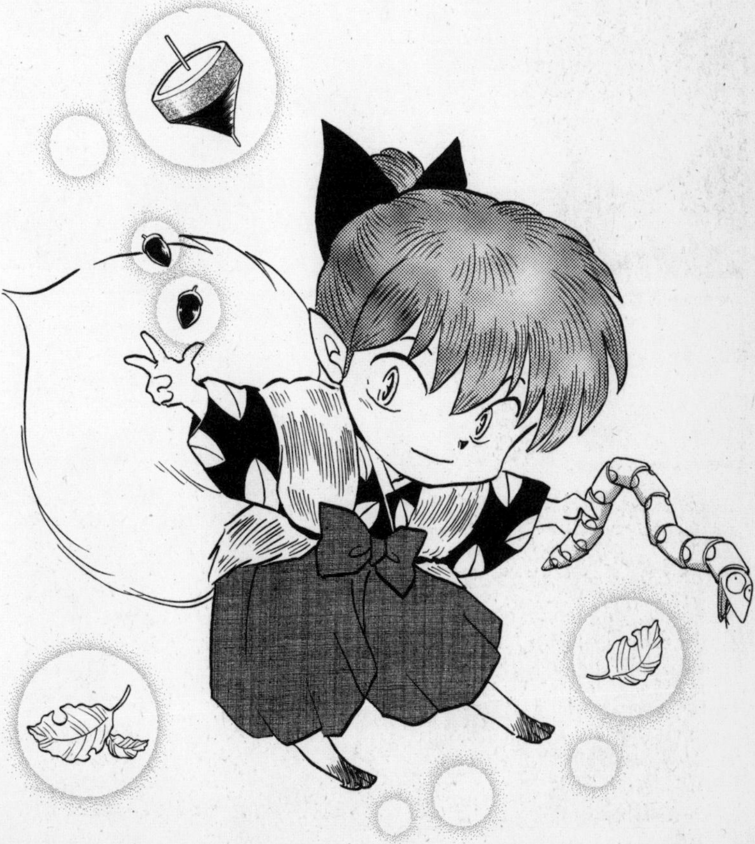

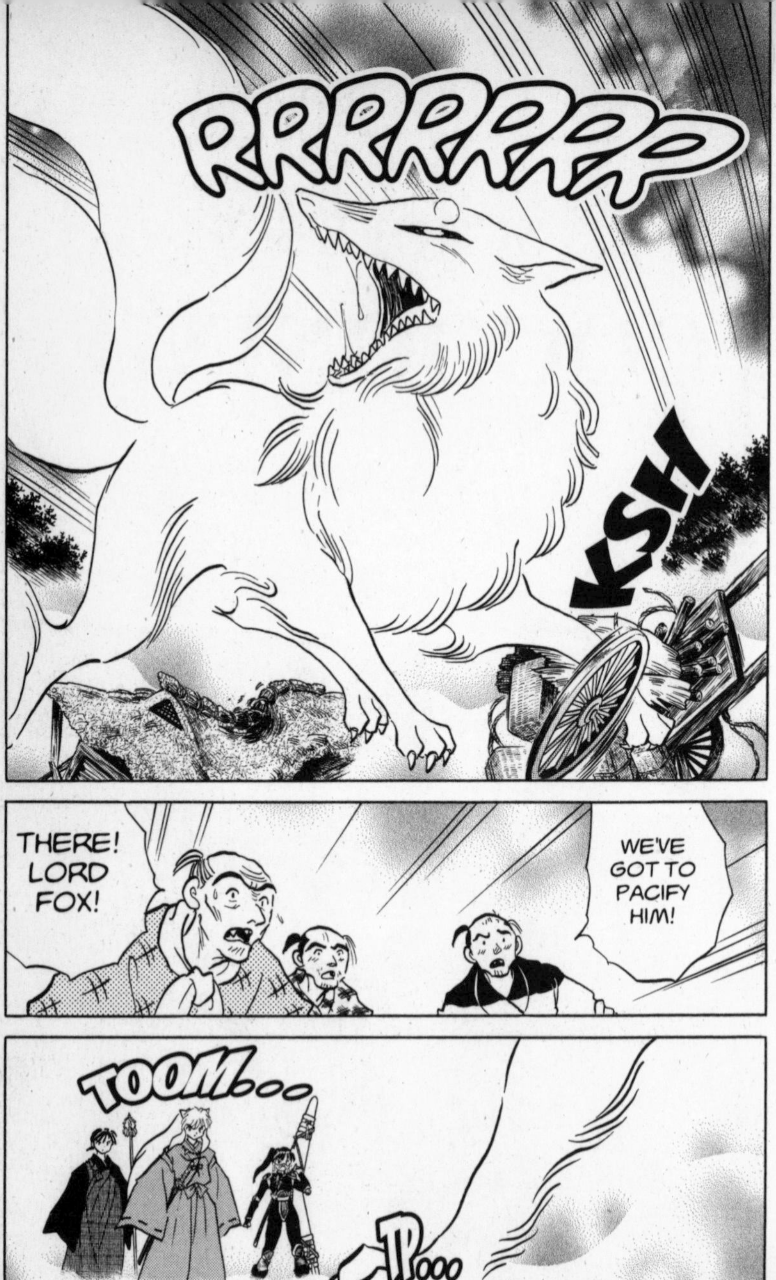
RRRRRRR
KSH
THERE! LORD FOX!
WE'VE GOT TO PACIFY HIM!
TOOM...
TP...

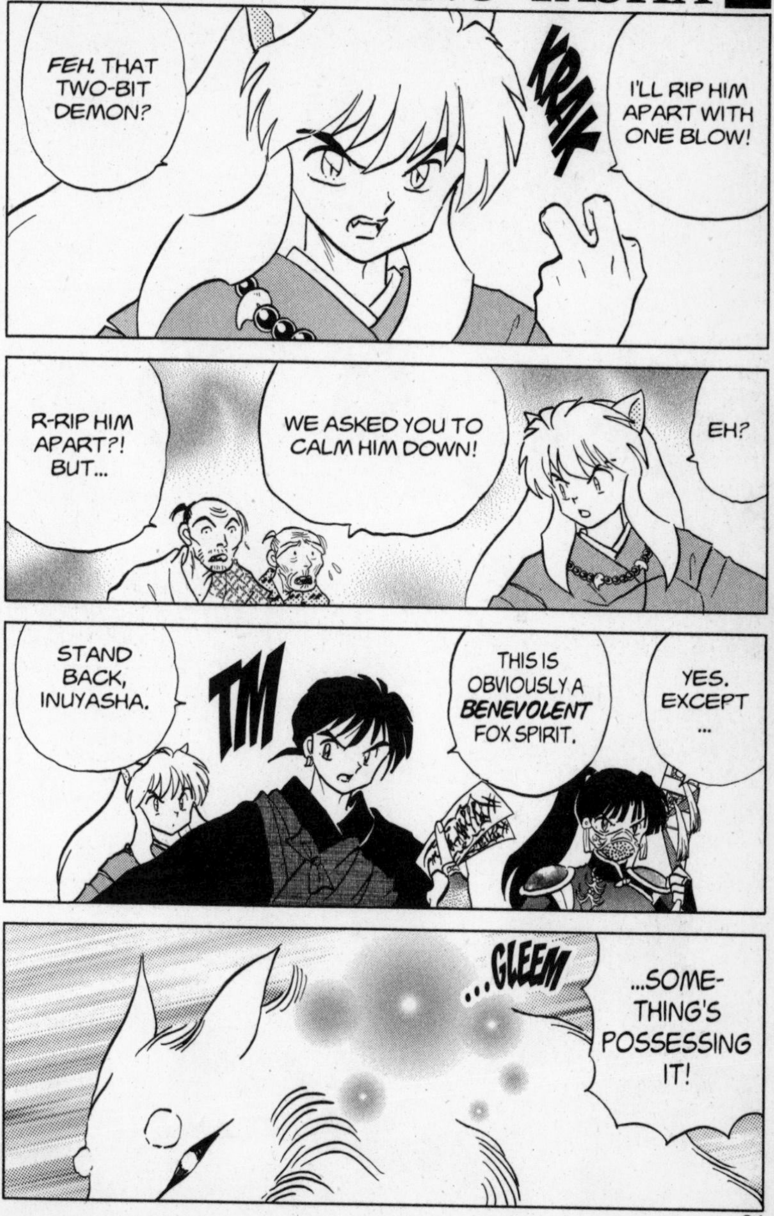
FEH. THAT TWO-BIT DEMON?
KRAK
I'LL RIP HIM APART WITH ONE BLOW!
R-RIP HIM APART?! BUT...
WE ASKED YOU TO CALM HIM DOWN!
EH?
STAND BACK, INUYASHA.
TM
THIS IS OBVIOUSLY A BENEVOLENT FOX SPIRIT.
YES. EXCEPT ...
...GLEEM
...SOME-THING'S POSSESSING IT!

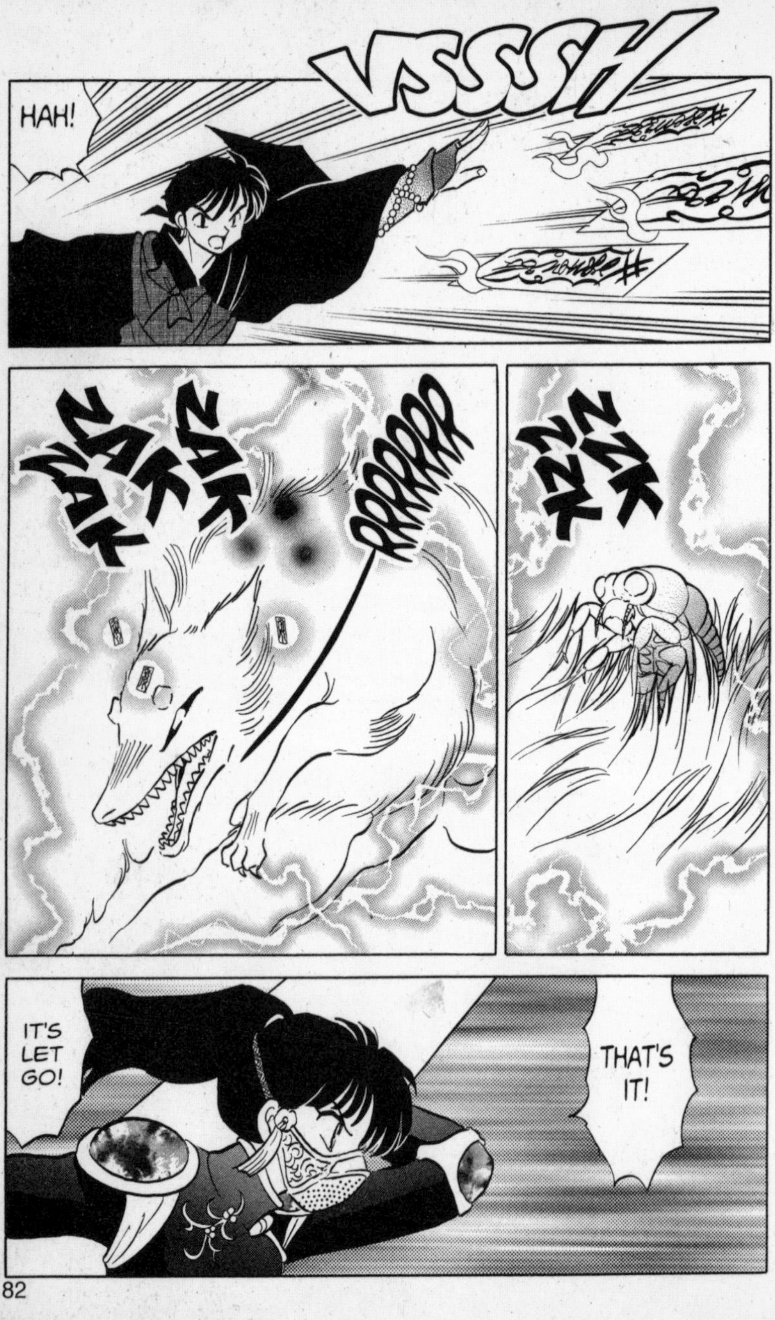
VSSSH
HAH!
ZAK ZAK ZAK
RRRRRRR
ZZK ZZK
IT'S LET GO!
THAT'S IT!

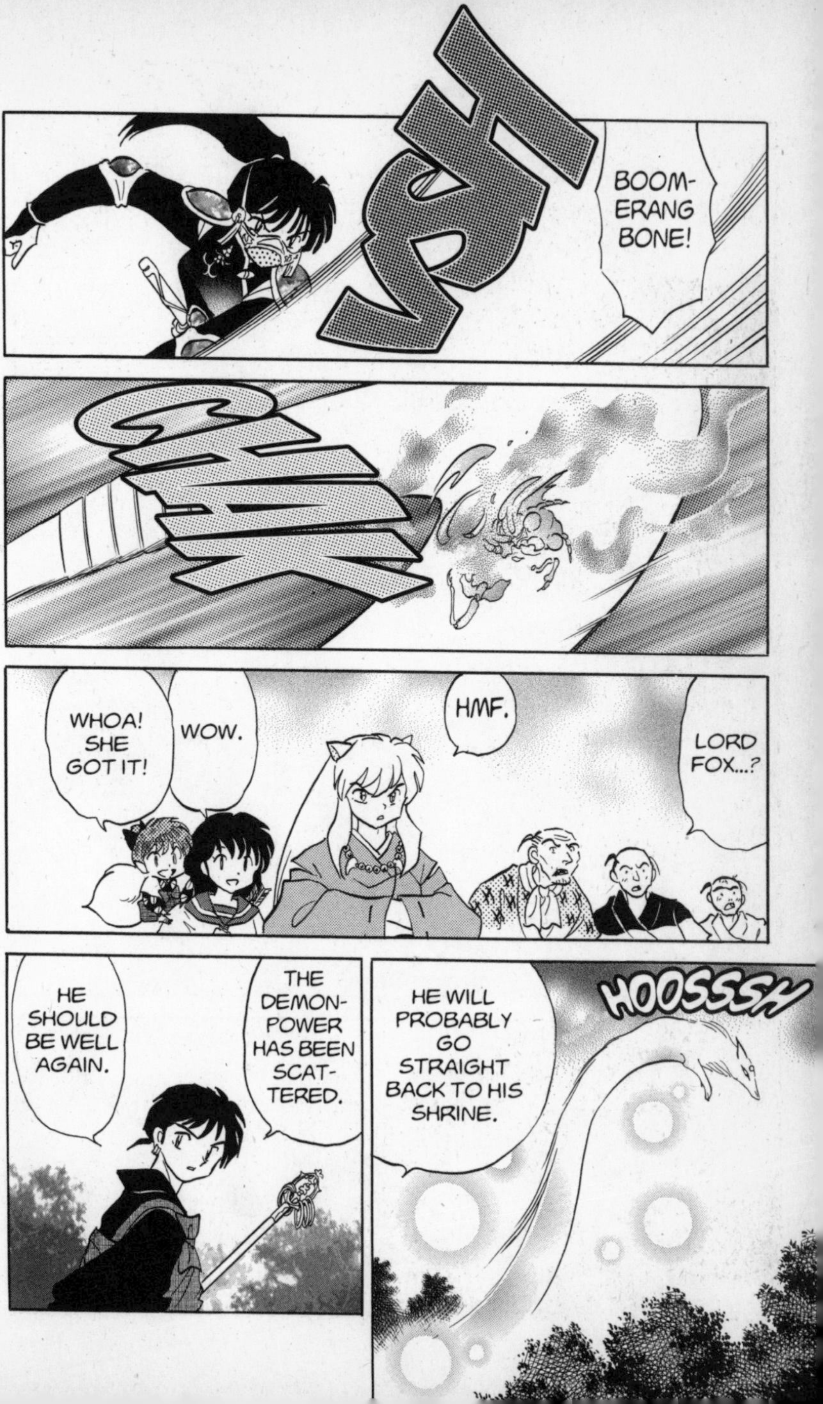
VSH
BOOM-ERANG BONE!
WHOA! SHE GOT IT!
WOW.
HMF.
LORD FOX...?
HE SHOULD BE WELL AGAIN.
THE DEMON-POWER HAS BEEN SCATTERED.
HE WILL PROBABLY GO STRAIGHT BACK TO HIS SHRINE.
HOOSSSH

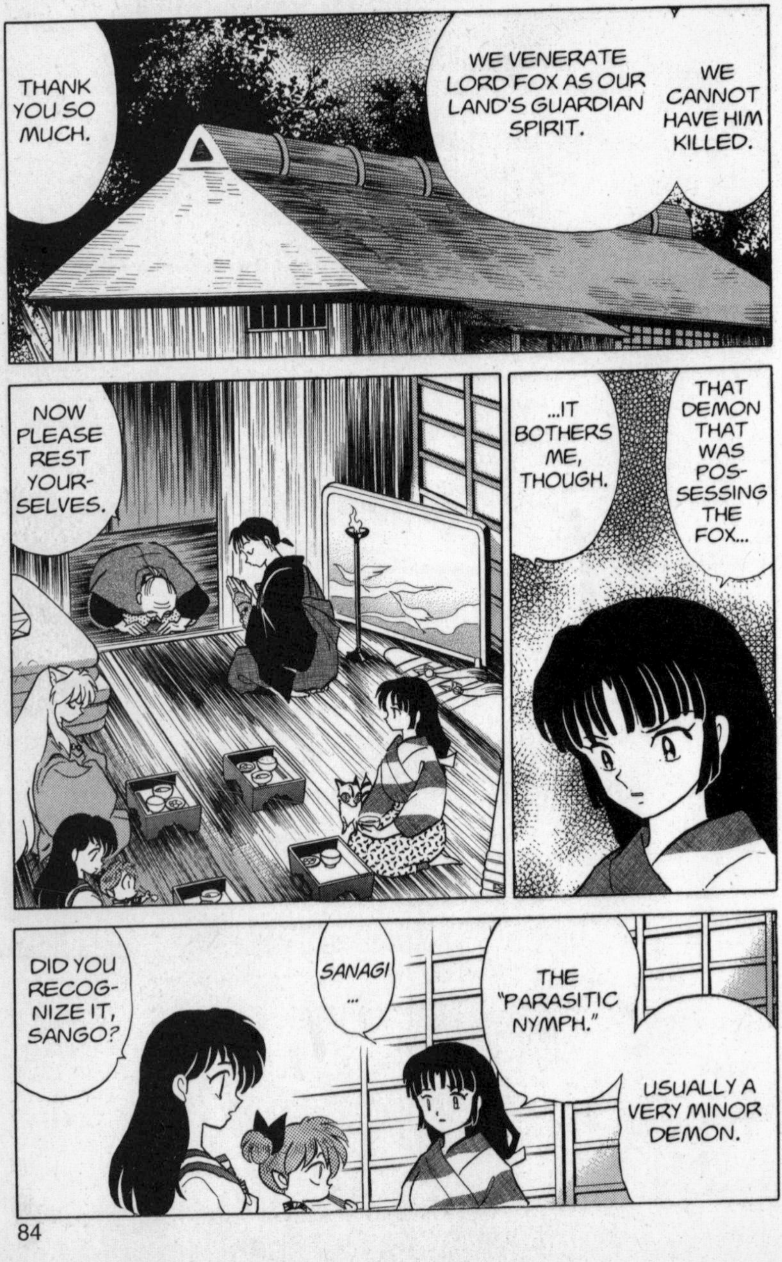
THANK YOU SO MUCH.
WE VENERATE LORD FOX AS OUR LAND'S GUARDIAN SPIRIT.
WE CANNOT HAVE HIM KILLED.
NOW PLEASE REST YOURSELVES.
...IT BOTHERS ME, THOUGH.
THAT DEMON THAT WAS POSSESSING THE FOX...
DID YOU RECOGNIZE IT, SANGO?
SANAGI ...
THE "PARASITIC NYMPH."
USUALLY A VERY MINOR DEMON.

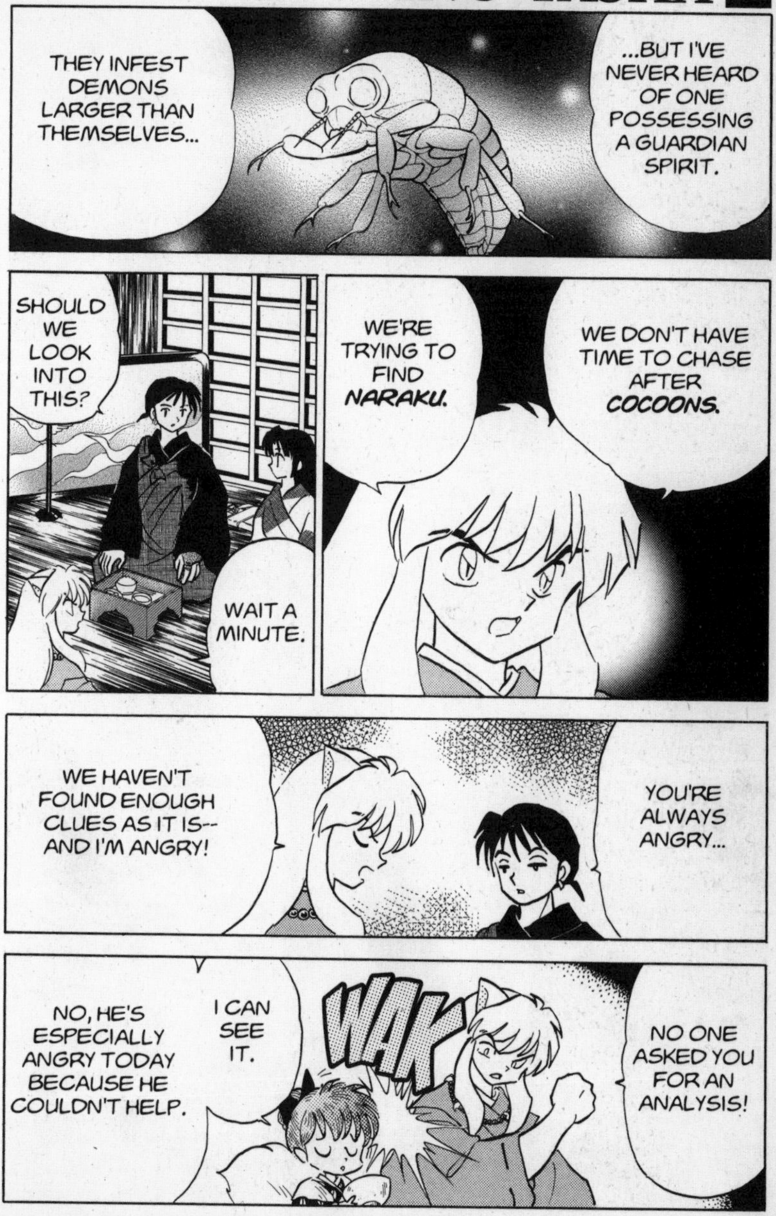
THEY INFEST DEMONS LARGER THAN THEMSELVES...
...BUT I'VE NEVER HEARD OF ONE POSSESSING A GUARDIAN SPIRIT.
SHOULD WE LOOK INTO THIS?
WAIT A MINUTE.
WE'RE TRYING TO FIND NARAKU.
WE DON'T HAVE TIME TO CHASE AFTER COCOONS.
WE HAVEN'T FOUND ENOUGH CLUES AS IT IS-- AND I'M ANGRY!
YOU'RE ALWAYS ANGRY...
NO, HE'S ESPECIALLY ANGRY TODAY BECAUSE HE COULDN'T HELP.
I CAN SEE IT.
WAK
NO ONE ASKED YOU FOR AN ANALYSIS!

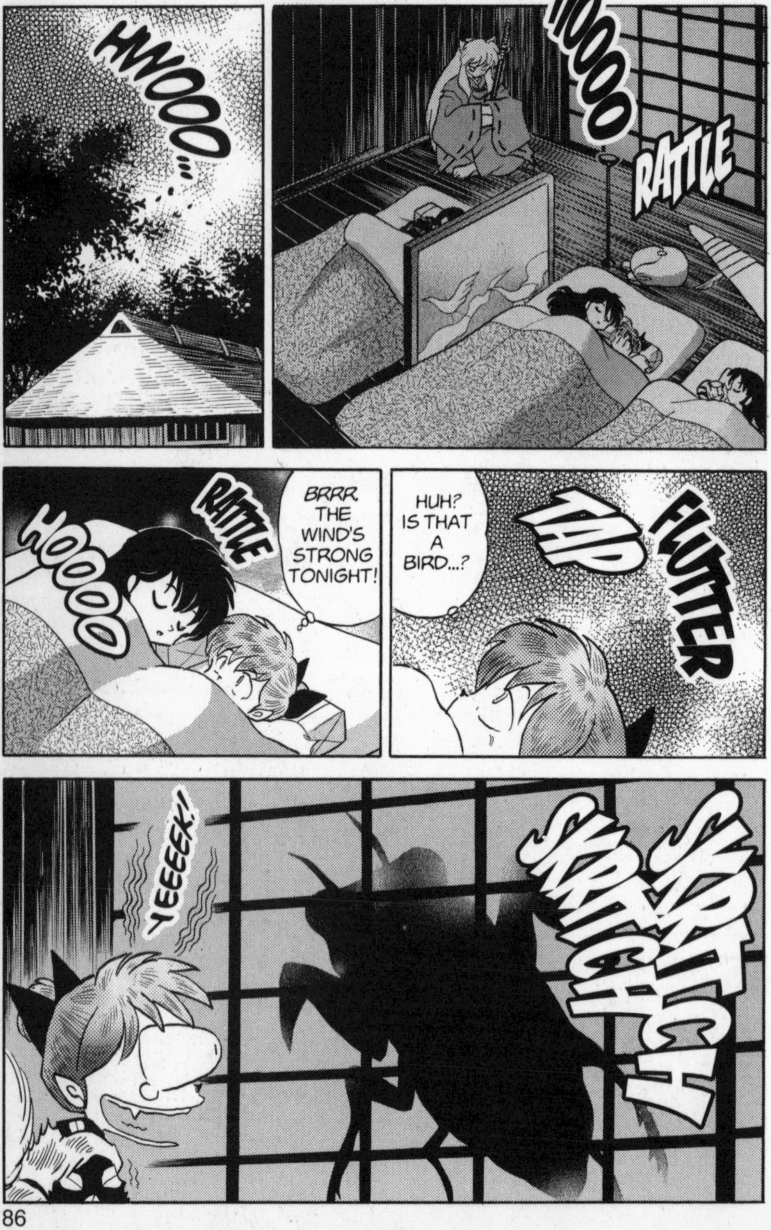
HWOOO...
HOOOO
RATTLE
RATTLE
HOOOO
BRRR. THE WIND'S STRONG TONIGHT!
HUH? IS THAT A BIRD...?
TAP
FLUTTER
YEEEEK!
SKRITCH
SKRITCH!

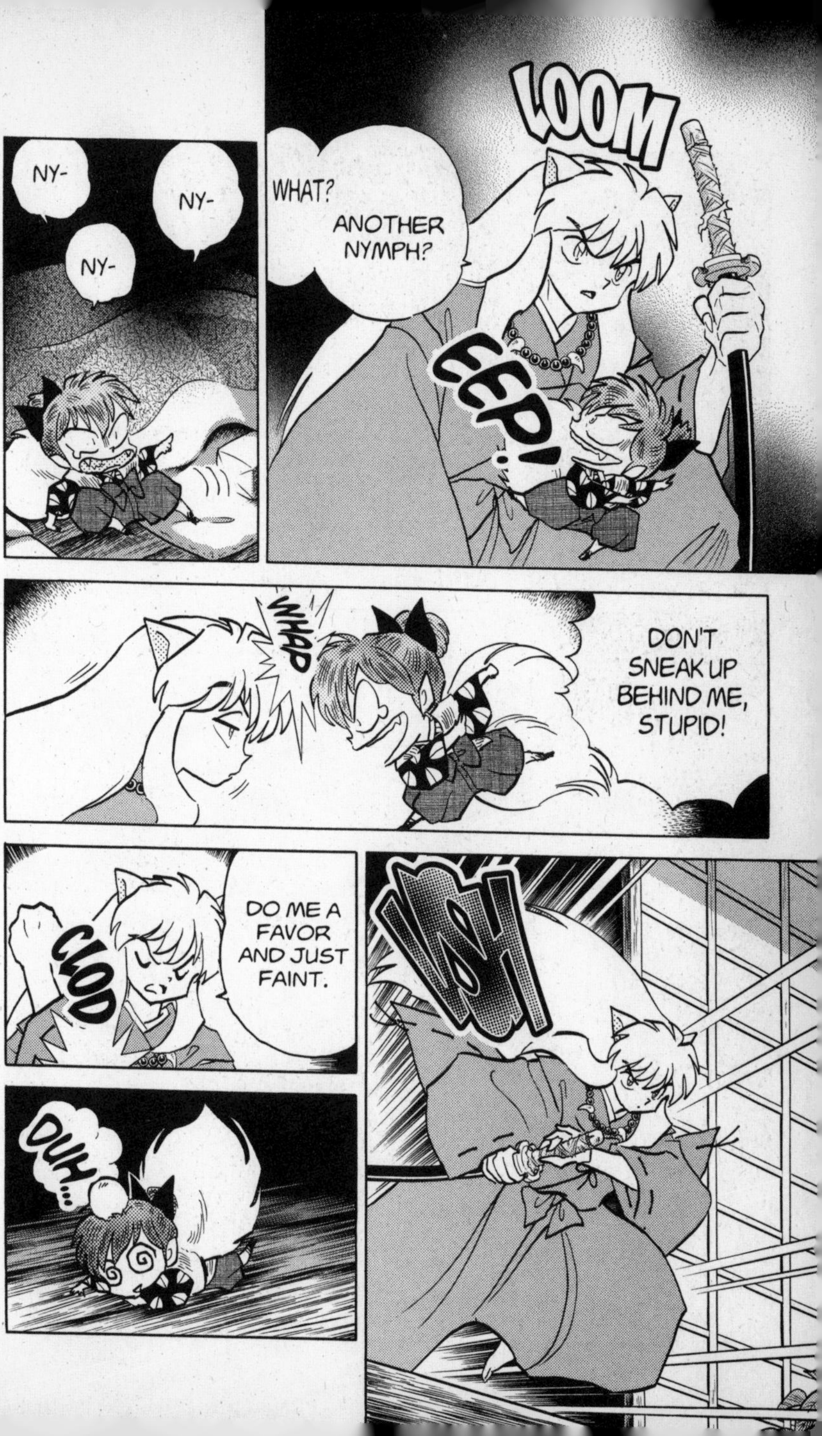
NY-
NY-
NY-
LOOM
WHAT?
ANOTHER NYMPH?
EEP!
WHAP
DON'T SNEAK UP BEHIND ME, STUPID!
CLOD
DO ME A FAVOR AND JUST FAINT.
DUH...
VSH

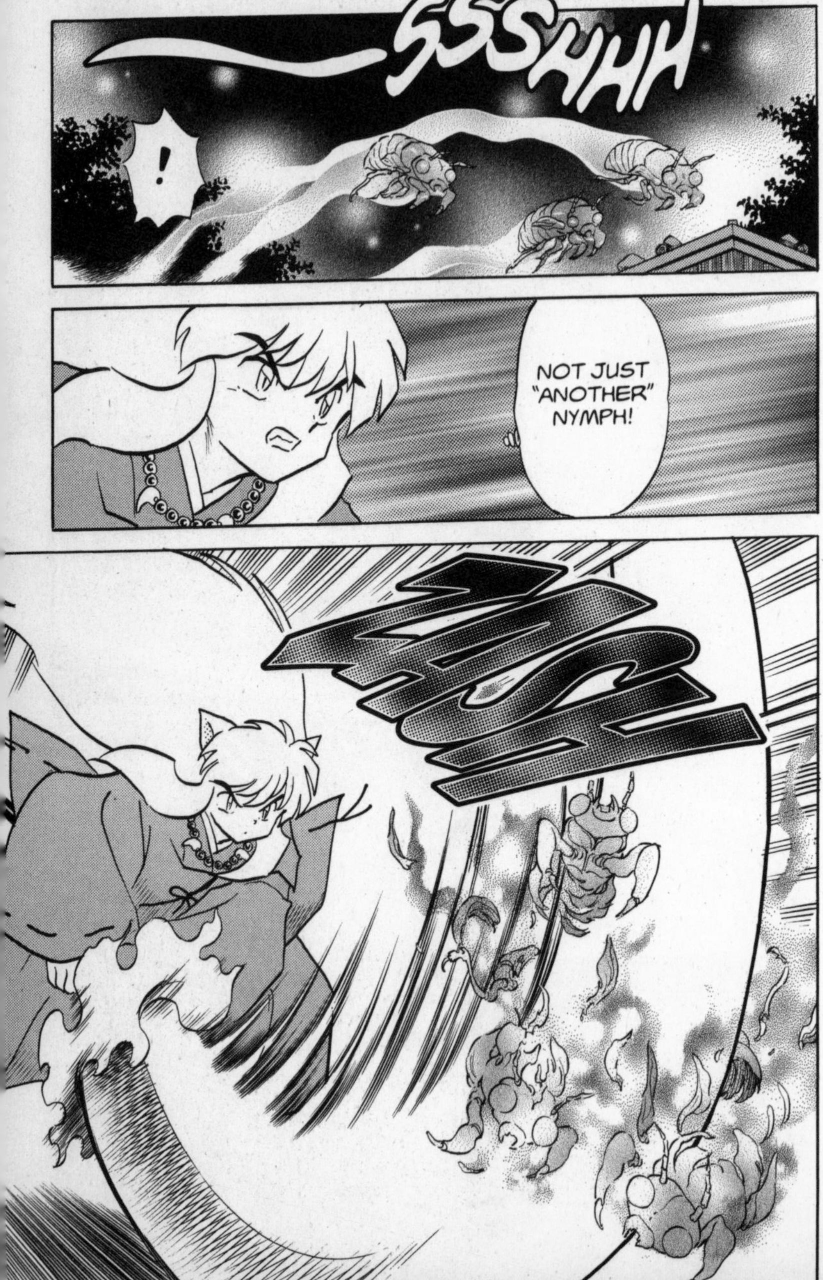
SSSHHH
!
NOT JUST "ANOTHER" NYMPH!
ZASH

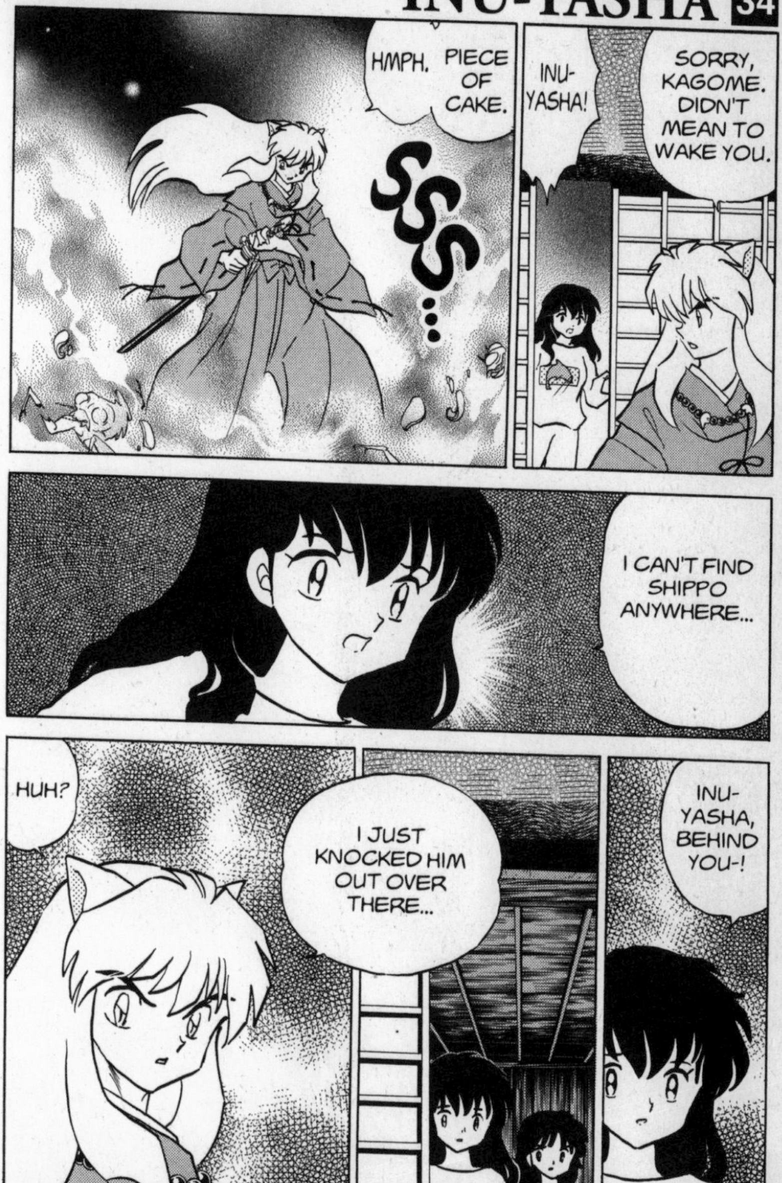
HMPH.
PIECE OF CAKE.
SSS...
INU-YASHA!
SORRY, KAGOME. DIDN'T MEAN TO WAKE YOU.
I CAN'T FIND SHIPPO ANYWHERE...
HUH?
I JUST KNOCKED HIM OUT OVER THERE...
INU-YASHA, BEHIND YOU-!

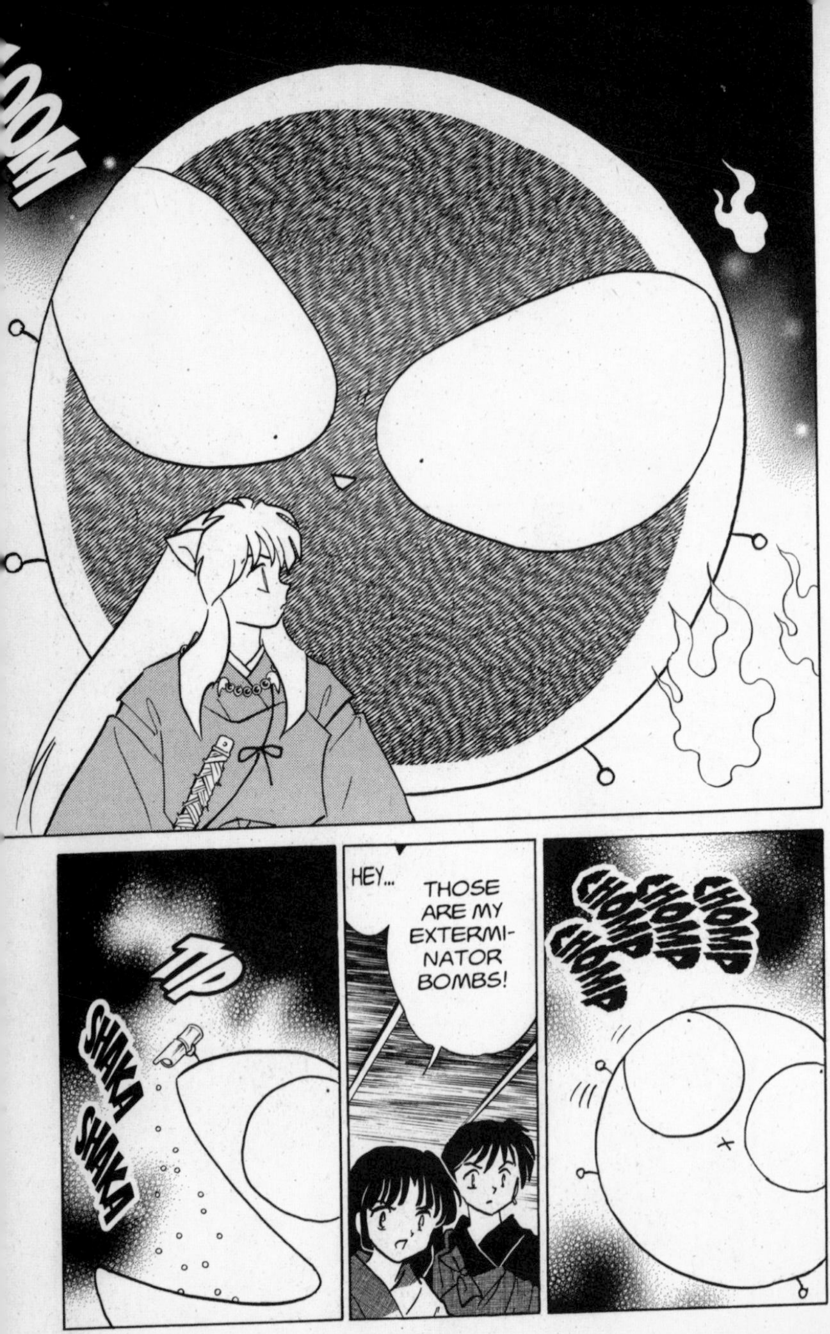
OOM
CHOMP CHOMP CHOMP CHOMP
HEY...
THOSE ARE MY EXTERMINATOR BOMBS!
TIP
SHAKA SHAKA SHAKA

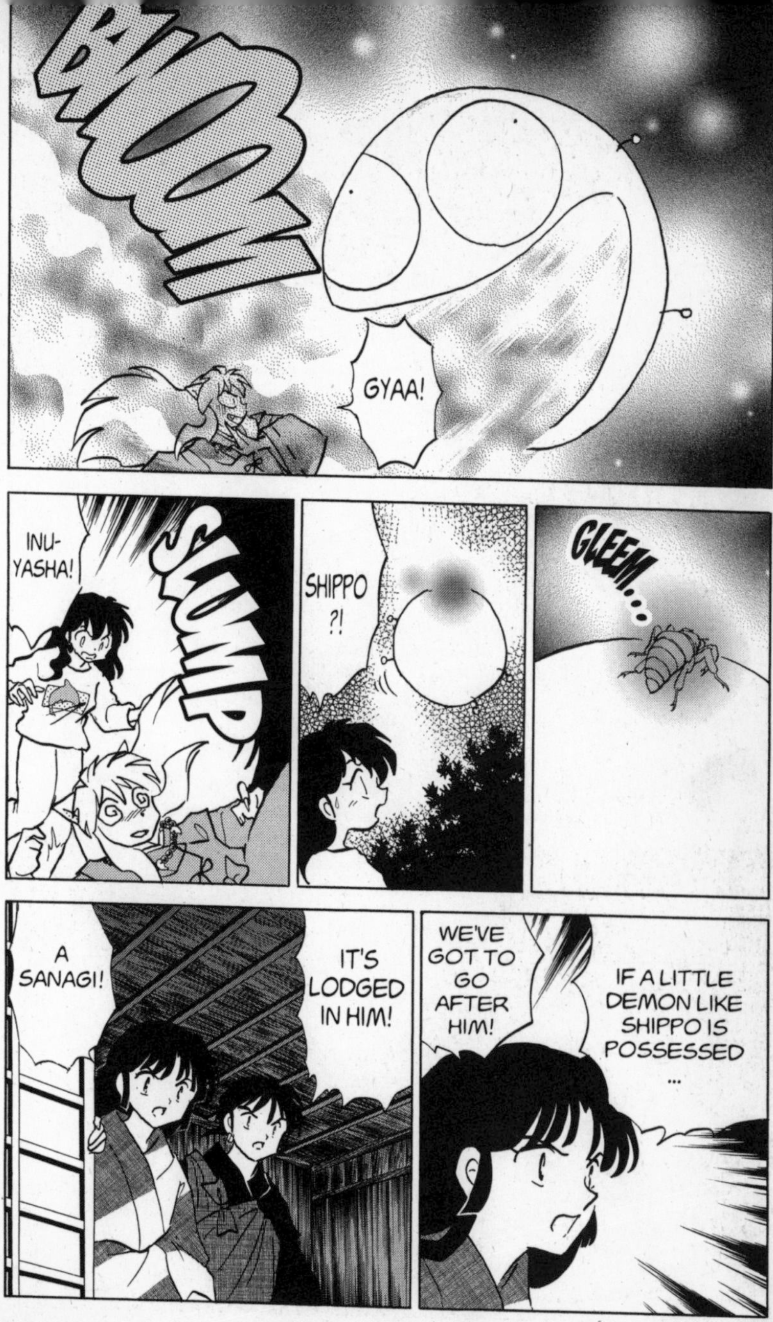
BAOOOM
GYAA!
INU-YASHA!
SLUMP
SHIPPO ?!
GLEEM...
A SANAGI!
IT'S LODGED IN HIM!
WE'VE GOT TO GO AFTER HIM!
IF A LITTLE DEMON LIKE SHIPPO IS POSSESSED ...

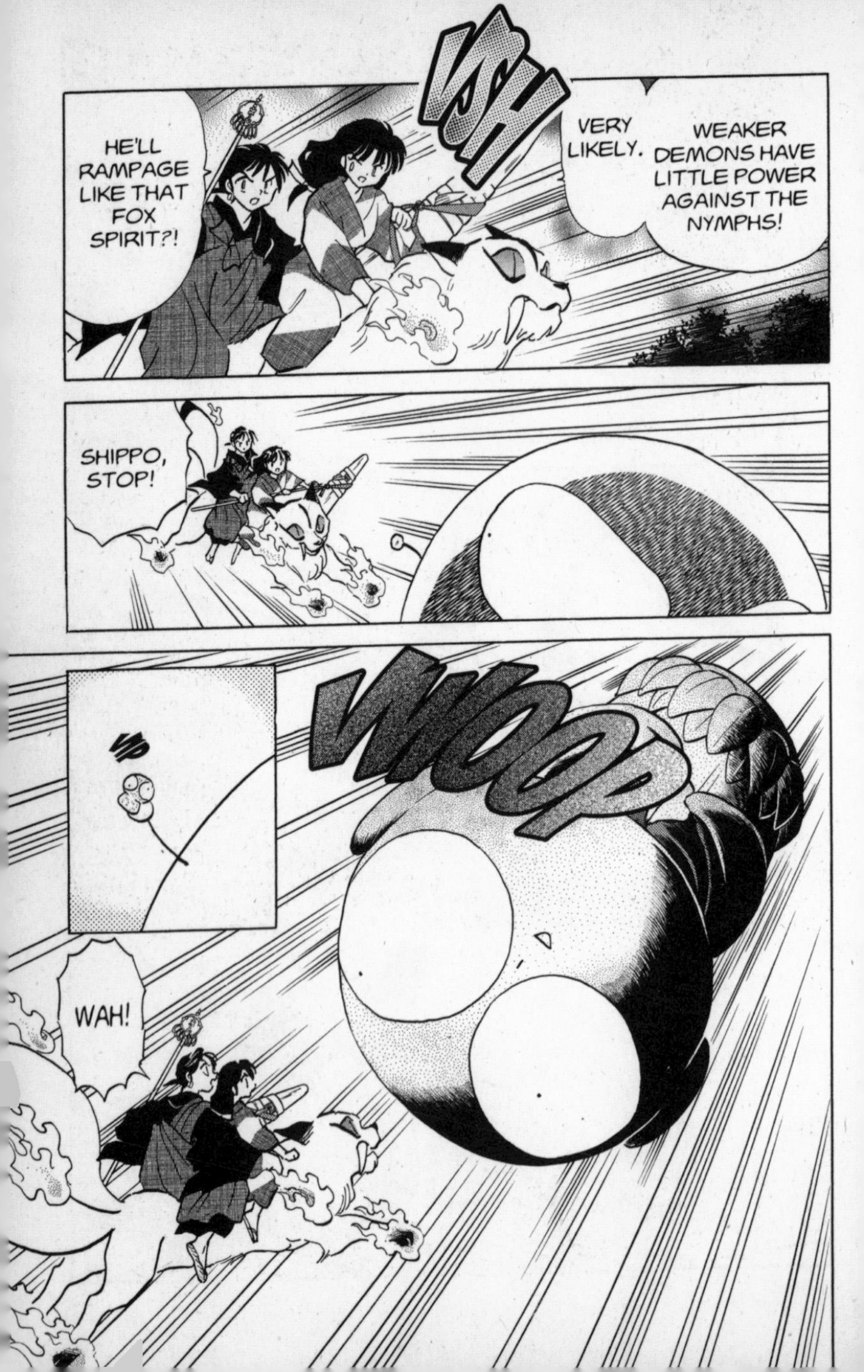
HE'LL RAMPAGE LIKE THAT FOX SPIRIT?!
VSH
VERY LIKELY.
WEAKER DEMONS HAVE LITTLE POWER AGAINST THE NYMPHS!
SHIPPO, STOP!
WHOOP
WAH!

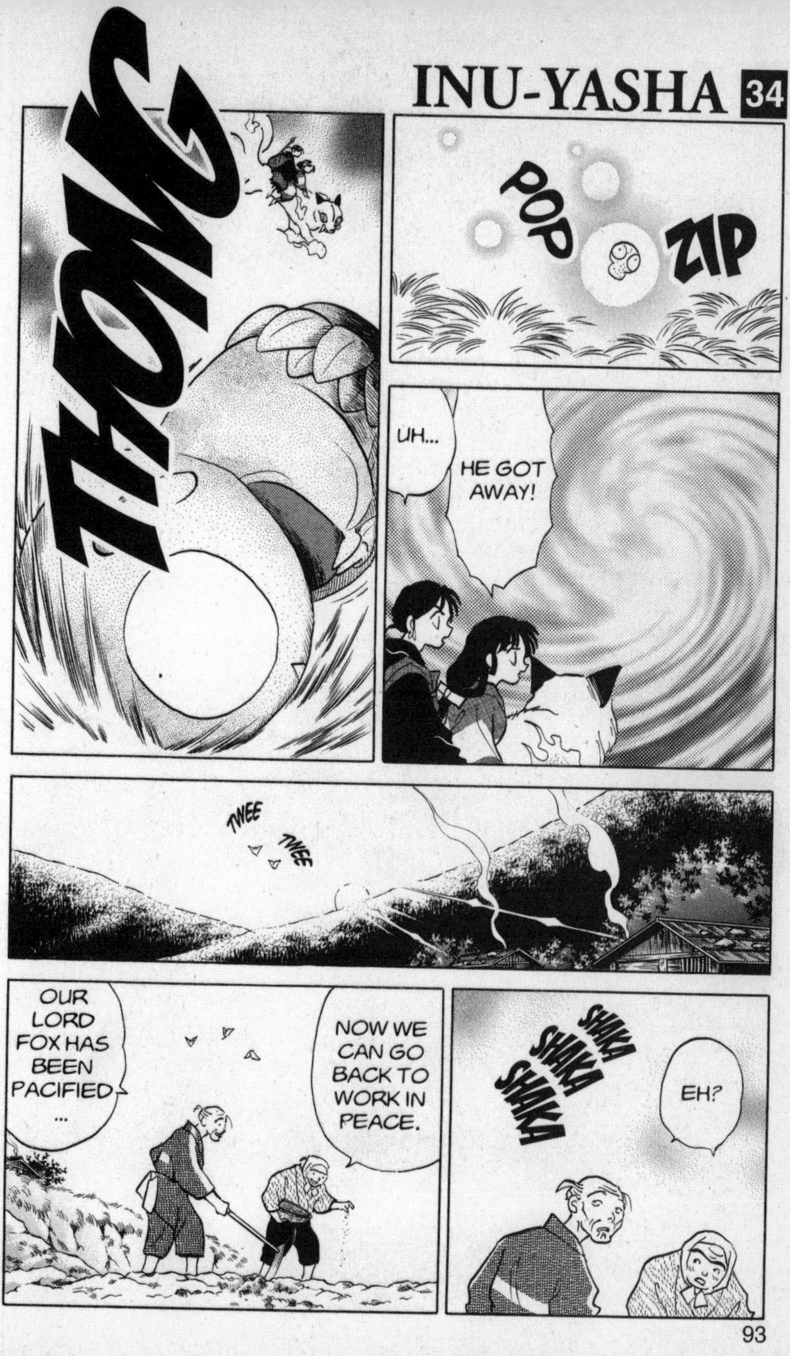
THONG
POP
ZIP
UH...
HE GOT AWAY!
TWEE
TWEE
OUR LORD FOX HAS BEEN PACIFIED...
NOW WE CAN GO BACK TO WORK IN PEACE.
SHAKA SHAKA SHAKA
EH?

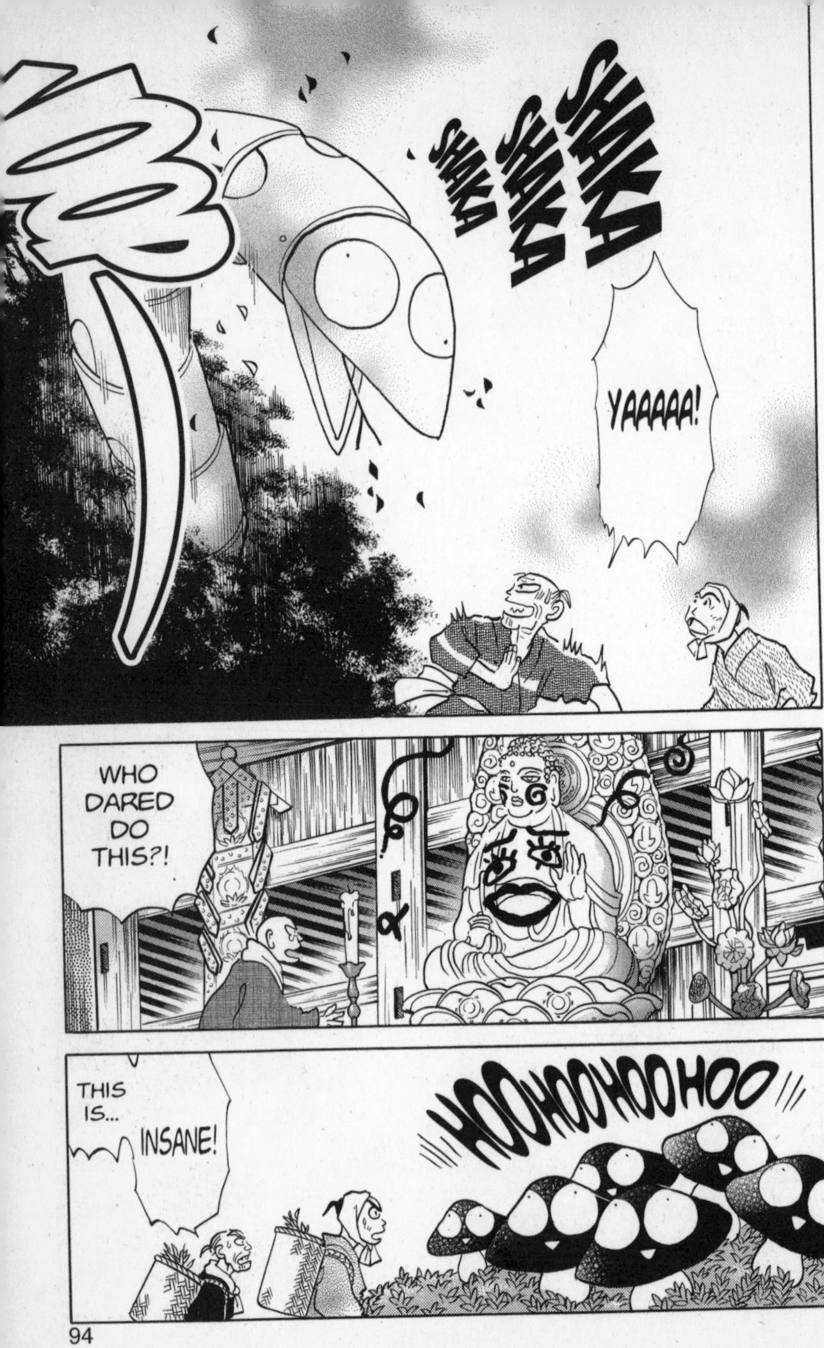
SHAKA SHAKA SHAKA
YAAAAA!
WHO DARED DO THIS?!
THIS IS... INSANE!
HOOHOOHOOHOO

VOOSH

THERE HE IS!

SHIPPO!

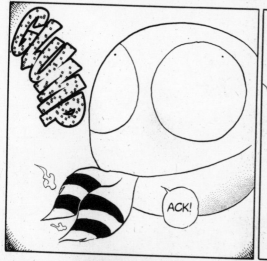

GLUMP

ACK!

A STICKY RICE TRAP!

GUORB

MIROKU AND SANGO HAVE SURE BEEN GONE A LONG TIME...

YAMMER YAMMER YAMMER

HUH?

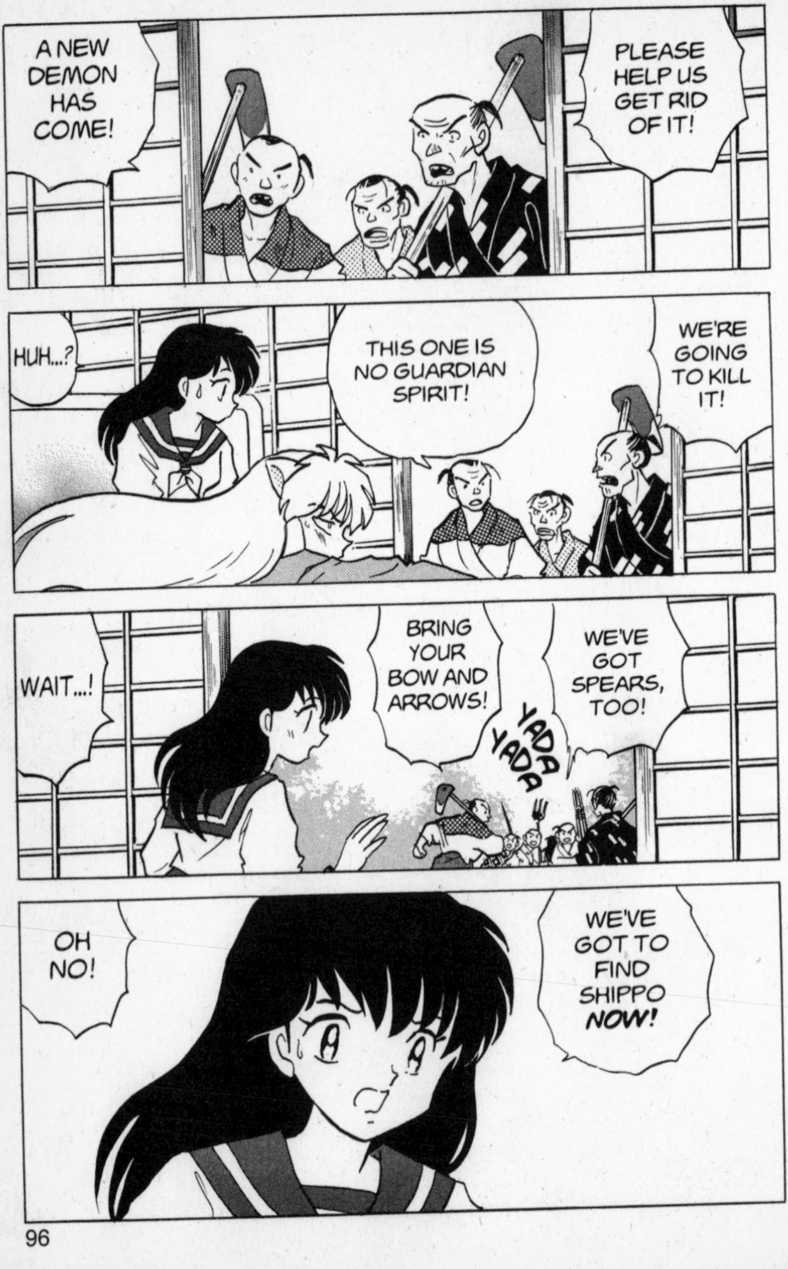
A NEW DEMON HAS COME!
PLEASE HELP US GET RID OF IT!
HUH...?
THIS ONE IS NO GUARDIAN SPIRIT!
WE'RE GOING TO KILL IT!
WAIT...!
BRING YOUR BOW AND ARROWS!
YADA YADA
WE'VE GOT SPEARS, TOO!
OH NO!
WE'VE GOT TO FIND SHIPPO *NOW!*

SCROLL 6

THE PERFECT HOST

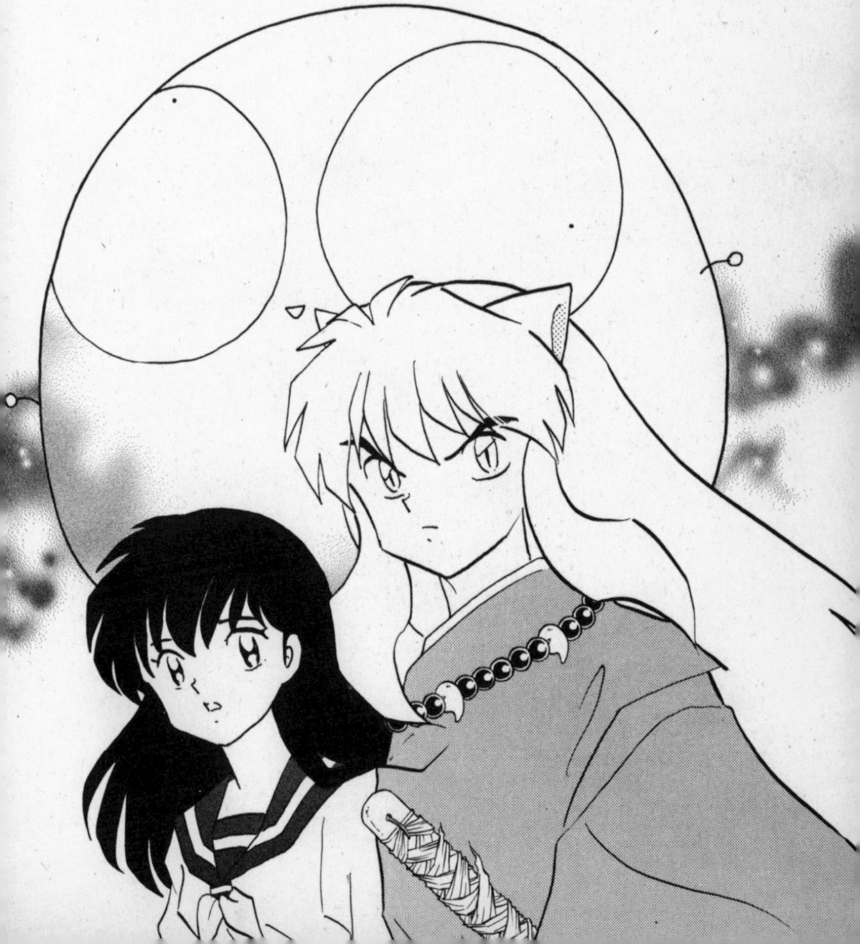

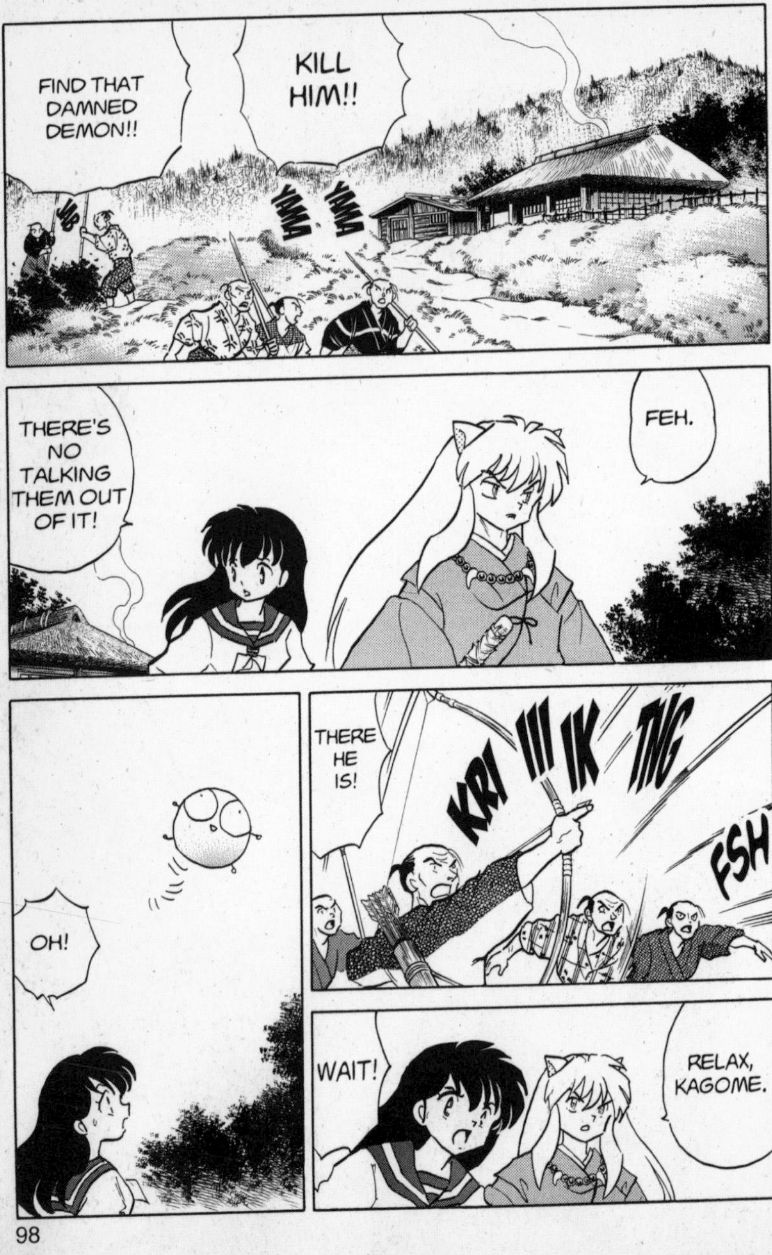
FIND THAT DAMNED DEMON!!
KILL HIM!!
THERE'S NO TALKING THEM OUT OF IT!
FEH.
OH!
THERE HE IS!
KRIIIIK
TNG
FSH
WAIT!
RELAX, KAGOME.

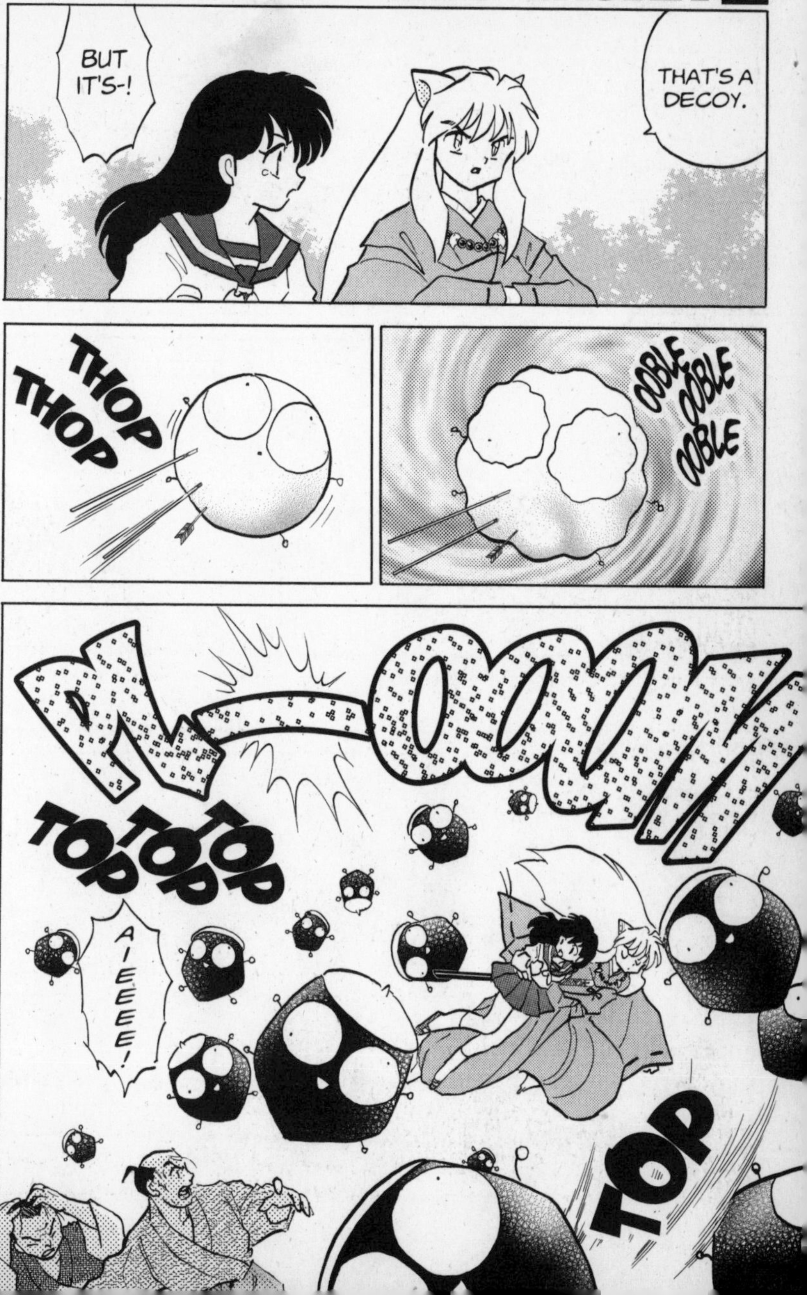
BUT IT'S-!
THAT'S A DECOY.
THOP THOP
OOBLE OOBLE OOBLE
TOP TOP TOP
AIEEEEE!
TOP

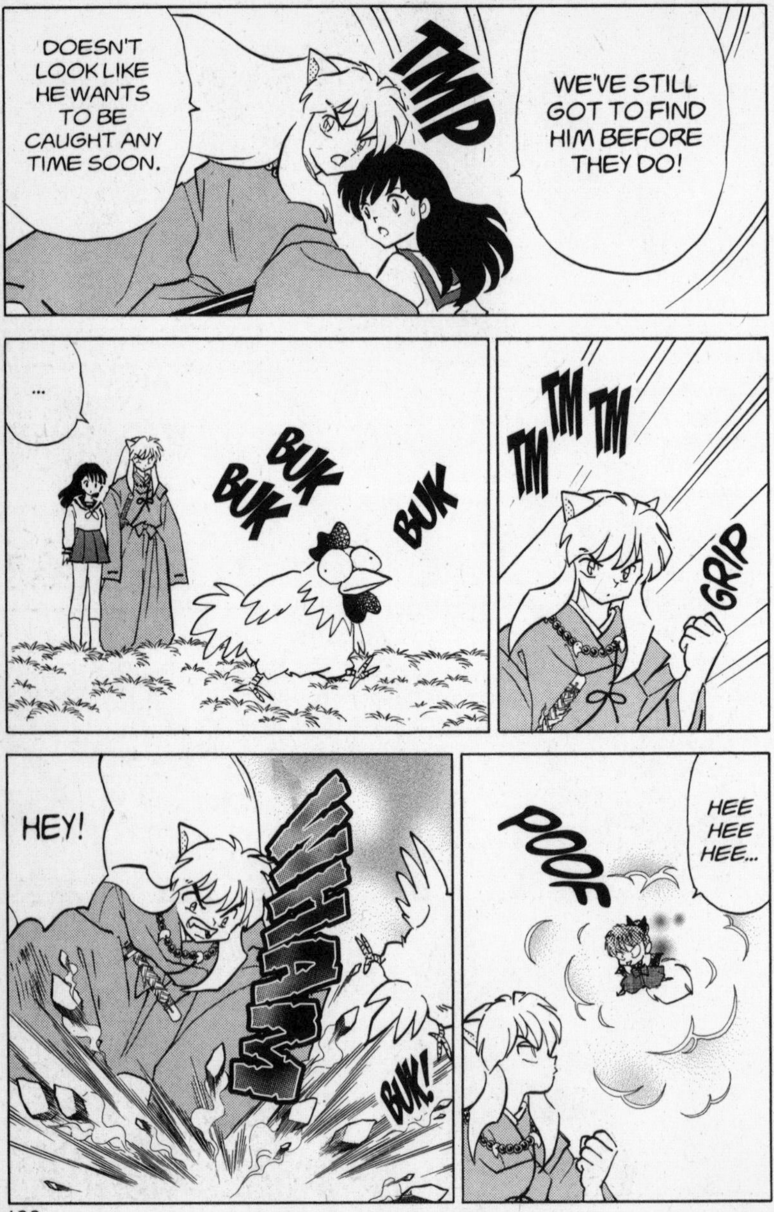
DOESN'T LOOK LIKE HE WANTS TO BE CAUGHT ANY TIME SOON.
TMP
WE'VE STILL GOT TO FIND HIM BEFORE THEY DO!
...
BUK BUK
BUK
TM TM TM
GRIP
HEY!
WHAM
BUK!
POOF
HEE HEE HEE...

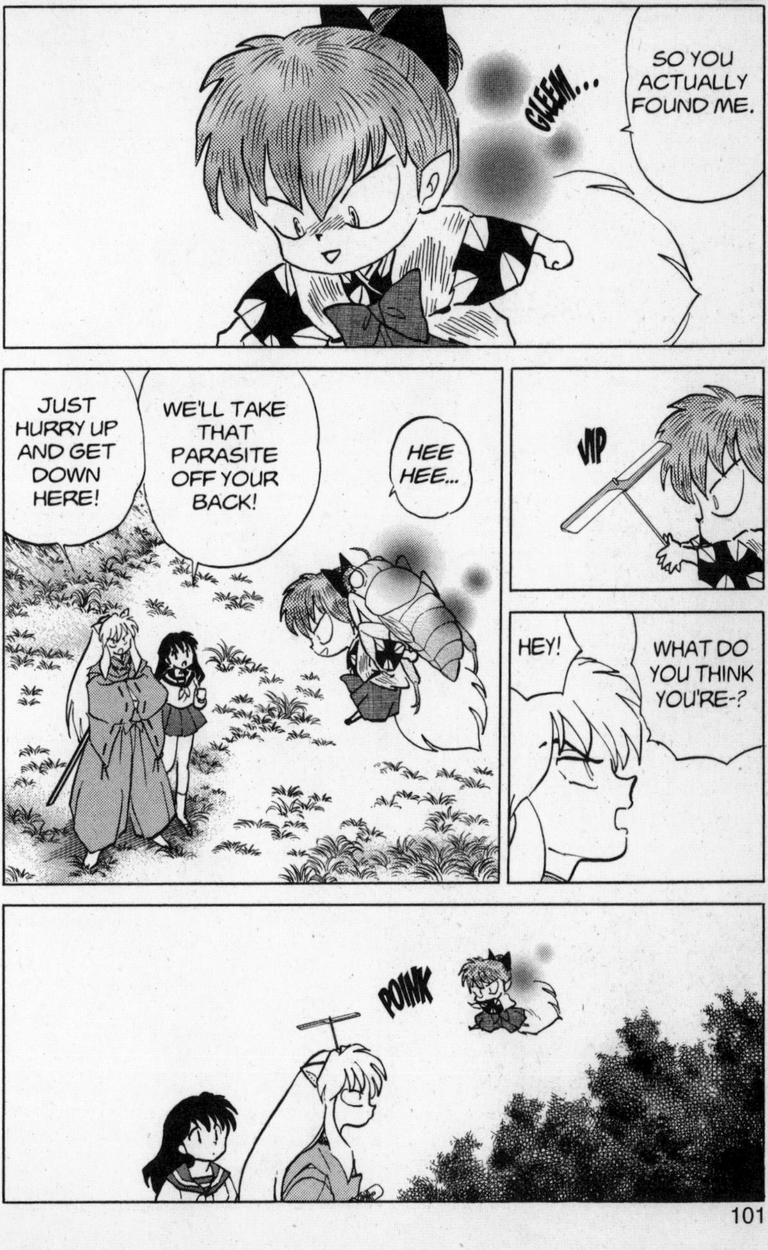
GLEEM...
SO YOU ACTUALLY FOUND ME.
JUST HURRY UP AND GET DOWN HERE!
WE'LL TAKE THAT PARASITE OFF YOUR BACK!
HEE HEE...
VIP
HEY!
WHAT DO YOU THINK YOU'RE-?
POINK

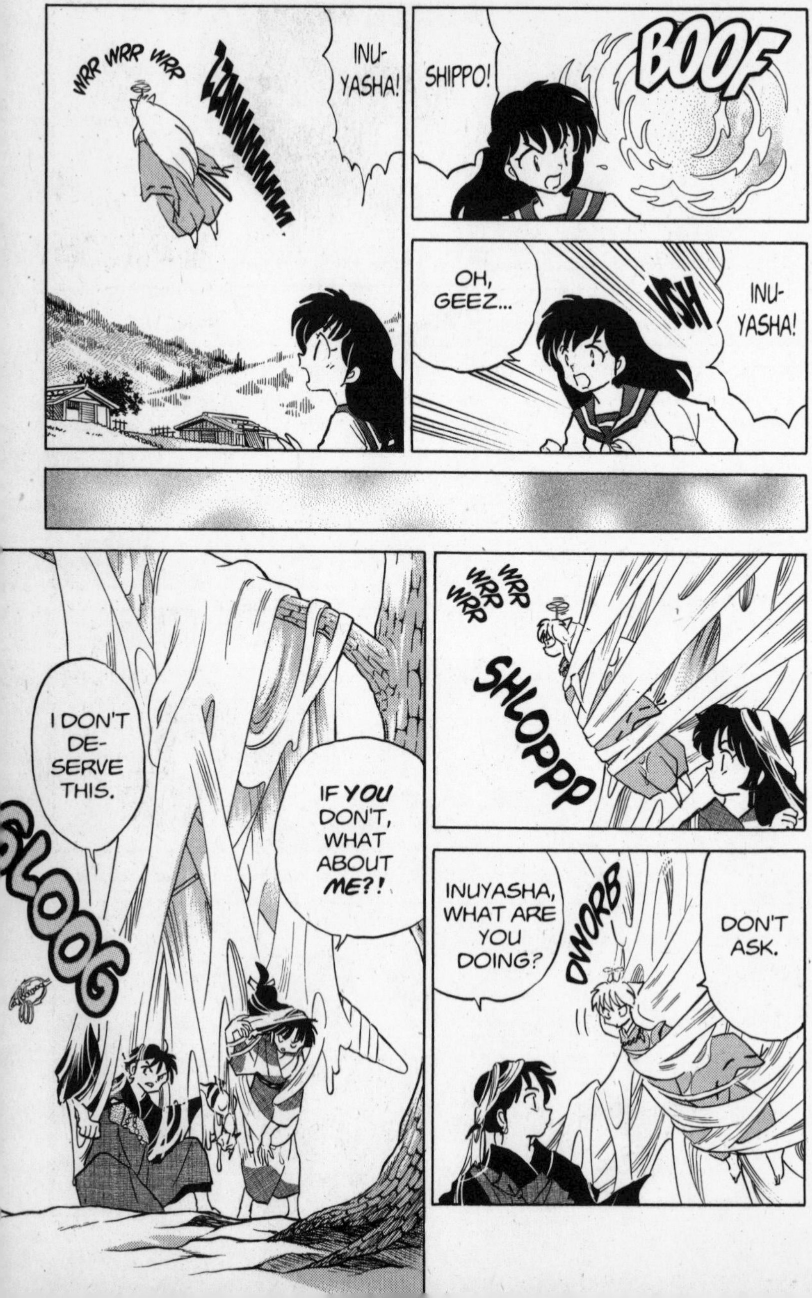
WRR WRR WRR
ZZMMMMMMM
INU-YASHA!
SHIPPO!
BOOF
OH, GEEZ...
VSH
INU-YASHA!
I DON'T DE-SERVE THIS.
IF YOU DON'T, WHAT ABOUT ME?!
GLOOG
WRR WRR WRR
SHLOPPP
INUYASHA, WHAT ARE YOU DOING?
DWORB
DON'T ASK.

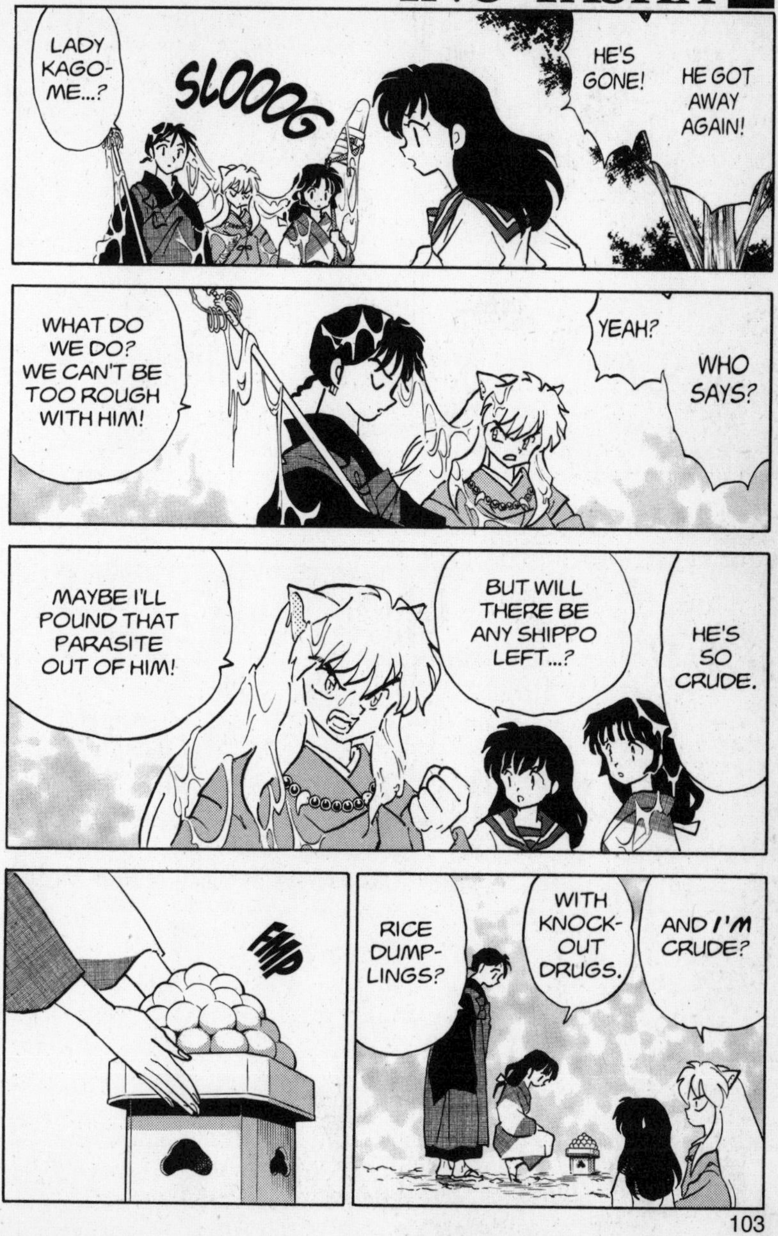
LADY KAGO-ME...?
SLOOOG
HE'S GONE!
HE GOT AWAY AGAIN!
WHAT DO WE DO? WE CAN'T BE TOO ROUGH WITH HIM!
YEAH?
WHO SAYS?
MAYBE I'LL POUND THAT PARASITE OUT OF HIM!
BUT WILL THERE BE ANY SHIPPO LEFT...?
HE'S SO CRUDE.
FMP
RICE DUMP-LINGS?
WITH KNOCK-OUT DRUGS.
AND *I'M* CRUDE?

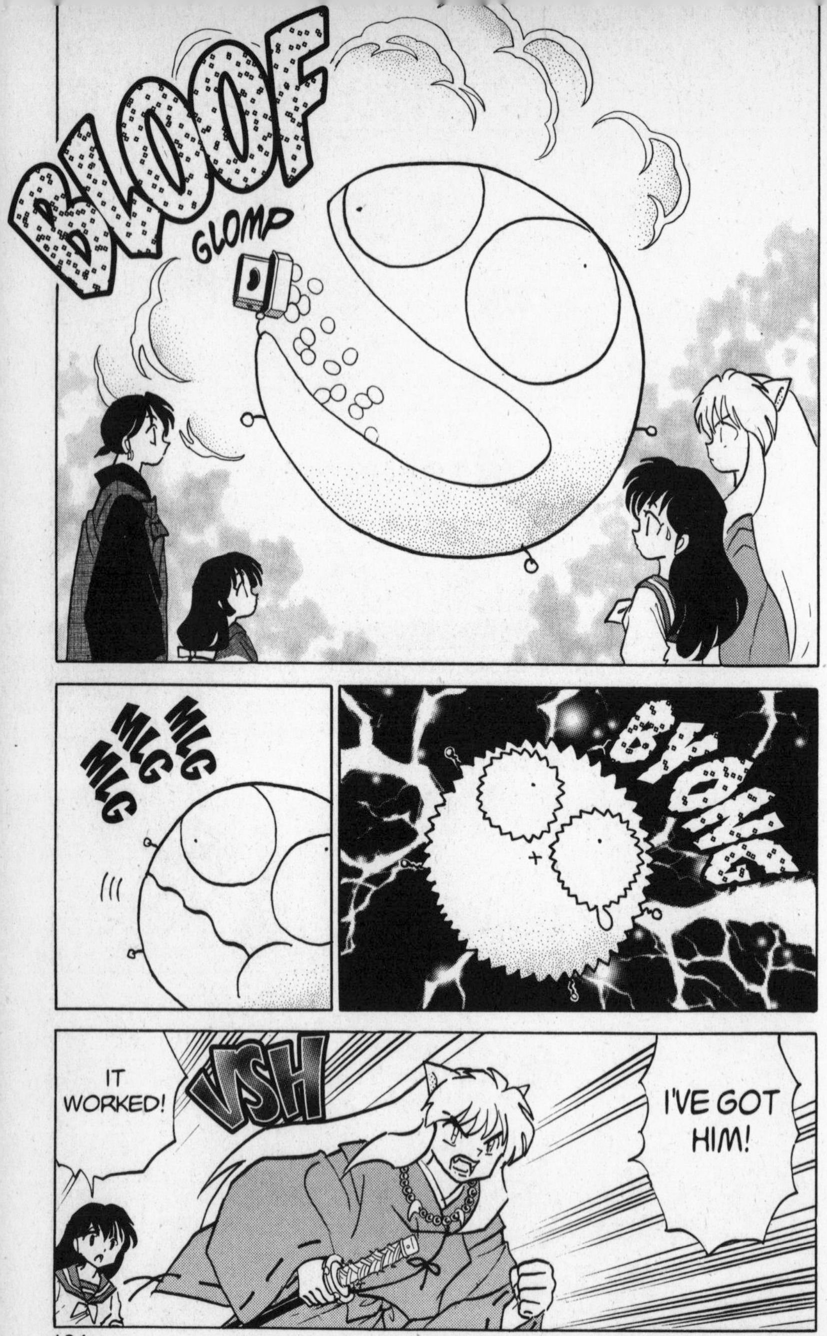
BLOOF
GLOMP
MLG MLG MLG
BYONG
IT WORKED!
VSH
I'VE GOT HIM!

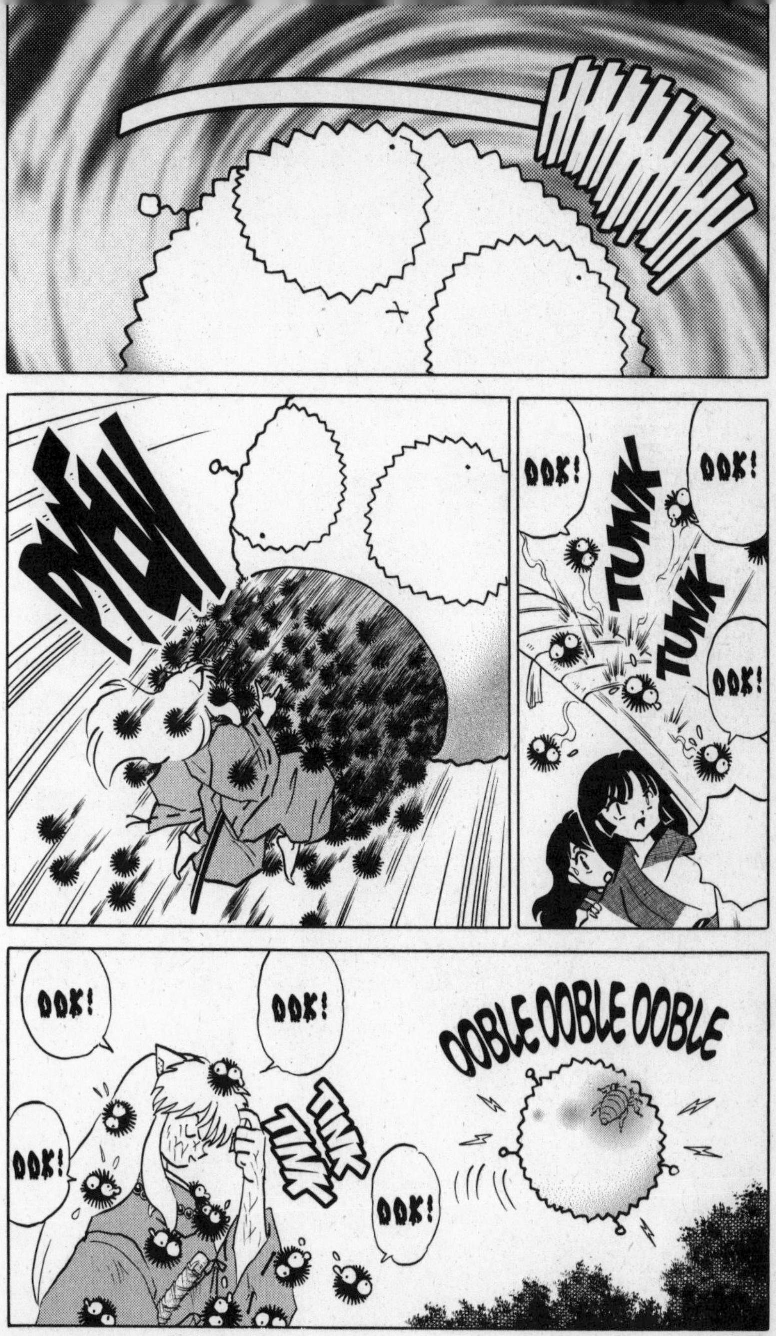
BAM!
OOK!
TUNK
OOK!
TUNK
OOK!
OOK!
OOK!
OOK!
TINK
TINK
OOK!
OOBLE OOBLE OOBLE

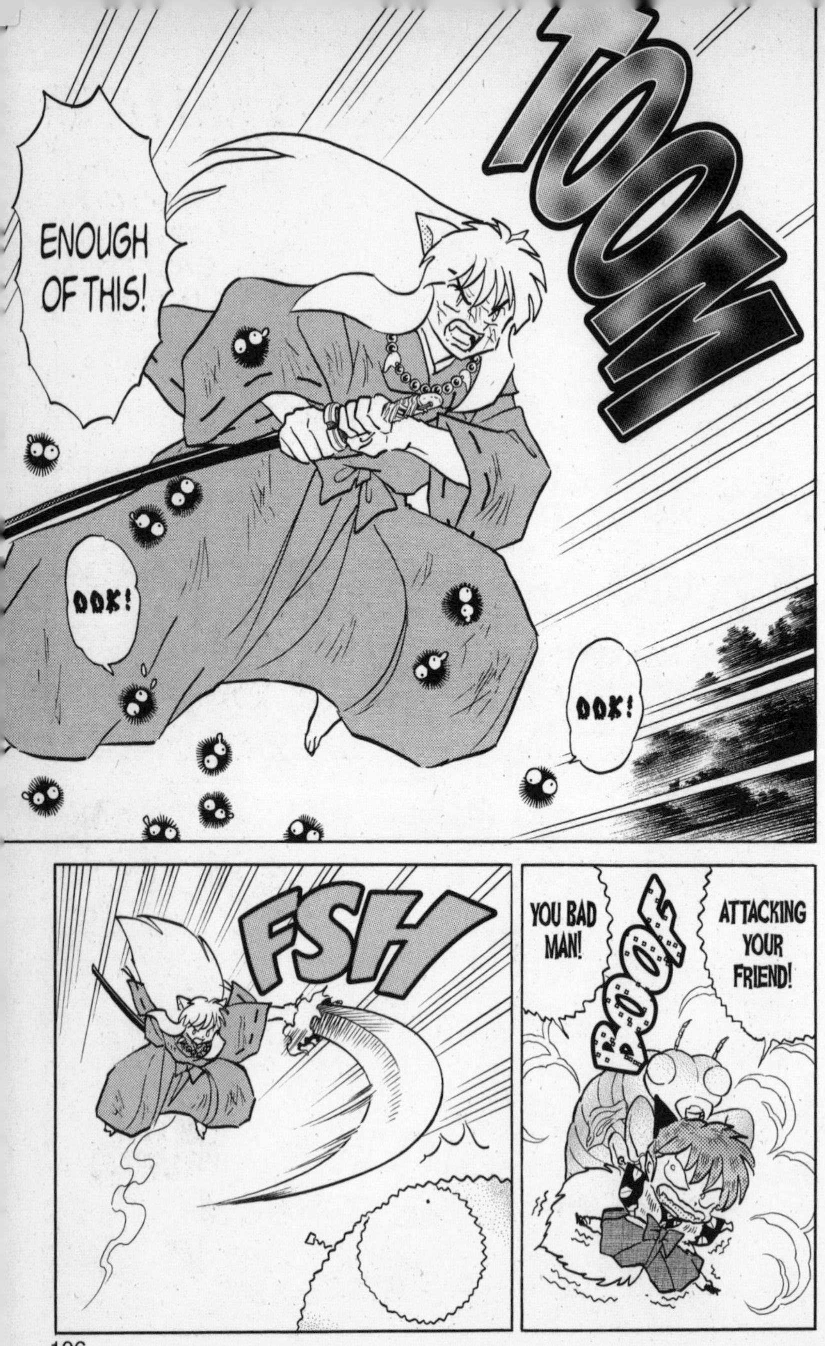
ENOUGH OF THIS!
TOOM
OOK!
OOK!
FSH
YOU BAD MAN!
BOOF
ATTACKING YOUR FRIEND!

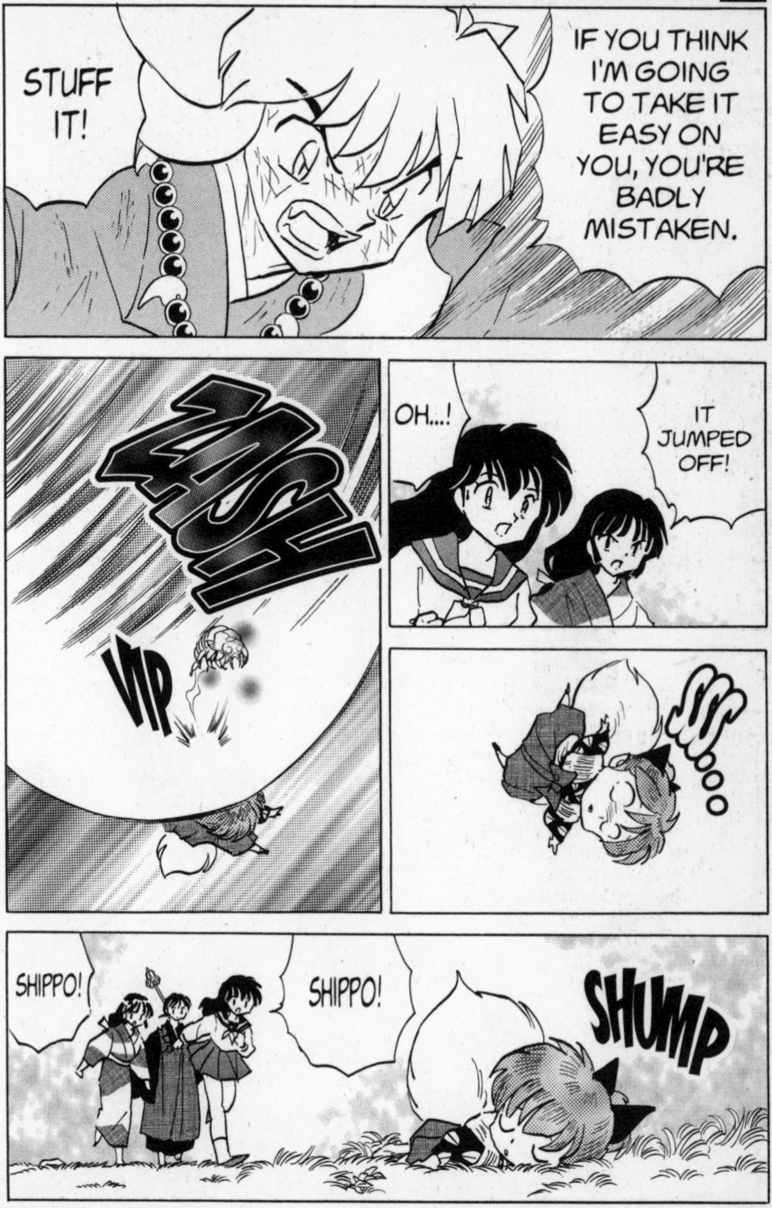
STUFF IT!
IF YOU THINK I'M GOING TO TAKE IT EASY ON YOU, YOU'RE BADLY MISTAKEN.
ZASH!
VIP
OH...!
IT JUMPED OFF!
SSOOOO
SHIPPO!
SHIPPO!
SHUMP

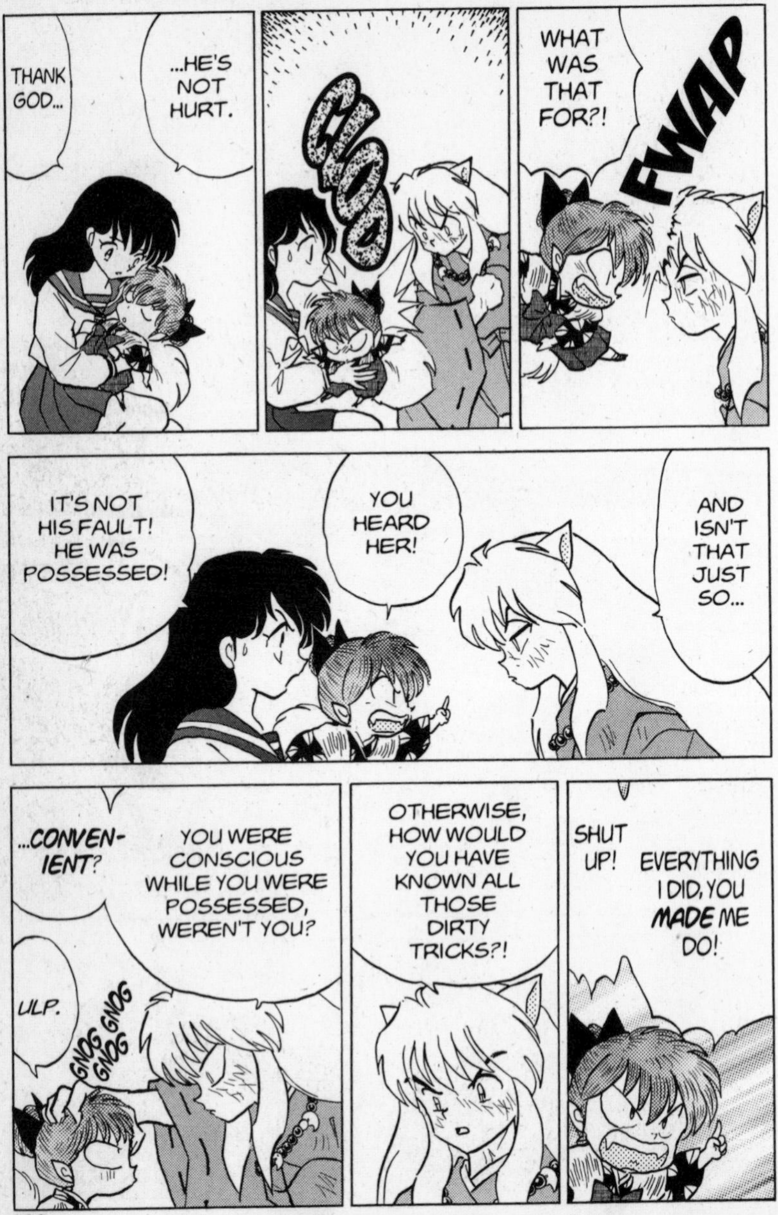
THANK GOD...
...HE'S NOT HURT.
CLOD
WHAT WAS THAT FOR?!
FWAP
IT'S NOT HIS FAULT! HE WAS POSSESSED!
YOU HEARD HER!
AND ISN'T THAT JUST SO...
...*CONVENIENT*?
YOU WERE CONSCIOUS WHILE YOU WERE POSSESSED, WEREN'T YOU?
ULP.
GNOG GNOG GNOG
OTHERWISE, HOW WOULD YOU HAVE KNOWN ALL THOSE DIRTY TRICKS?!
SHUT UP!
EVERYTHING I DID, YOU *MADE* ME DO!

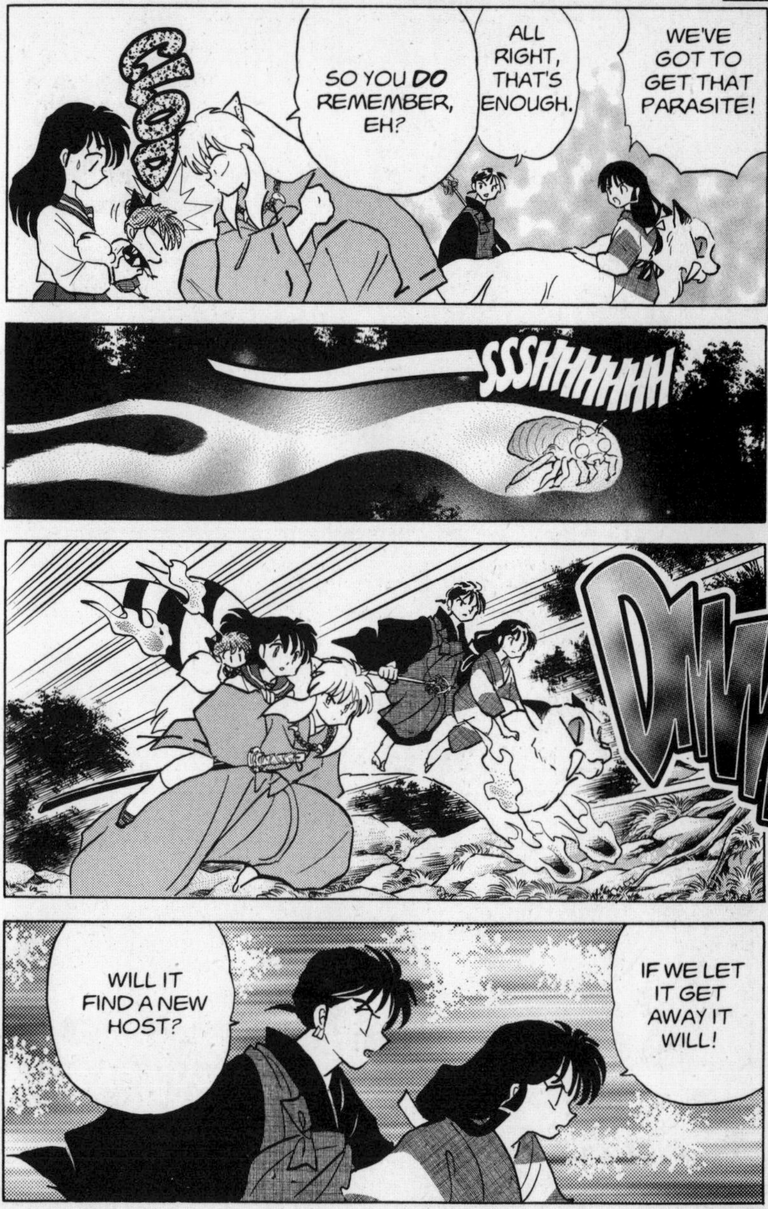
CLOD
SO YOU **DO** REMEMBER, EH?
ALL RIGHT, THAT'S ENOUGH.
WE'VE GOT TO GET THAT PARASITE!
SSSHHHHHHH
DMM
WILL IT FIND A NEW HOST?
IF WE LET IT GET AWAY IT WILL!

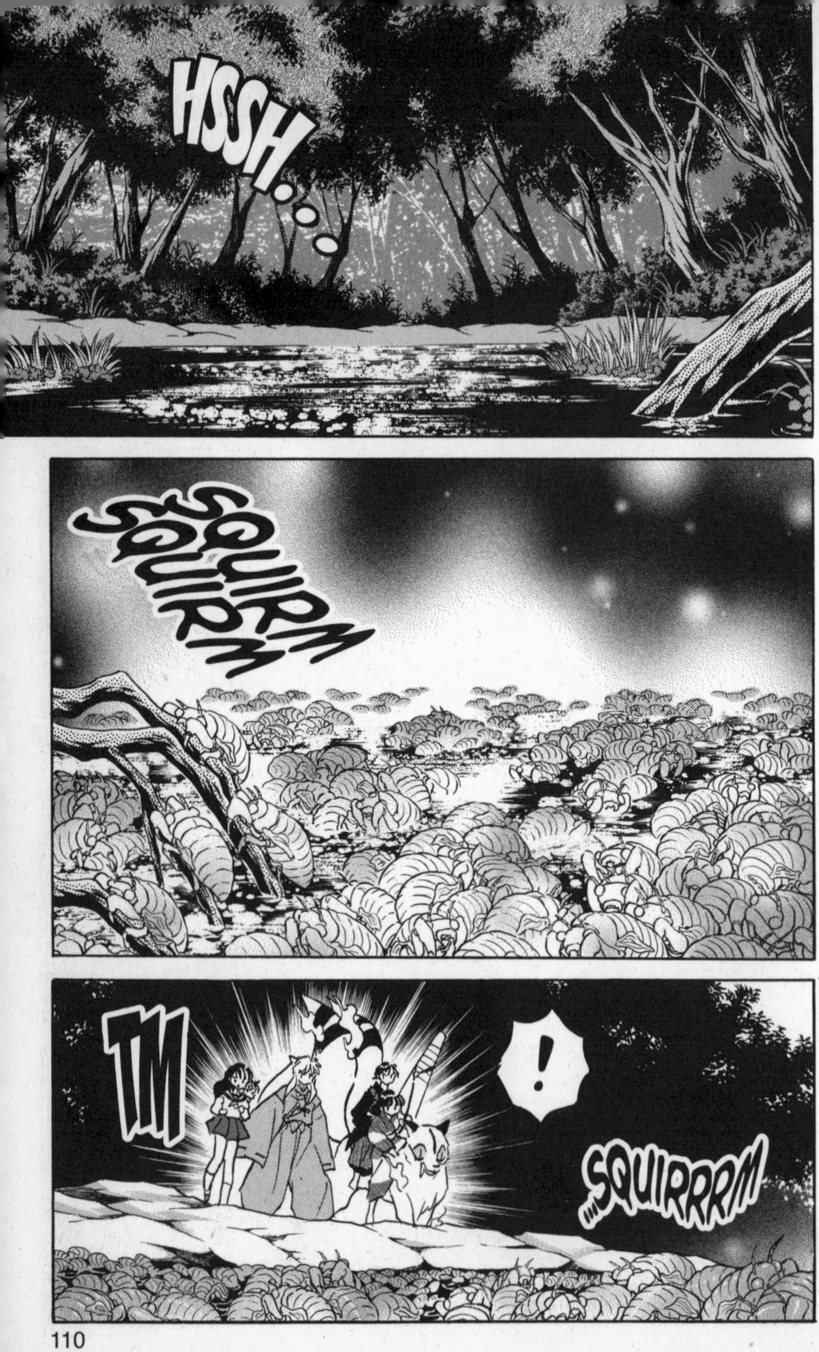
HSSH...
SQUIRM SQUIRM
TM
!
...SQUIRRRM

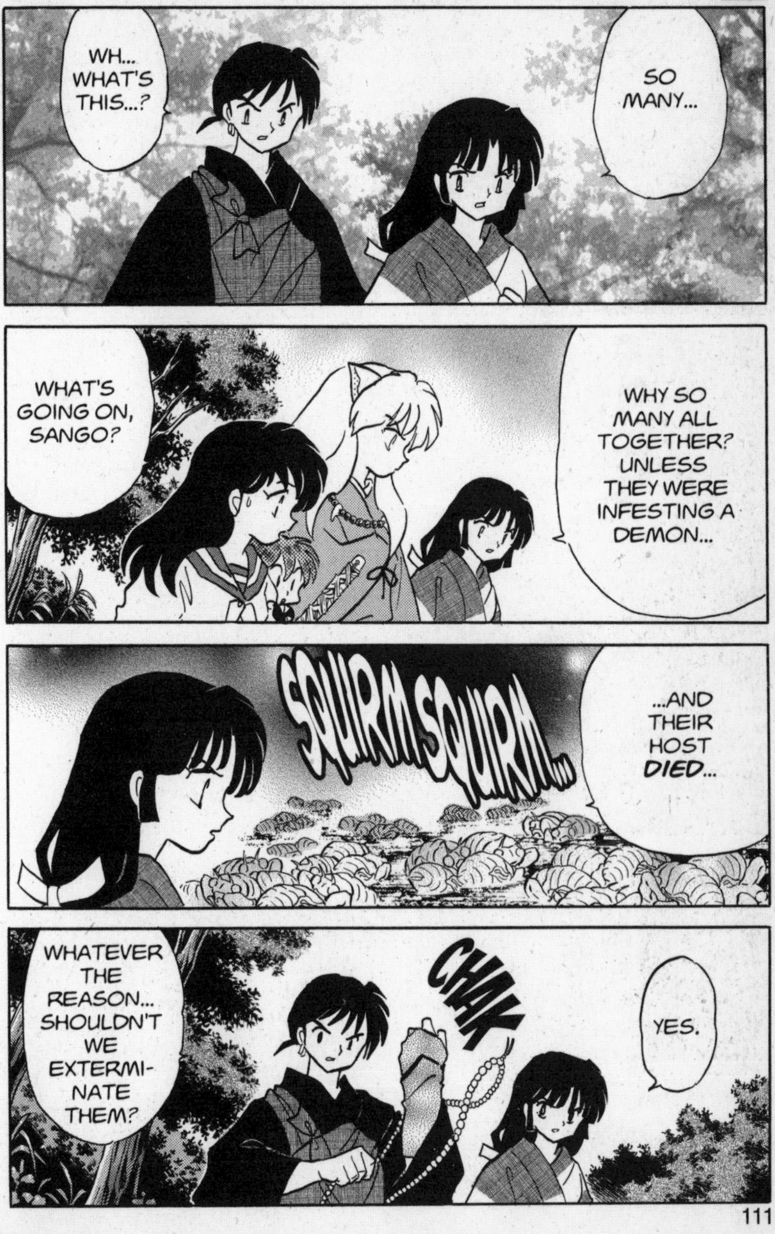
WH... WHAT'S THIS...?
SO MANY...
WHAT'S GOING ON, SANGO?
WHY SO MANY ALL TOGETHER? UNLESS THEY WERE INFESTING A DEMON...
SQUIRM SQUIRM...
...AND THEIR HOST **DIED**...
WHATEVER THE REASON... SHOULDN'T WE EXTERMI-NATE THEM?
CHAK
YES.

HSSH...

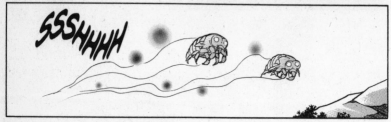

SSSHHHH

SHP

CHAK

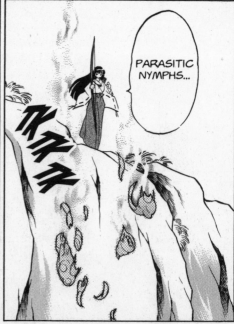

TK TK TK

PARASITIC NYMPHS...

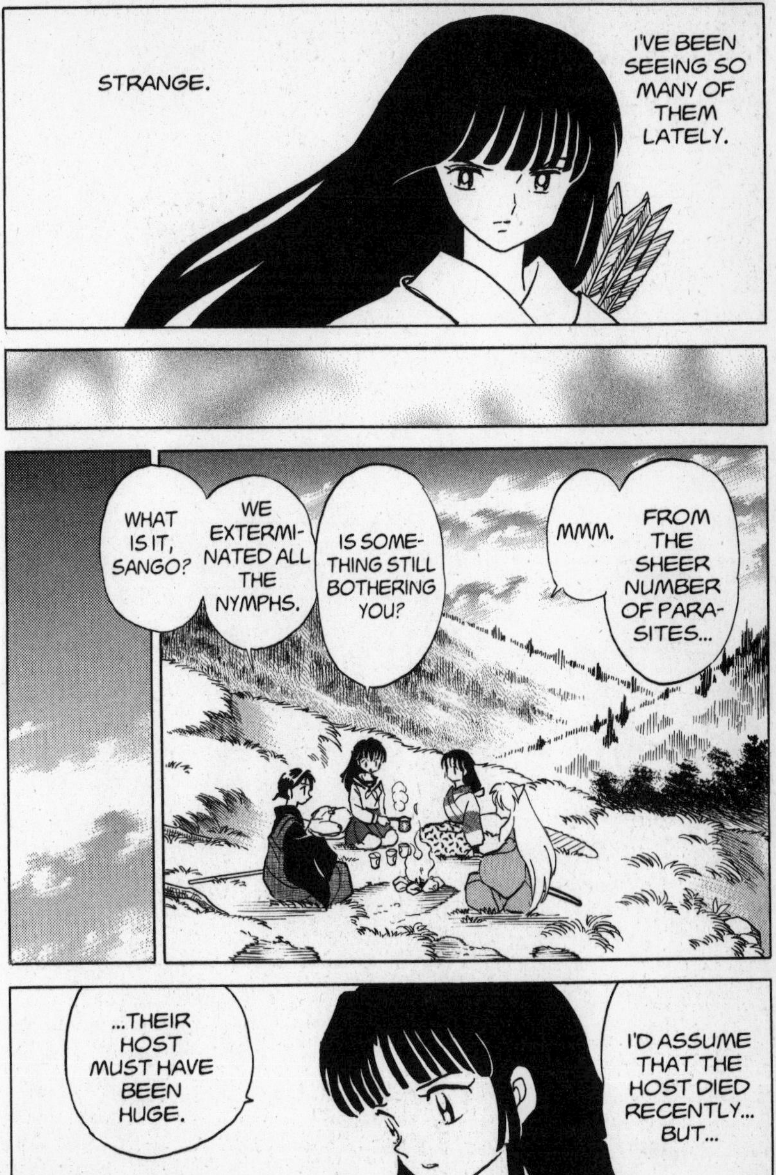
STRANGE.
I'VE BEEN SEEING SO MANY OF THEM LATELY.
WHAT IS IT, SANGO?
WE EXTERMINATED ALL THE NYMPHS.
IS SOMETHING STILL BOTHERING YOU?
MMM.
FROM THE SHEER NUMBER OF PARASITES...
...THEIR HOST MUST HAVE BEEN HUGE.
I'D ASSUME THAT THE HOST DIED RECENTLY... BUT...

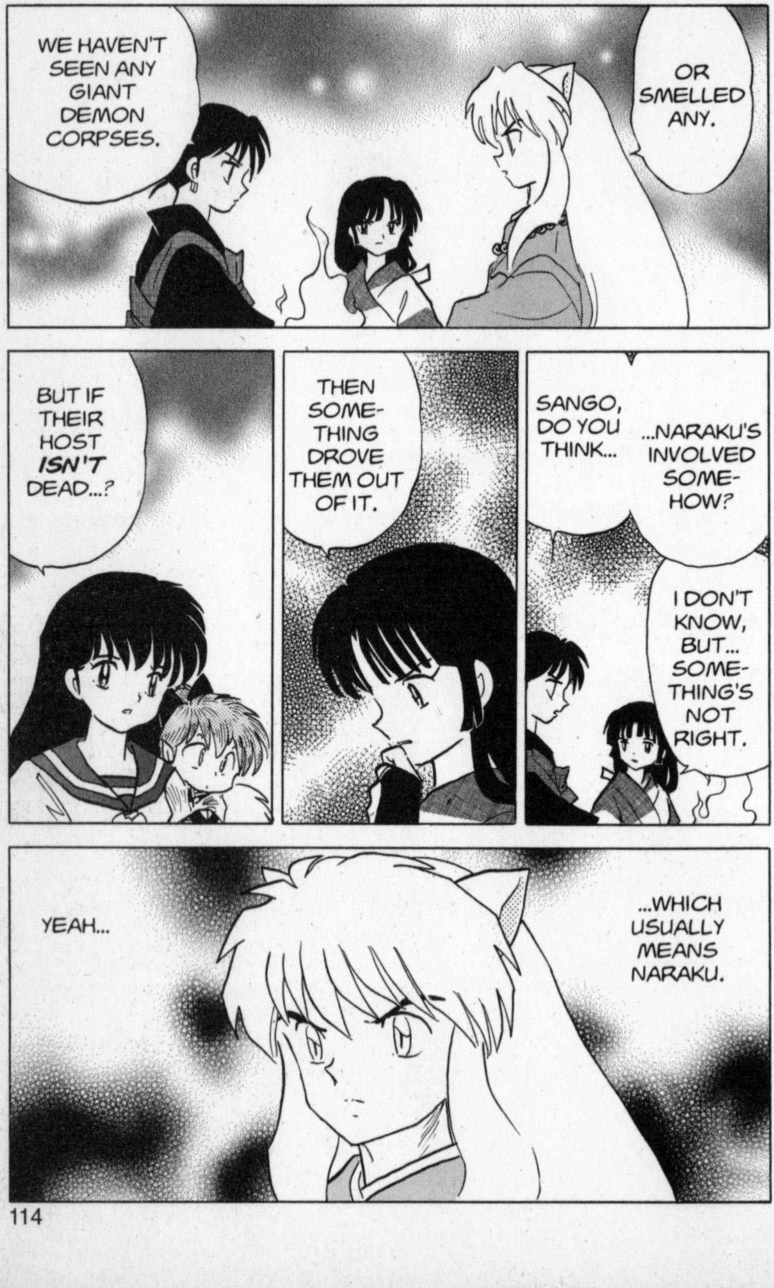
WE HAVEN'T SEEN ANY GIANT DEMON CORPSES.
OR SMELLED ANY.
BUT IF THEIR HOST *ISN'T* DEAD...?
THEN SOME-THING DROVE THEM OUT OF IT.
SANGO, DO YOU THINK...
...NARAKU'S INVOLVED SOME-HOW?
I DON'T KNOW, BUT... SOME-THING'S NOT RIGHT.
YEAH...
...WHICH USUALLY MEANS NARAKU.

SCROLL 7
THE LOST MOUNTAIN

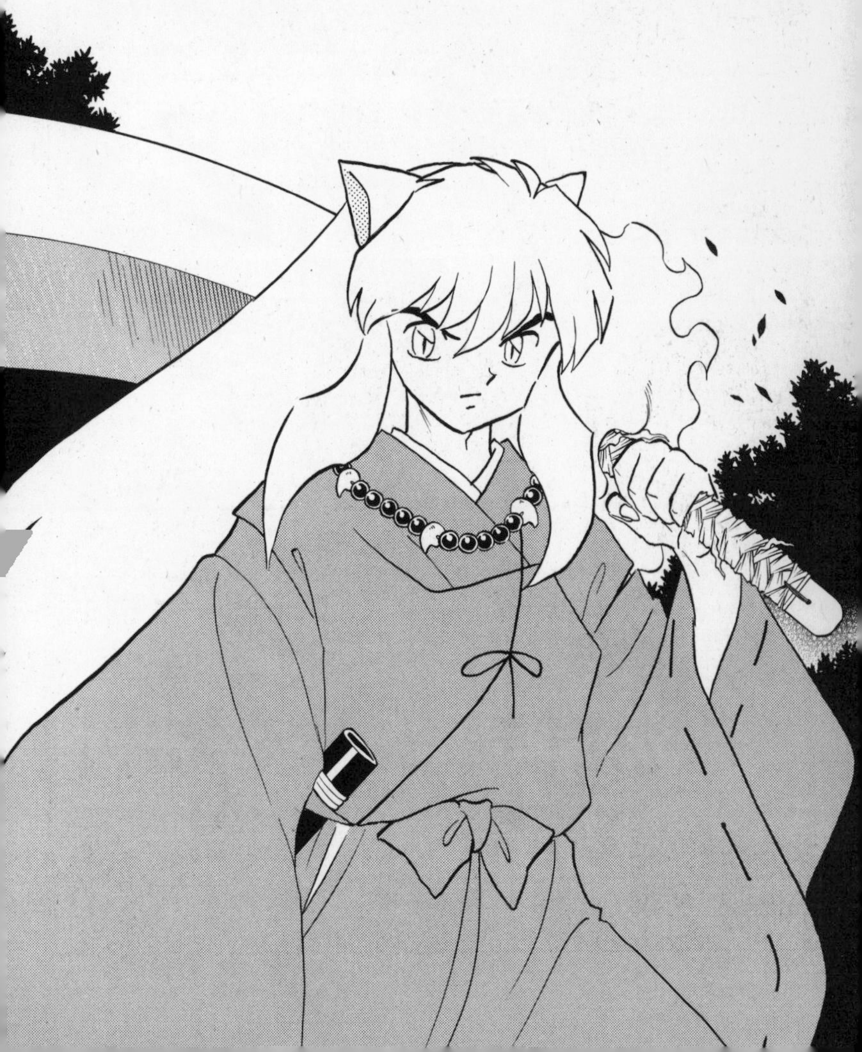

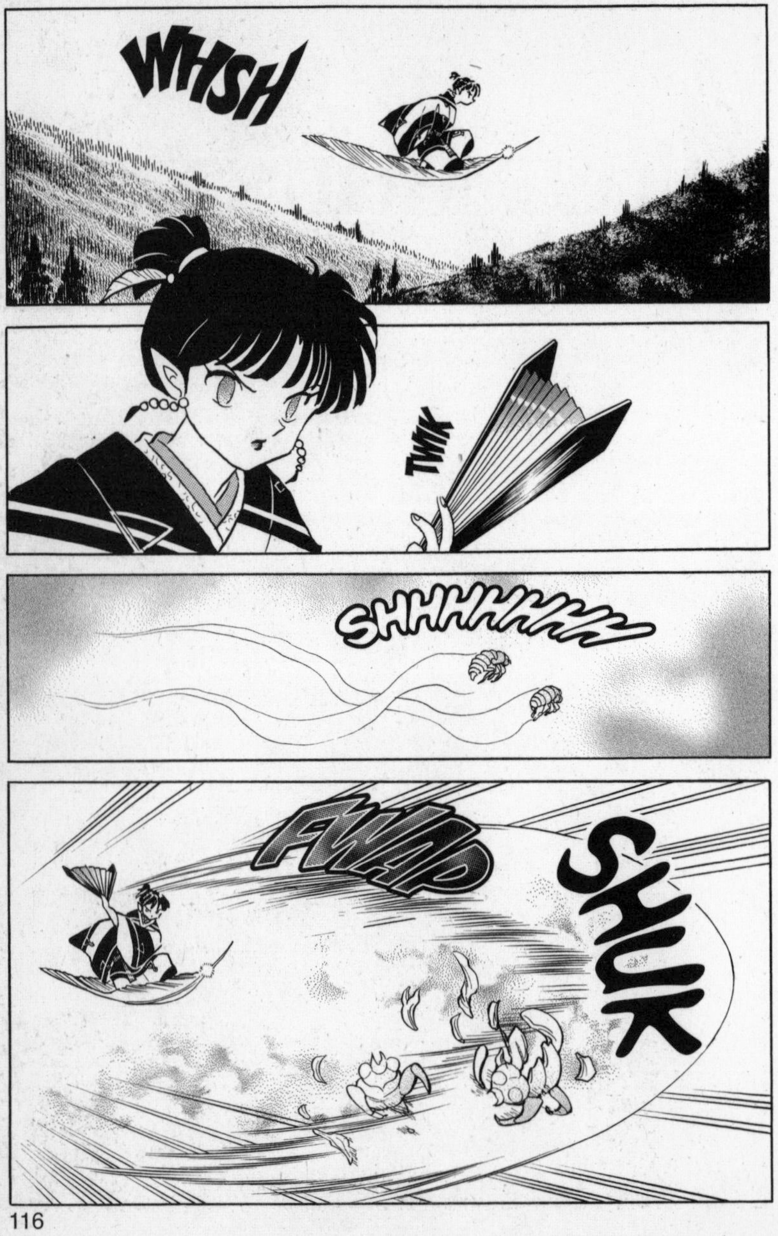
WHSH
TWIK
SHHHHHHH
FWAP
SHUK

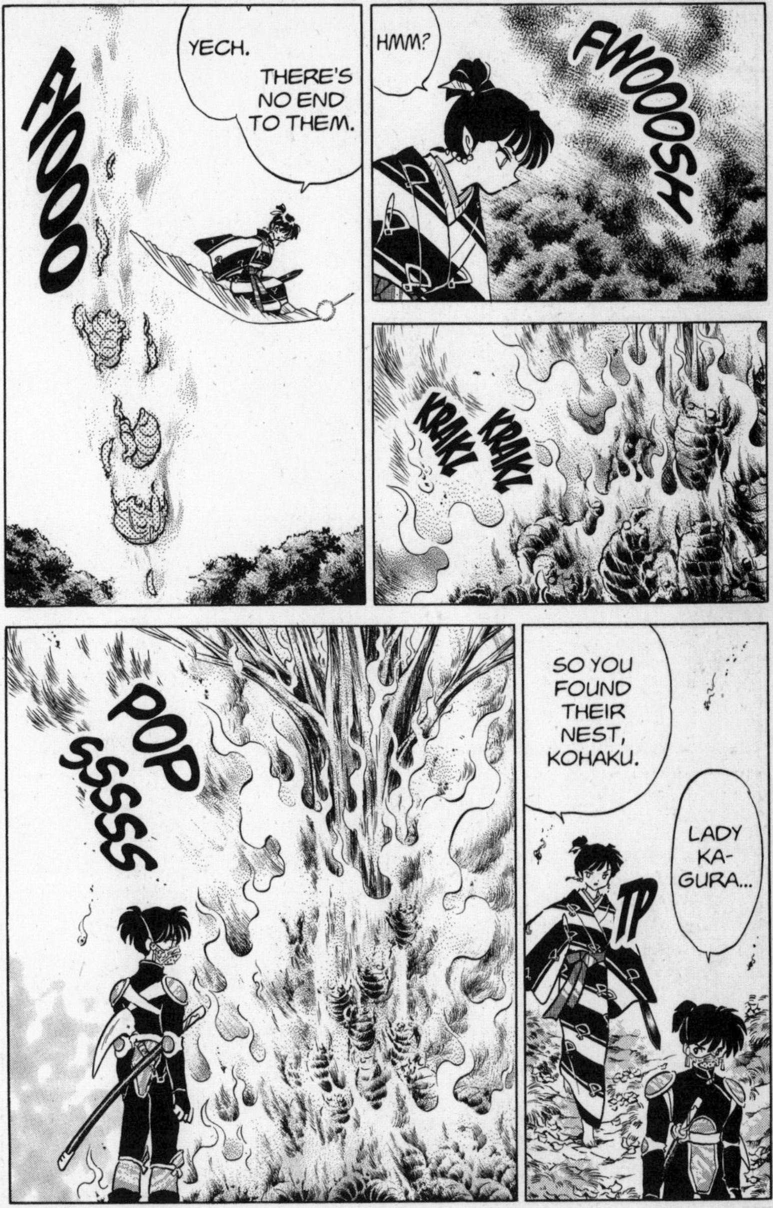
FYOOO
YECH.
THERE'S NO END TO THEM.
HMM?
FWOOOSH
KRAK! KRAK!
POP
SSSSS
SO YOU FOUND THEIR NEST, KOHAKU.
TP
LADY KA-GURA...

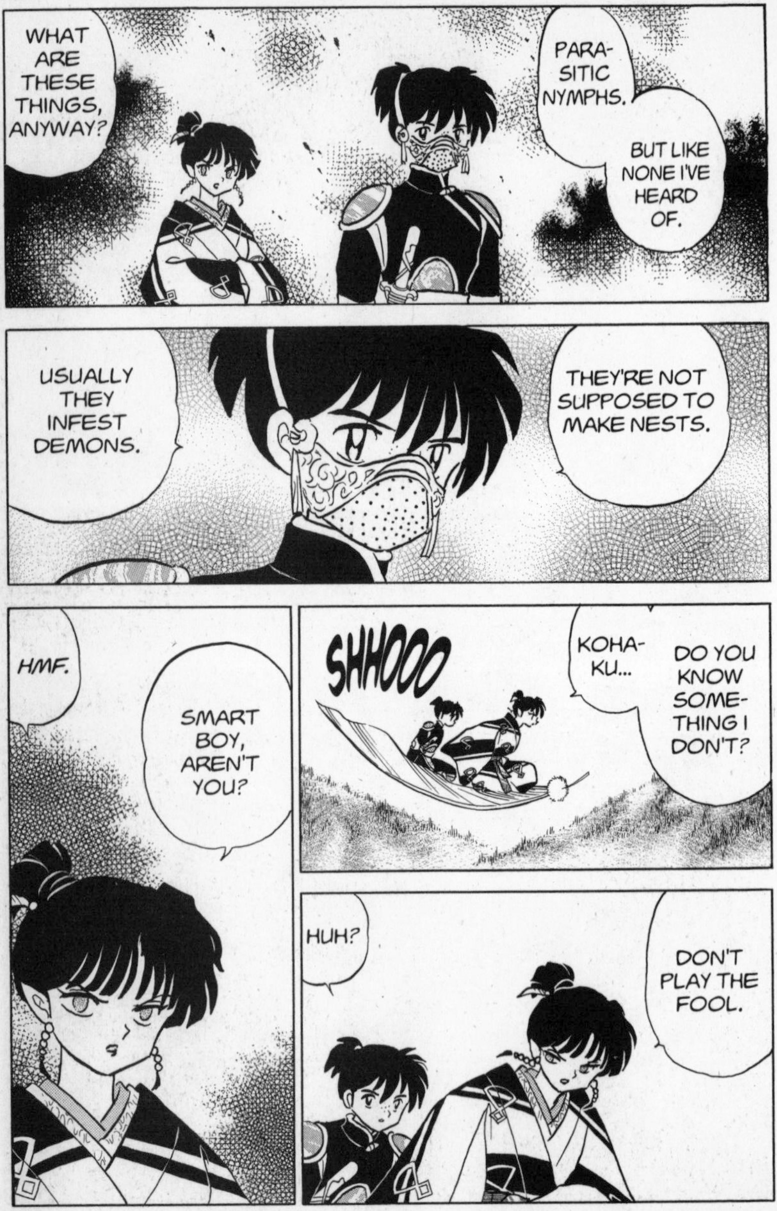
WHAT ARE THESE THINGS, ANYWAY?
PARA-SITIC NYMPHS.
BUT LIKE NONE I'VE HEARD OF.
USUALLY THEY INFEST DEMONS.
THEY'RE NOT SUPPOSED TO MAKE NESTS.
HMF.
SMART BOY, AREN'T YOU?
SHHOOO
KOHA-KU...
DO YOU KNOW SOMETHING I DON'T?
HUH?
DON'T PLAY THE FOOL.

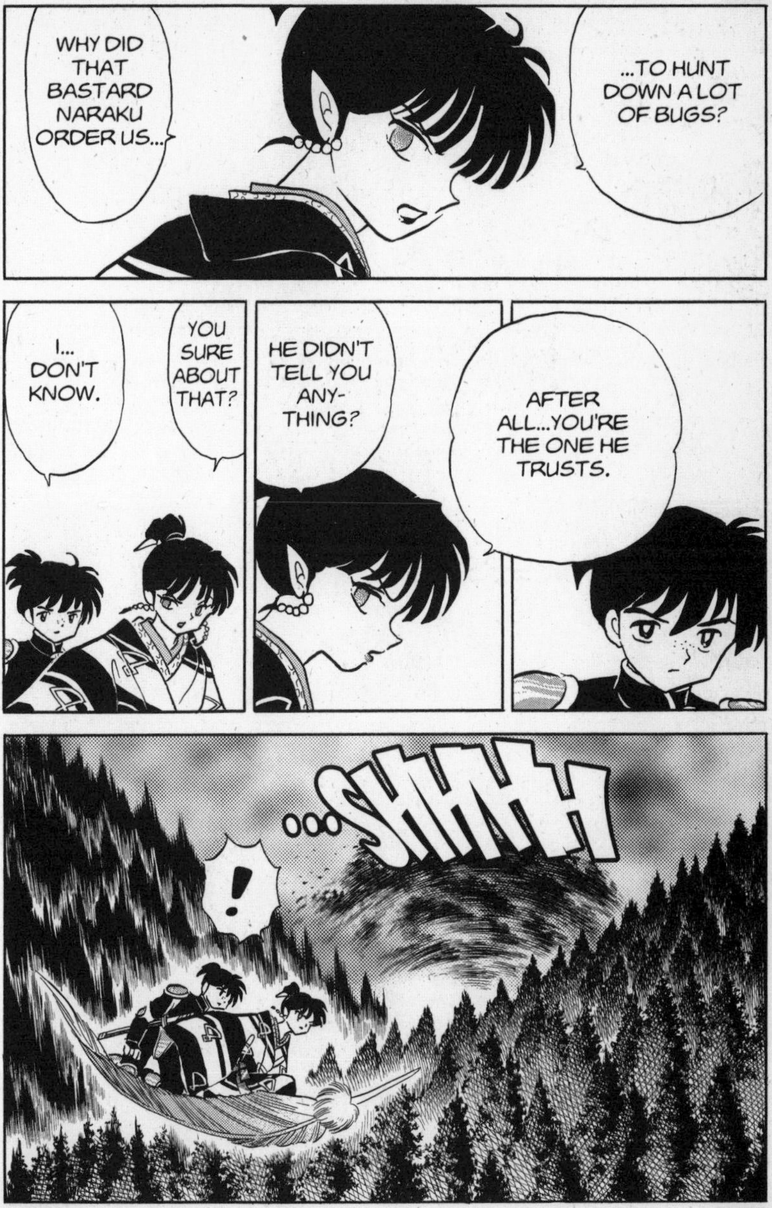
WHY DID THAT BASTARD NARAKU ORDER US...
...TO HUNT DOWN A LOT OF BUGS?
I... DON'T KNOW.
YOU SURE ABOUT THAT?
HE DIDN'T TELL YOU ANY-THING?
AFTER ALL...YOU'RE THE ONE HE TRUSTS.
...SHHHH
!

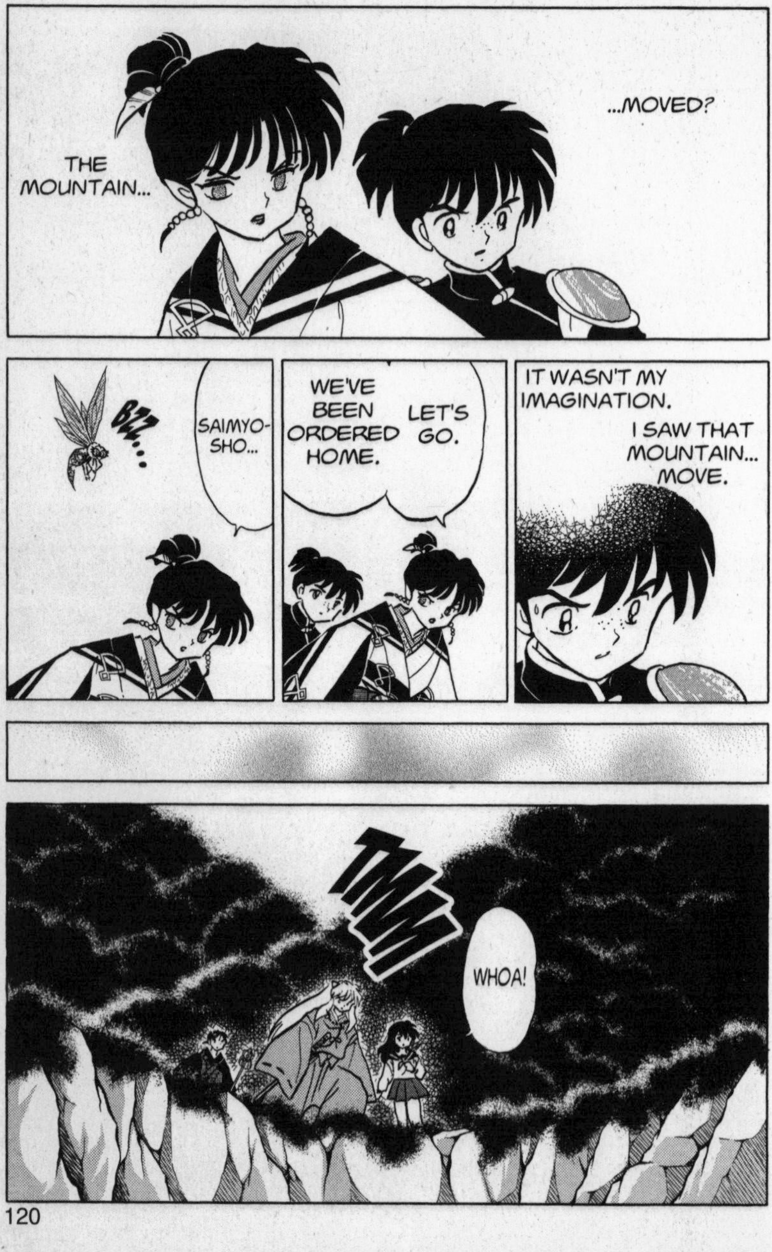
THE MOUNTAIN...
...MOVED?
BZZ...
SAIMYO-SHO...
WE'VE BEEN ORDERED HOME.
LET'S GO.
IT WASN'T MY IMAGINATION.
I SAW THAT MOUNTAIN... MOVE.
TMM
WHOA!

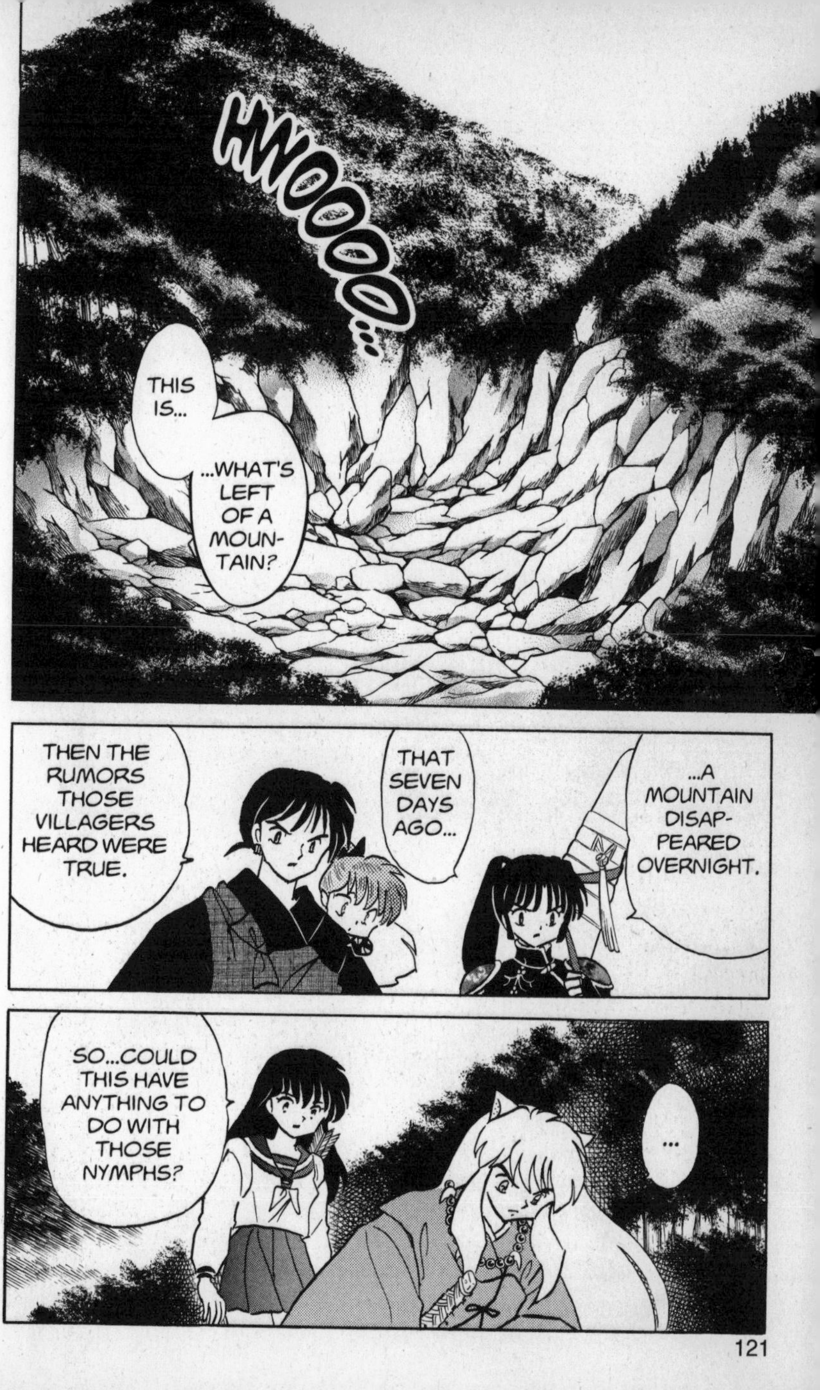
HWOOOO...
THIS IS...
...WHAT'S LEFT OF A MOUNTAIN?
THEN THE RUMORS THOSE VILLAGERS HEARD WERE TRUE.
THAT SEVEN DAYS AGO...
...A MOUNTAIN DISAPPEARED OVERNIGHT.
SO...COULD THIS HAVE ANYTHING TO DO WITH THOSE NYMPHS?
...

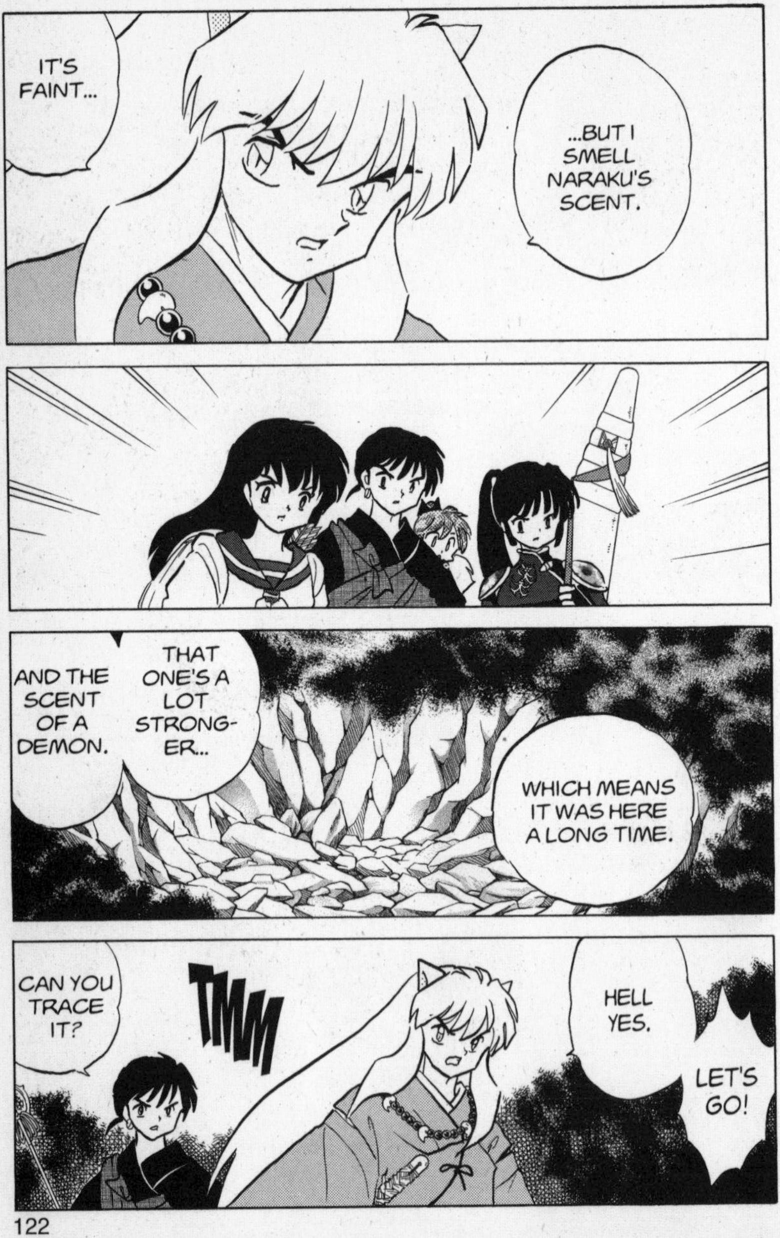

IT'S FAINT...
...BUT I SMELL NARAKU'S SCENT.
AND THE SCENT OF A DEMON.
THAT ONE'S A LOT STRONGER...
WHICH MEANS IT WAS HERE A LONG TIME.
CAN YOU TRACE IT?
TMM
HELL YES.
LET'S GO!

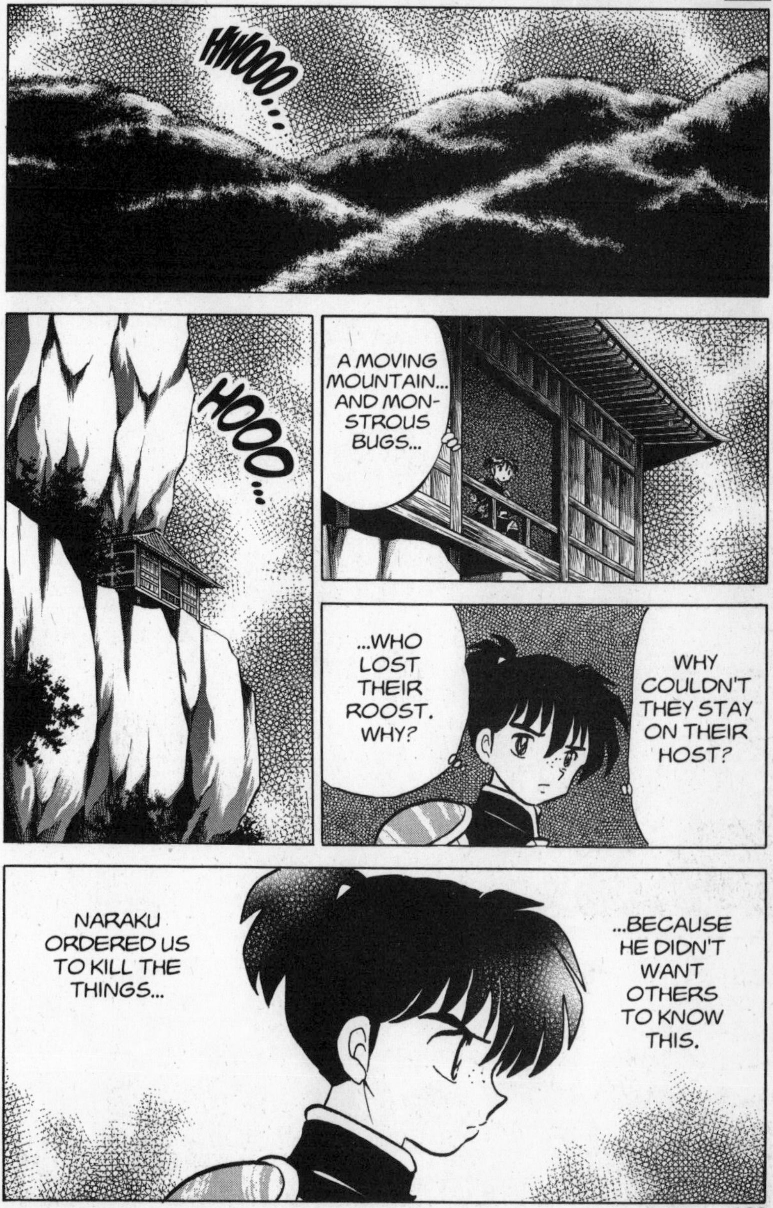
HWOOO...
HOOOO...
A MOVING MOUNTAIN... AND MON-STROUS BUGS...
...WHO LOST THEIR ROOST. WHY?
WHY COULDN'T THEY STAY ON THEIR HOST?
NARAKU ORDERED US TO KILL THE THINGS...
...BECAUSE HE DIDN'T WANT OTHERS TO KNOW THIS.

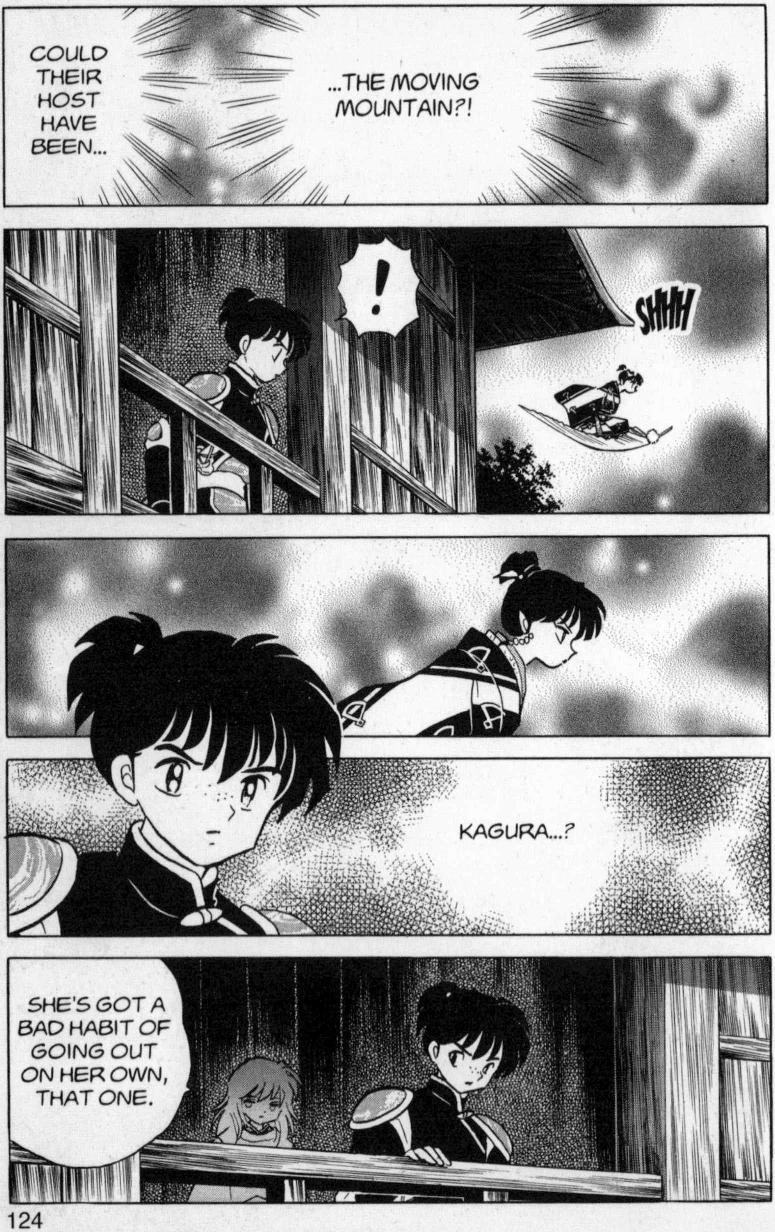
COULD THEIR HOST HAVE BEEN...
...THE MOVING MOUNTAIN?!
!
SHHH
KAGURA...?
SHE'S GOT A BAD HABIT OF GOING OUT ON HER OWN, THAT ONE.

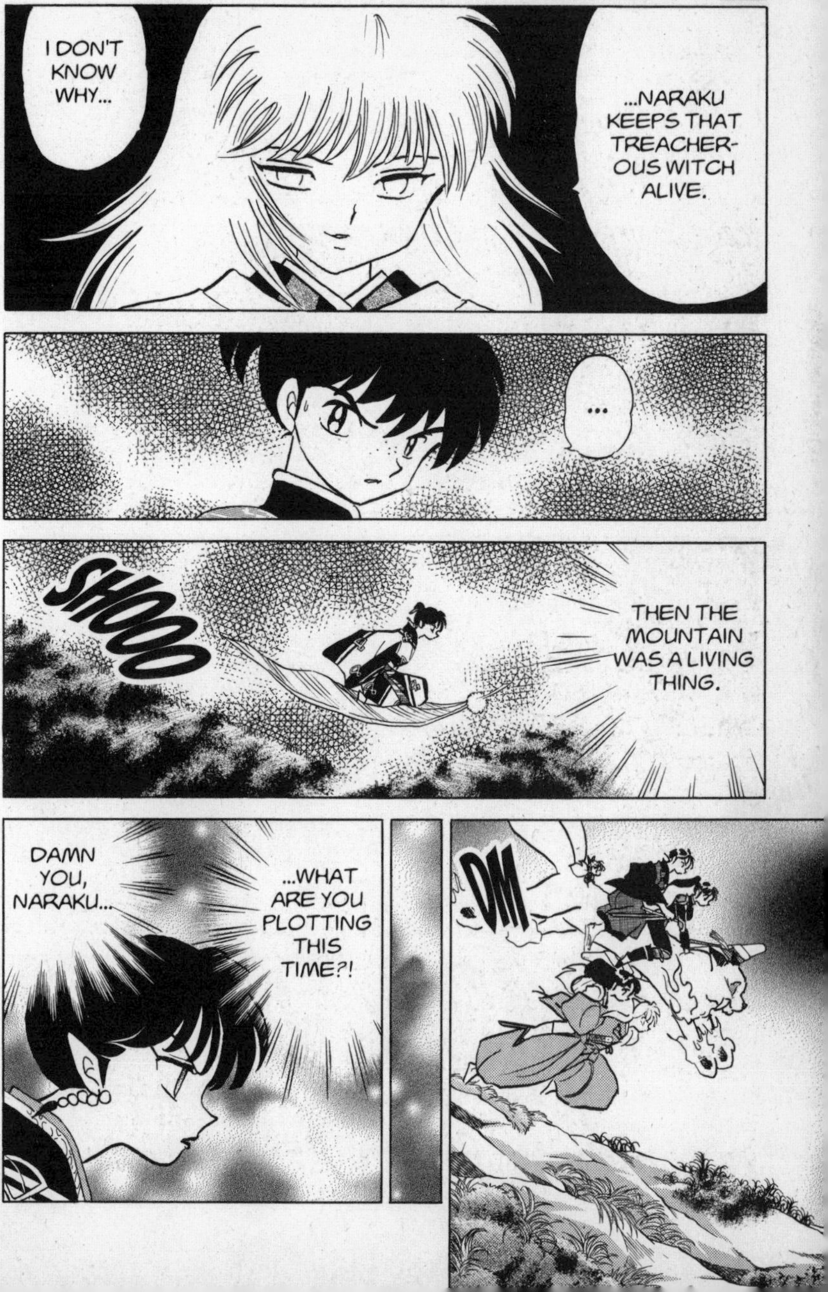
I DON'T KNOW WHY...
...NARAKU KEEPS THAT TREACHER-OUS WITCH ALIVE.
...
SHOOO
THEN THE MOUNTAIN WAS A LIVING THING.
DAMN YOU, NARAKU...
...WHAT ARE YOU PLOTTING THIS TIME?!
DM

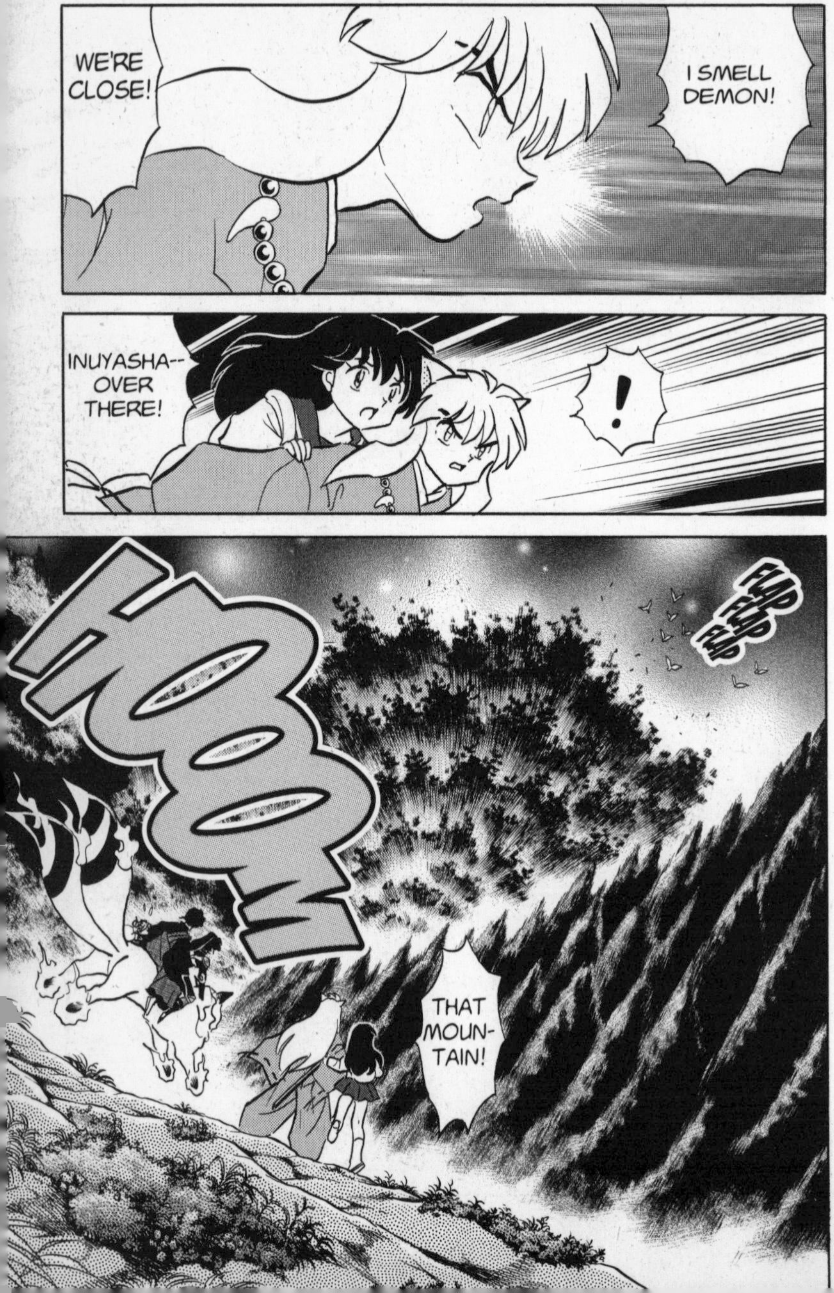
WE'RE CLOSE!
I SMELL DEMON!
INUYASHA-- OVER THERE!
!
FOOOM!
FLAP FLAP FLAP
THAT MOUN-TAIN!

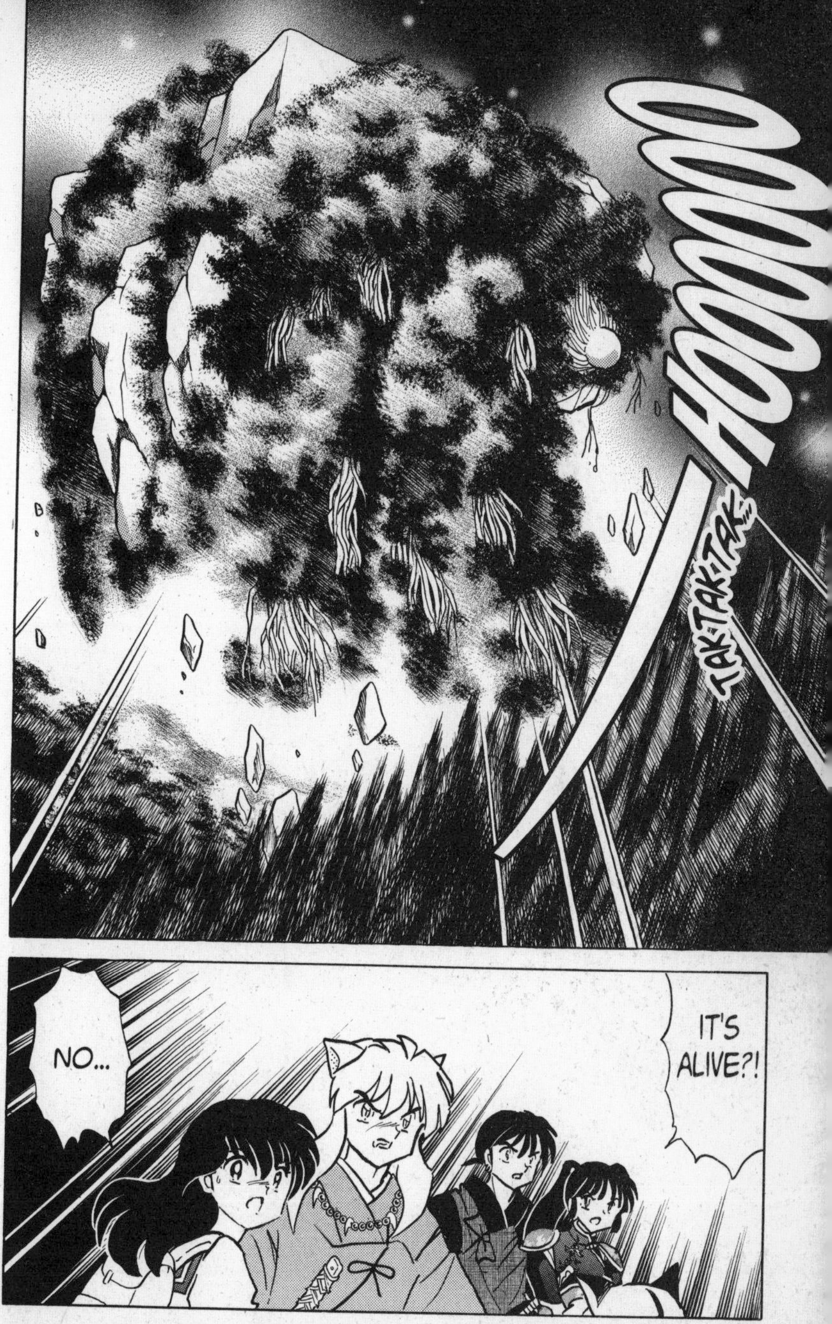
HOOOOOO
TAK TAK TAK...
NO...
IT'S ALIVE?!

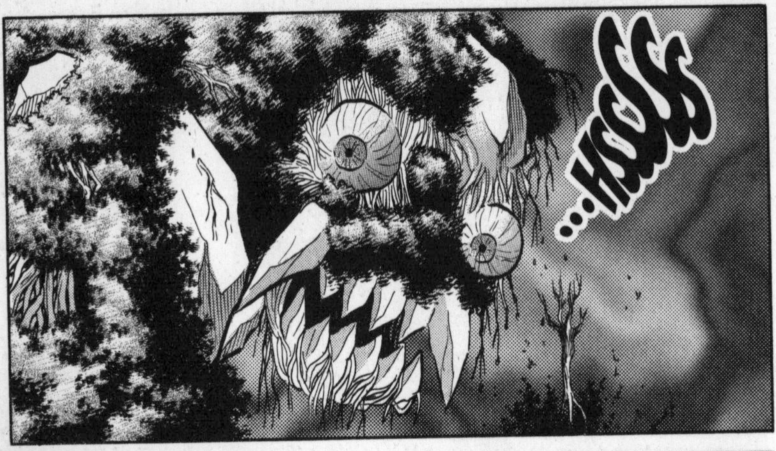
...HOSSS

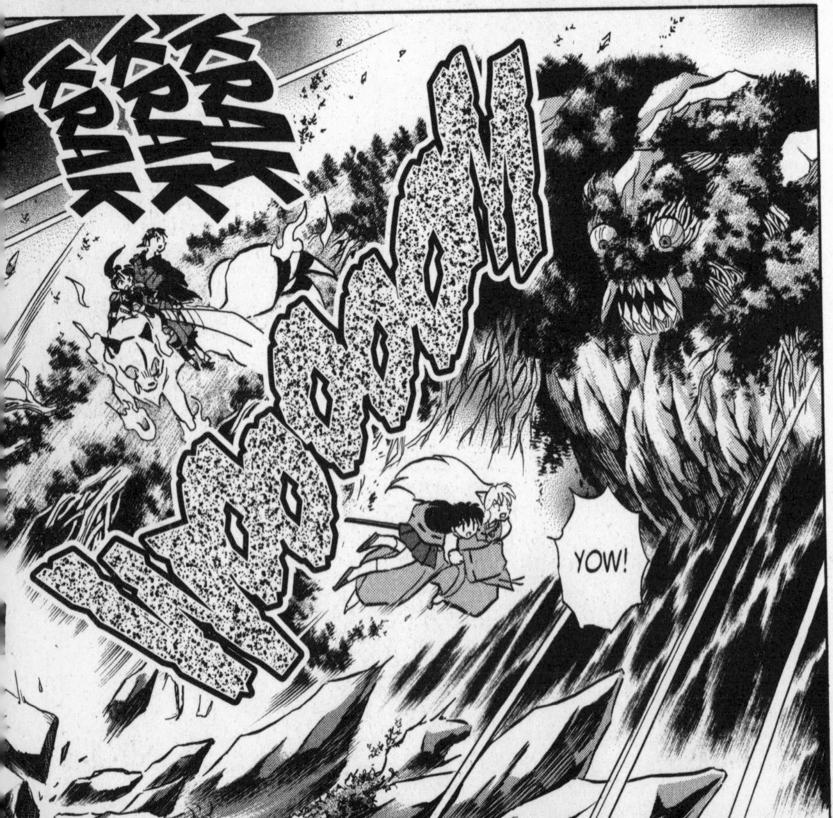
KRAK KRAK KRAK
BOOOM
YOW!

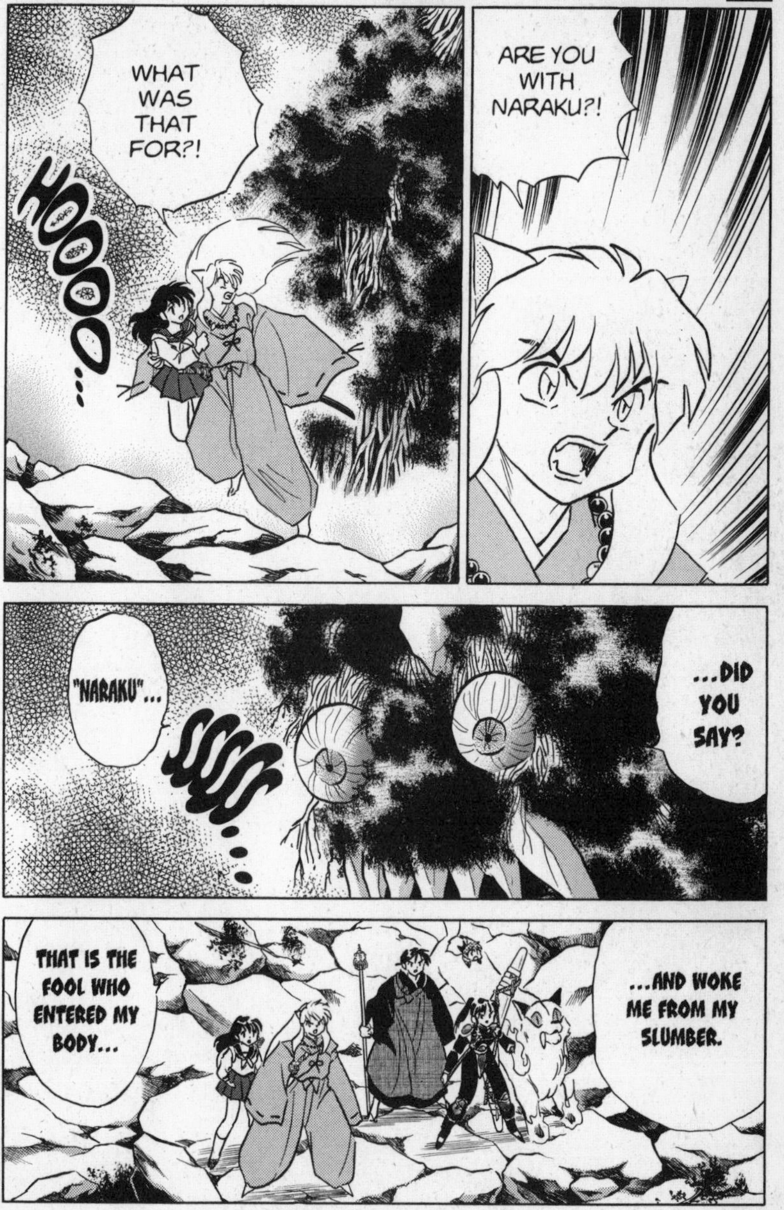
WHAT WAS THAT FOR?!
HOOOOO...
ARE YOU WITH NARAKU?!
"NARAKU"...
SSSS...
...DID YOU SAY?
THAT IS THE FOOL WHO ENTERED MY BODY...
...AND WOKE ME FROM MY SLUMBER.

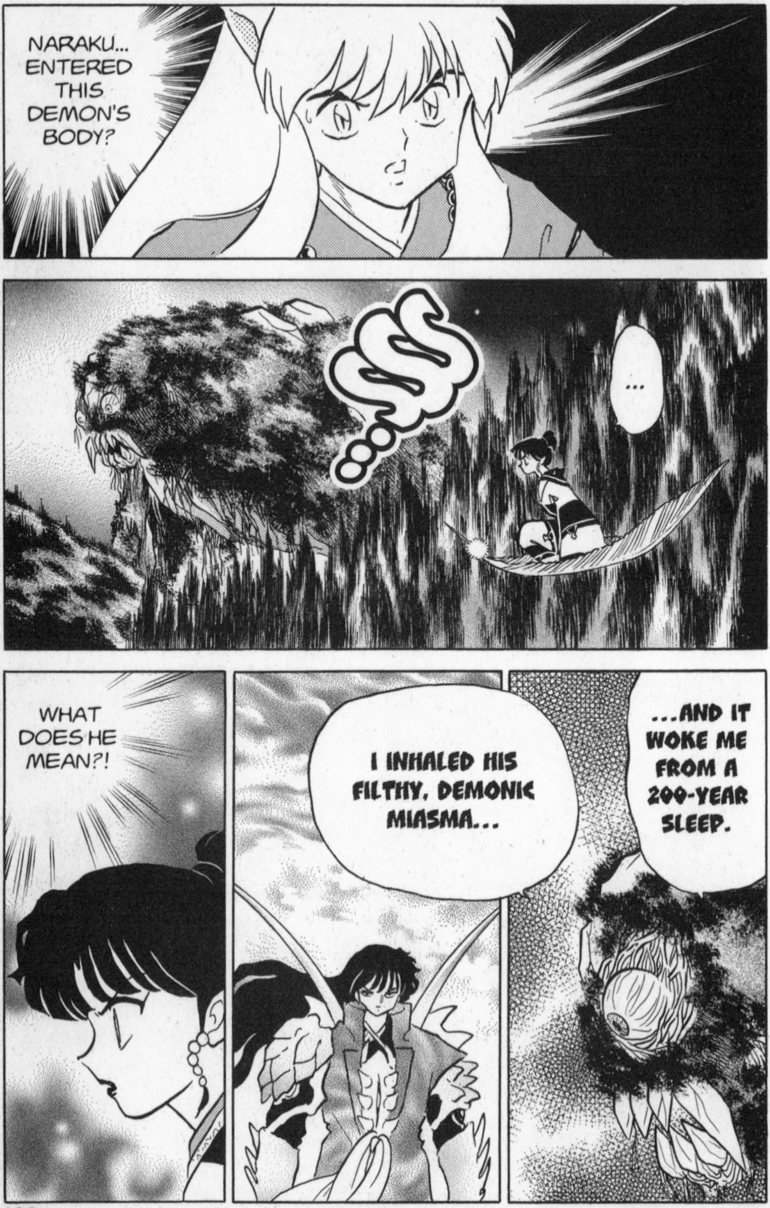
NARAKU... ENTERED THIS DEMON'S BODY?
...
WHAT DOES HE MEAN?!
I INHALED HIS FILTHY, DEMONIC MIASMA...
...AND IT WOKE ME FROM A 200-YEAR SLEEP.

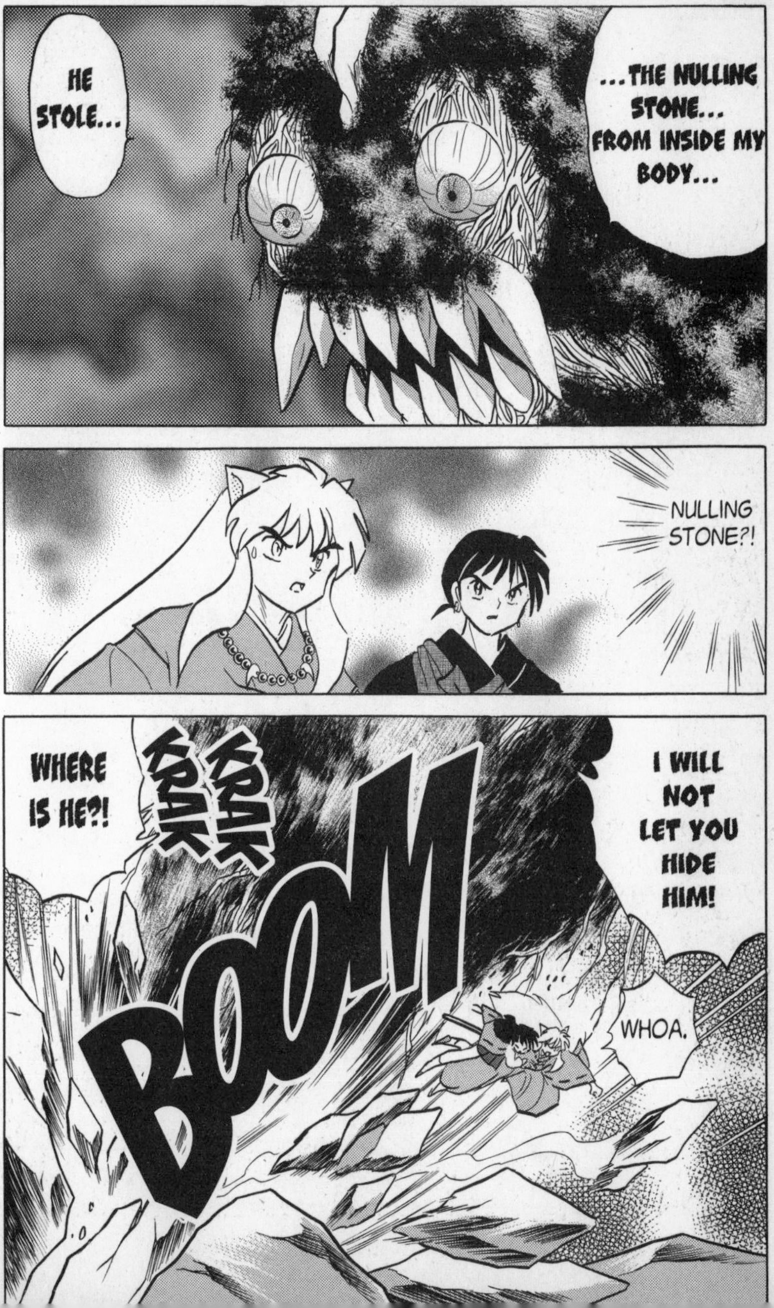
HE STOLE...
...THE NULLING STONE... FROM INSIDE MY BODY...
NULLING STONE?!
WHERE IS HE?!
KRAK KRAK
I WILL NOT LET YOU HIDE HIM!
BOOM
WHOA.

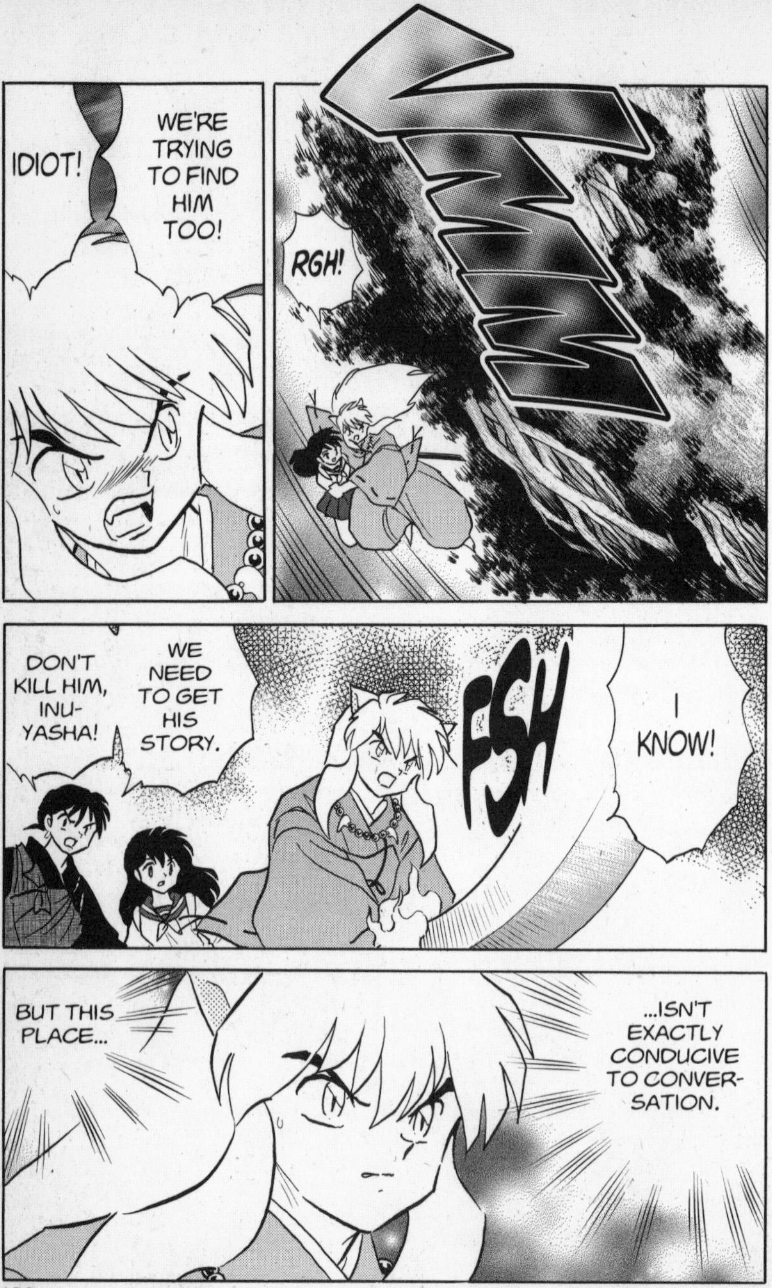
IDIOT!
WE'RE TRYING TO FIND HIM TOO!
RGH!
DON'T KILL HIM, INU-YASHA!
WE NEED TO GET HIS STORY.
FSH
I KNOW!
BUT THIS PLACE...
...ISN'T EXACTLY CONDUCIVE TO CONVER-SATION.

SCROLL 8
THE MOUNTAIN MAN

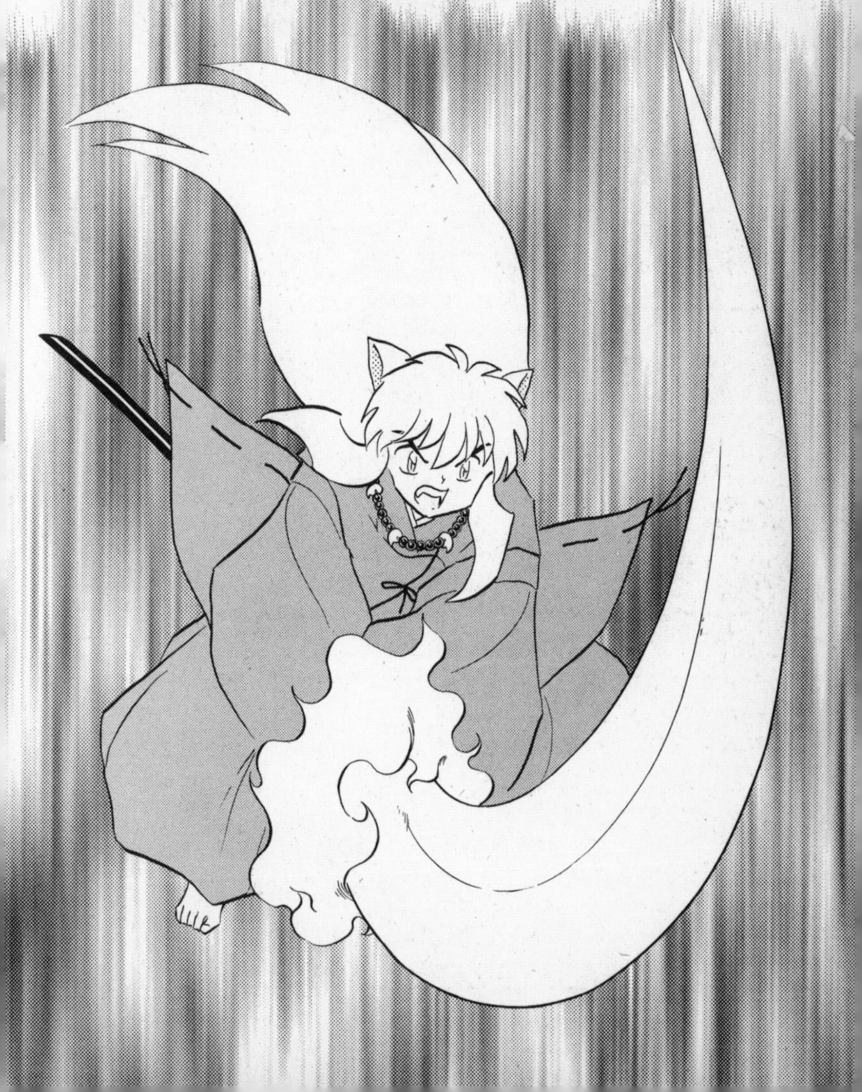

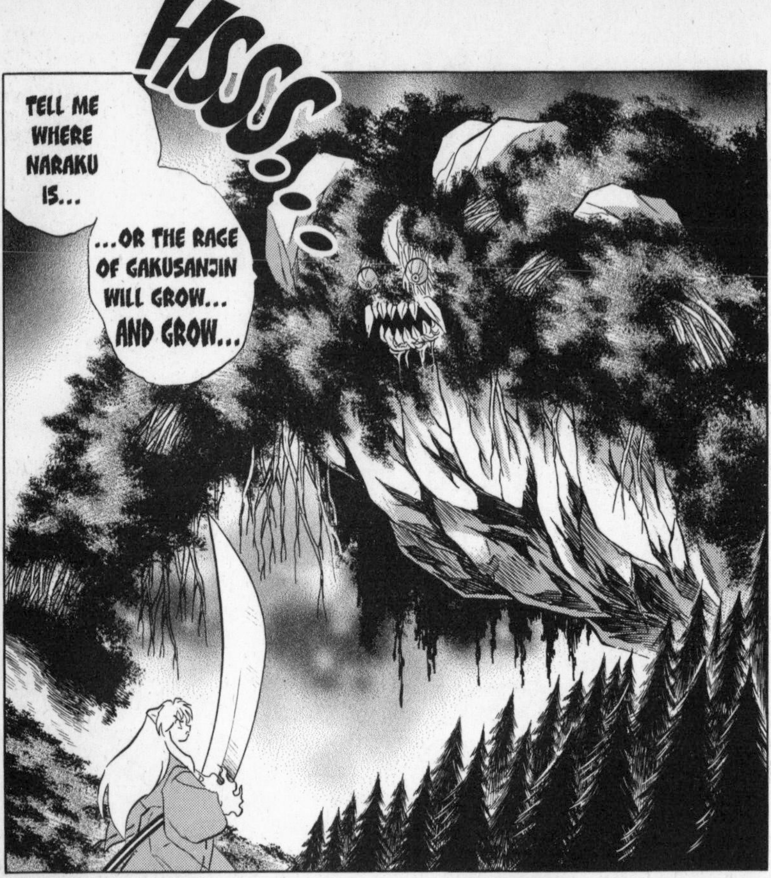
HSSS...
TELL ME WHERE NARAKU IS...
...OR THE RAGE OF GAKUSANJIN WILL GROW... AND GROW...
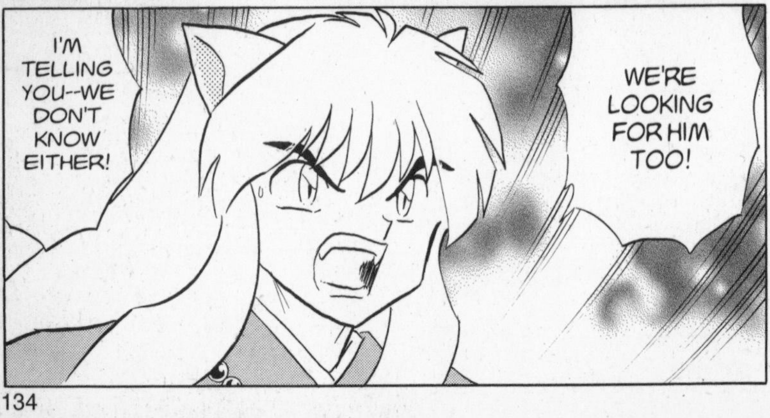
I'M TELLING YOU--WE DON'T KNOW EITHER!
WE'RE LOOKING FOR HIM TOO!

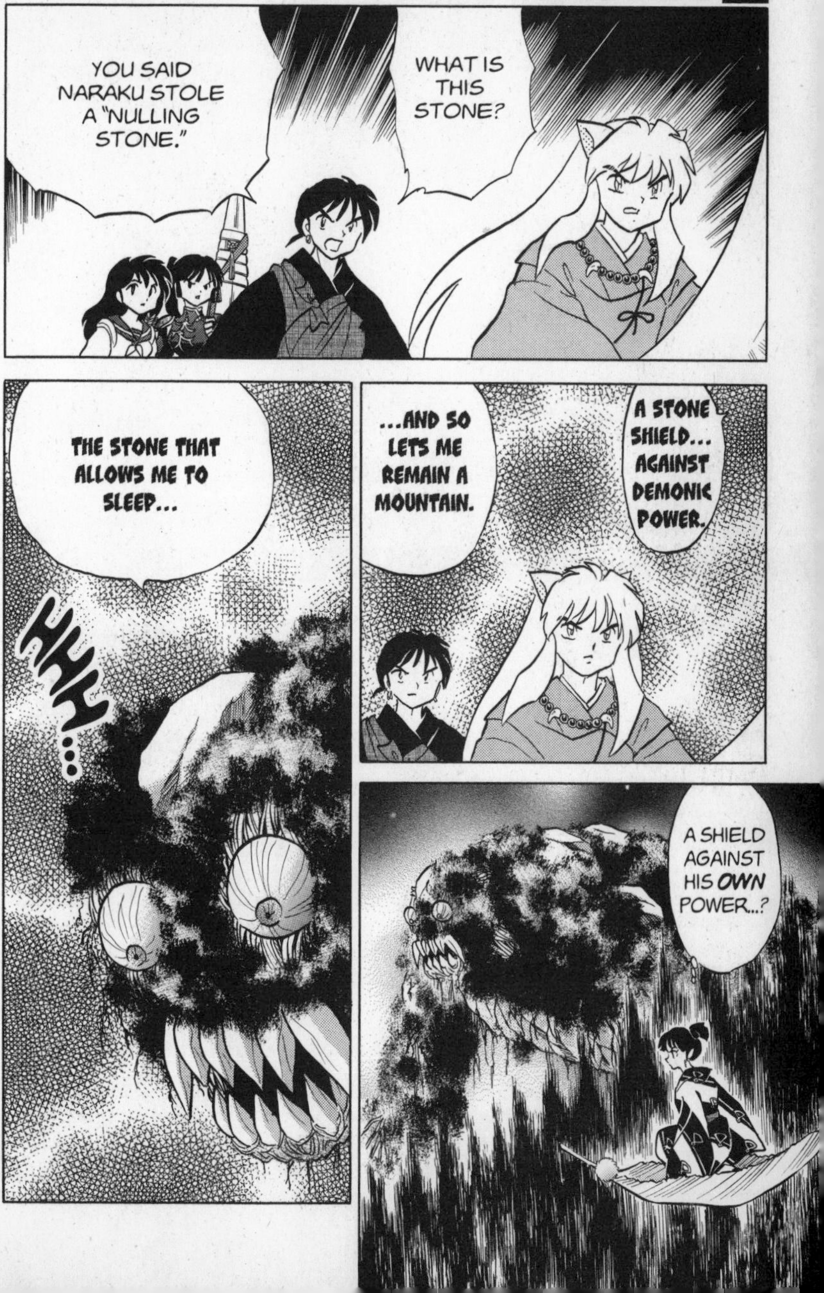
YOU SAID NARAKU STOLE A "NULLING STONE."
WHAT IS THIS STONE?
THE STONE THAT ALLOWS ME TO SLEEP...
HHH...
...AND SO LETS ME REMAIN A MOUNTAIN.
A STONE SHIELD... AGAINST DEMONIC POWER.
A SHIELD AGAINST HIS *OWN* POWER...?

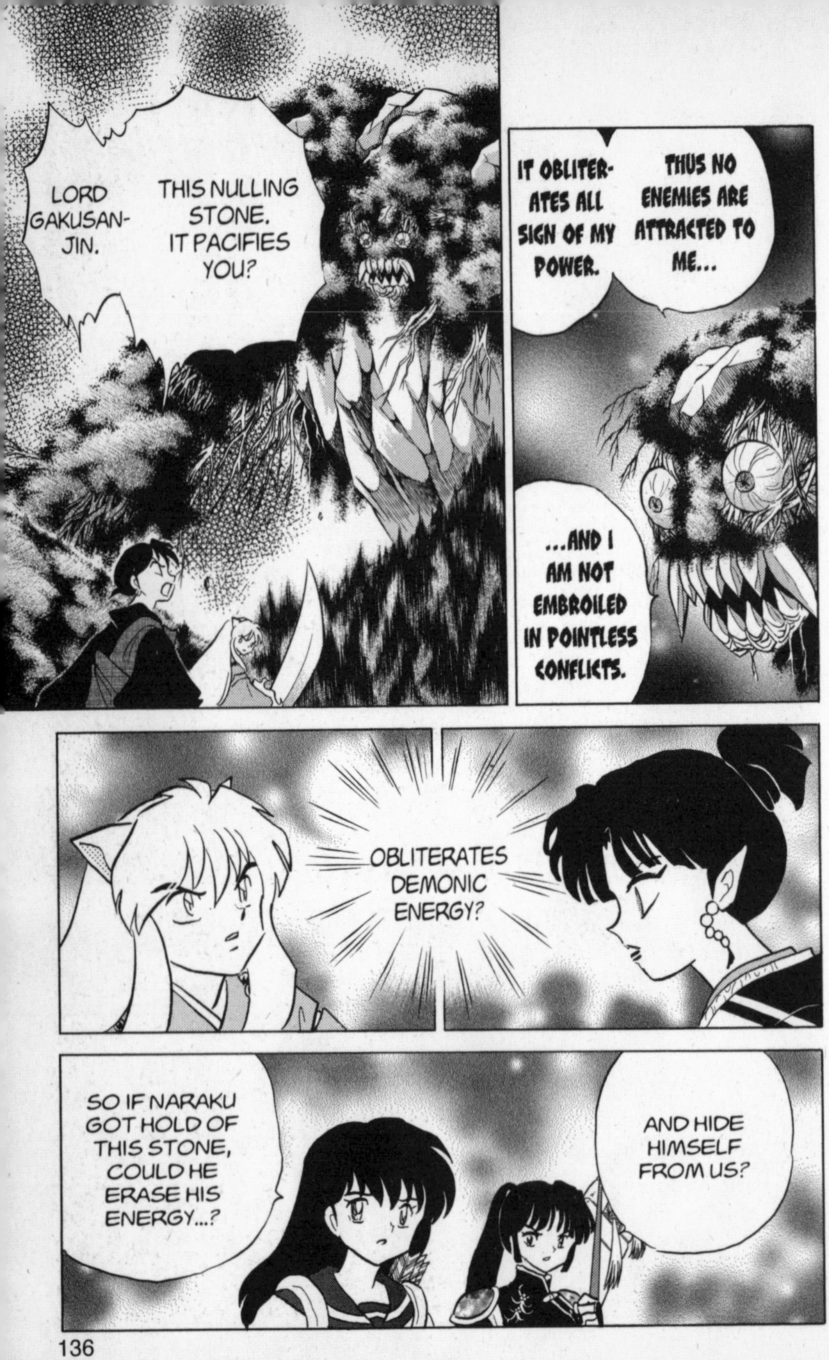

LORD GAKUSAN-JIN.
THIS NULLING STONE. IT PACIFIES YOU?
IT OBLITER-ATES ALL SIGN OF MY POWER.
THUS NO ENEMIES ARE ATTRACTED TO ME...
...AND I AM NOT EMBROILED IN POINTLESS CONFLICTS.
OBLITERATES DEMONIC ENERGY?
SO IF NARAKU GOT HOLD OF THIS STONE, COULD HE ERASE HIS ENERGY...?
AND HIDE HIMSELF FROM US?

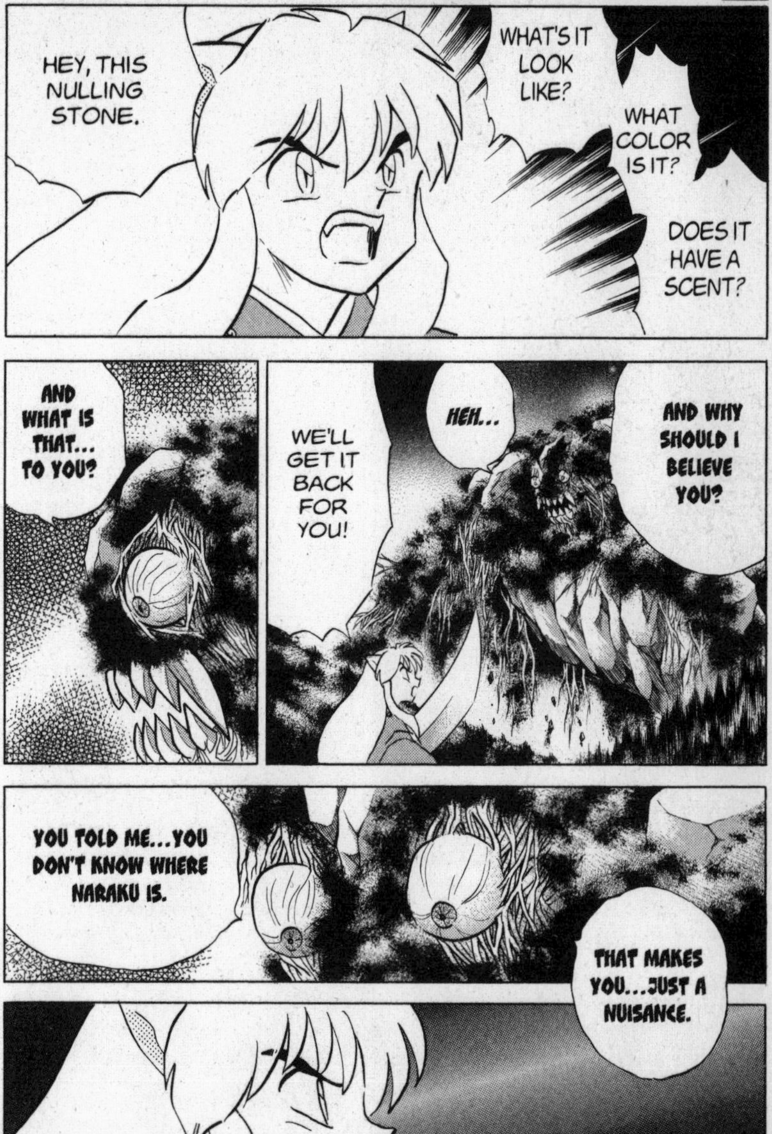
HEY, THIS NULLING STONE.
WHAT'S IT LOOK LIKE?
WHAT COLOR IS IT?
DOES IT HAVE A SCENT?
AND WHAT IS THAT... TO YOU?
WE'LL GET IT BACK FOR YOU!
HEH...
AND WHY SHOULD I BELIEVE YOU?
YOU TOLD ME...YOU DON'T KNOW WHERE NARAKU IS.
THAT MAKES YOU...JUST A NUISANCE.

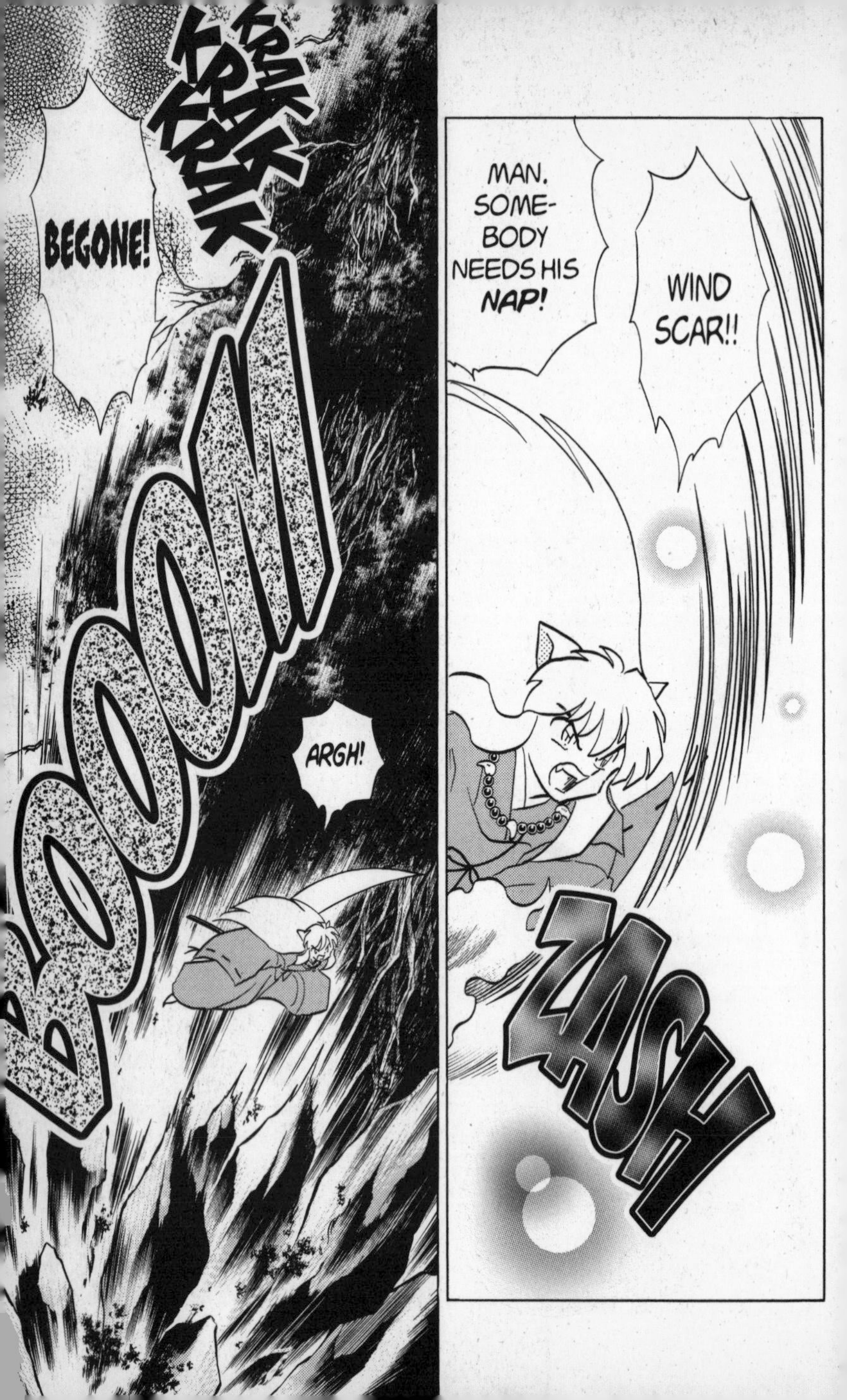
BEGONE!
KRAK KRAK KRAK
BOOOM
ARGH!
MAN. SOME-BODY NEEDS HIS *NAP!*
WIND SCAR!!
ZASH

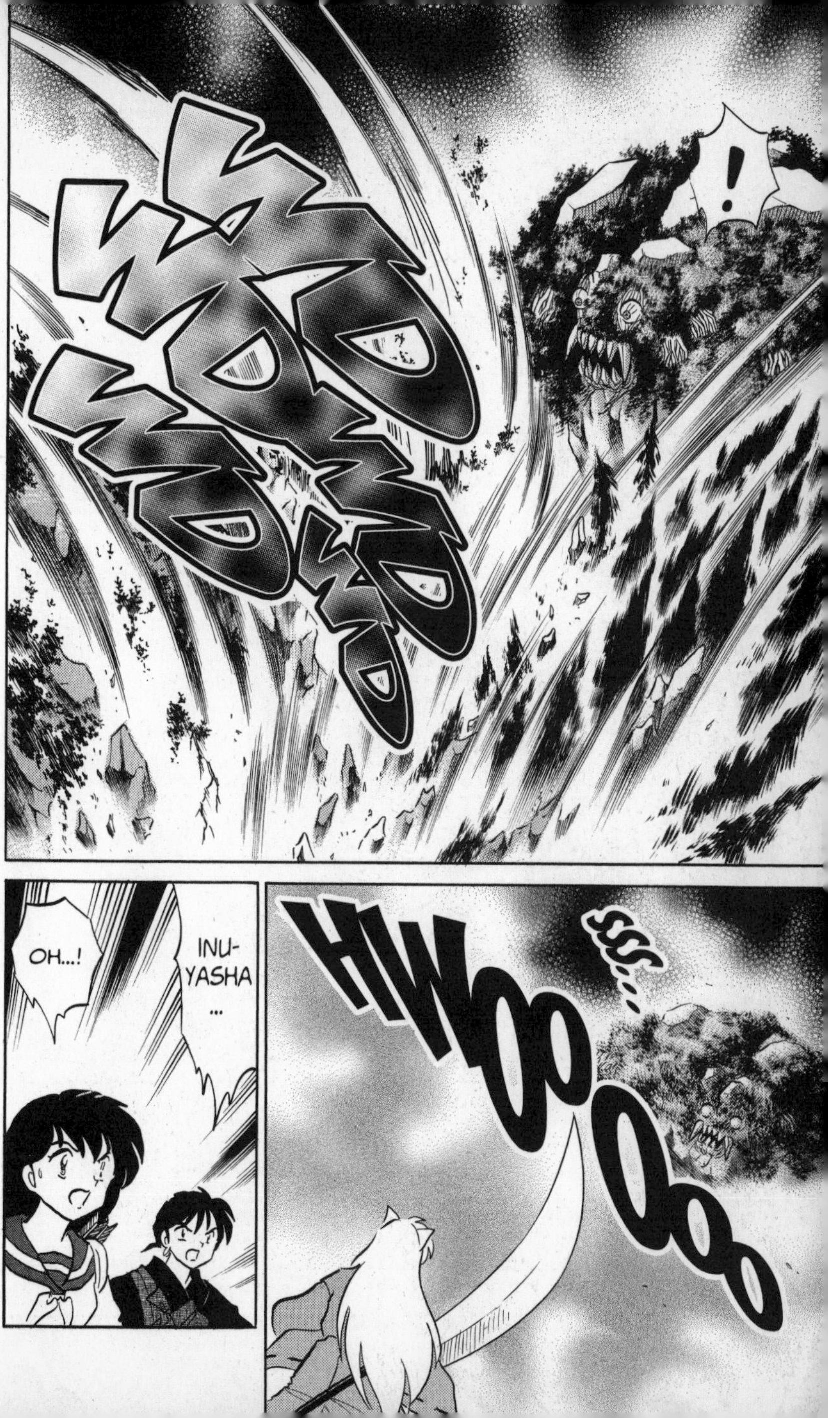
!
OH...!
INU-YASHA ...
HIWOOOOOO
SSS...

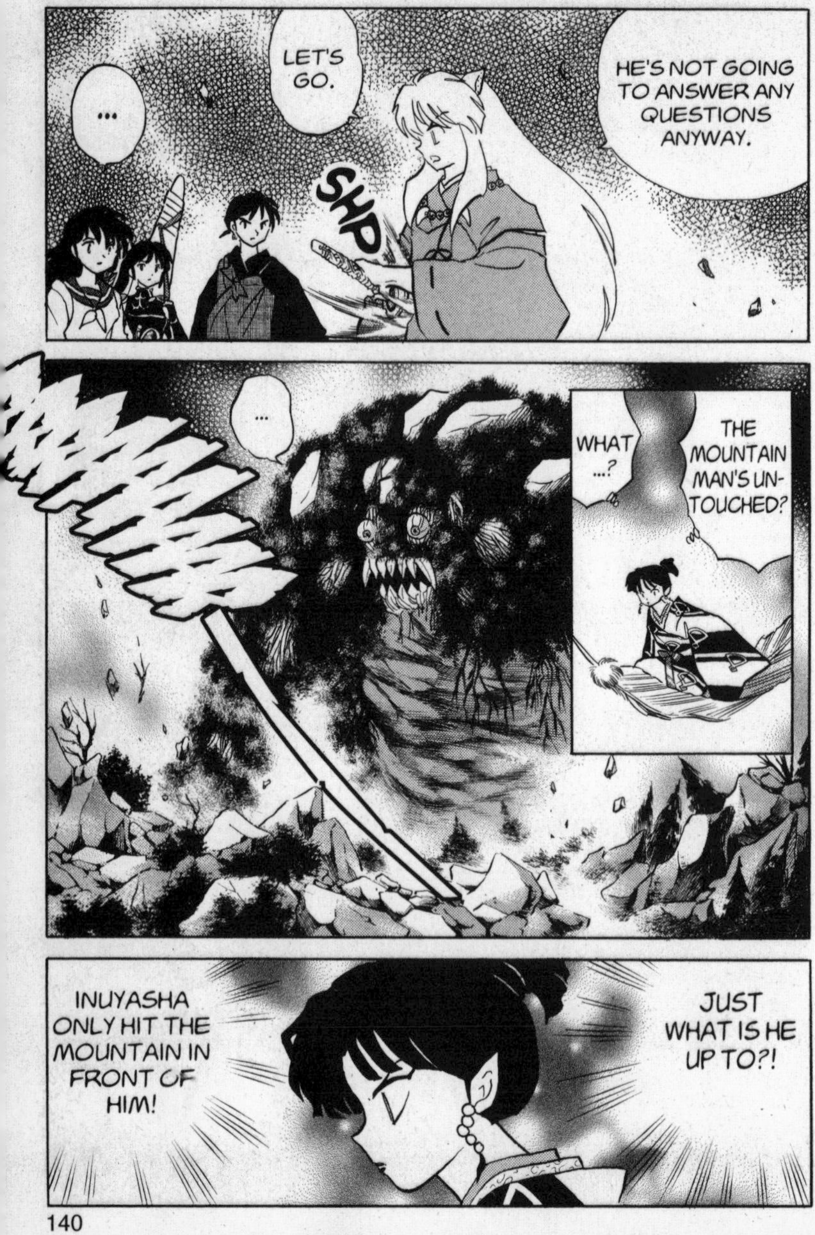
...
LET'S GO.
SHP
HE'S NOT GOING TO ANSWER ANY QUESTIONS ANYWAY.
...
WHAT ...?
THE MOUNTAIN MAN'S UN-TOUCHED?
INUYASHA ONLY HIT THE MOUNTAIN IN FRONT OF HIM!
JUST WHAT IS HE UP TO?!

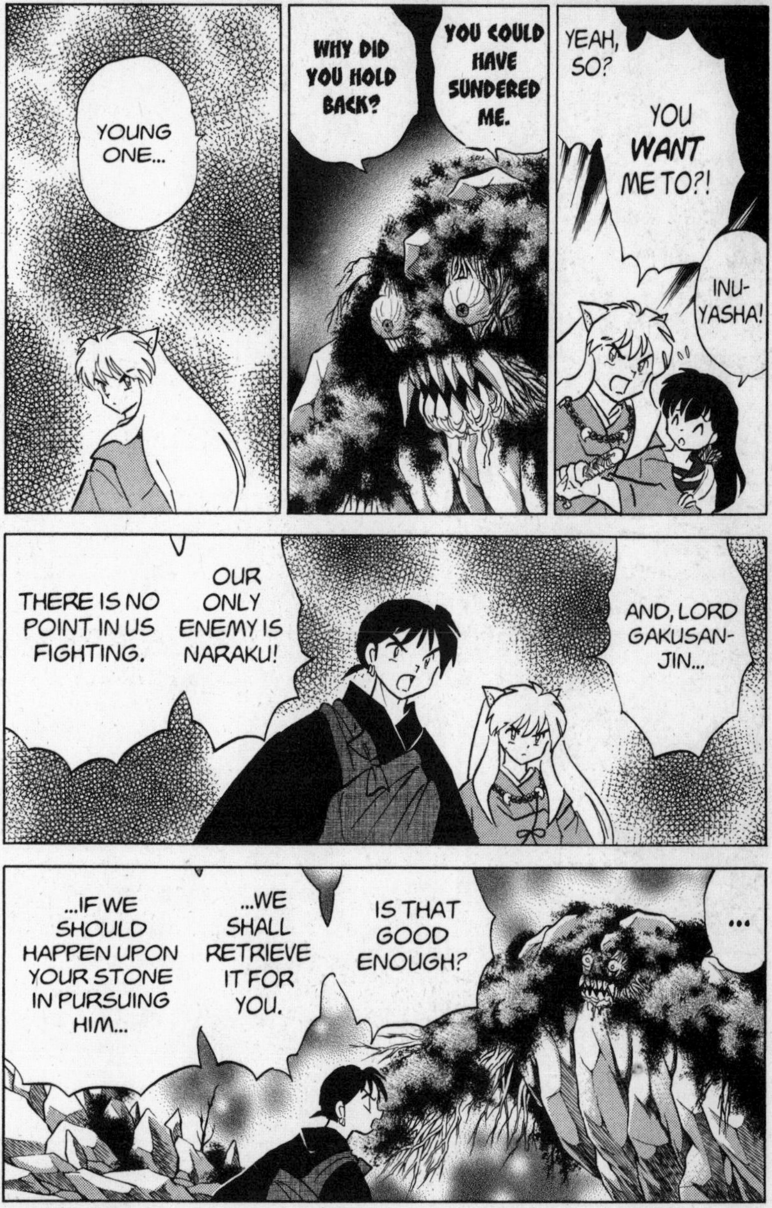
YOUNG ONE...
WHY DID YOU HOLD BACK?
YOU COULD HAVE SUNDERED ME.
YEAH, SO?
YOU WANT ME TO?!
INU-YASHA!
THERE IS NO POINT IN US FIGHTING.
OUR ONLY ENEMY IS NARAKU!
AND, LORD GAKUSAN-JIN...
...IF WE SHOULD HAPPEN UPON YOUR STONE IN PURSUING HIM...
...WE SHALL RETRIEVE IT FOR YOU.
IS THAT GOOD ENOUGH?
...

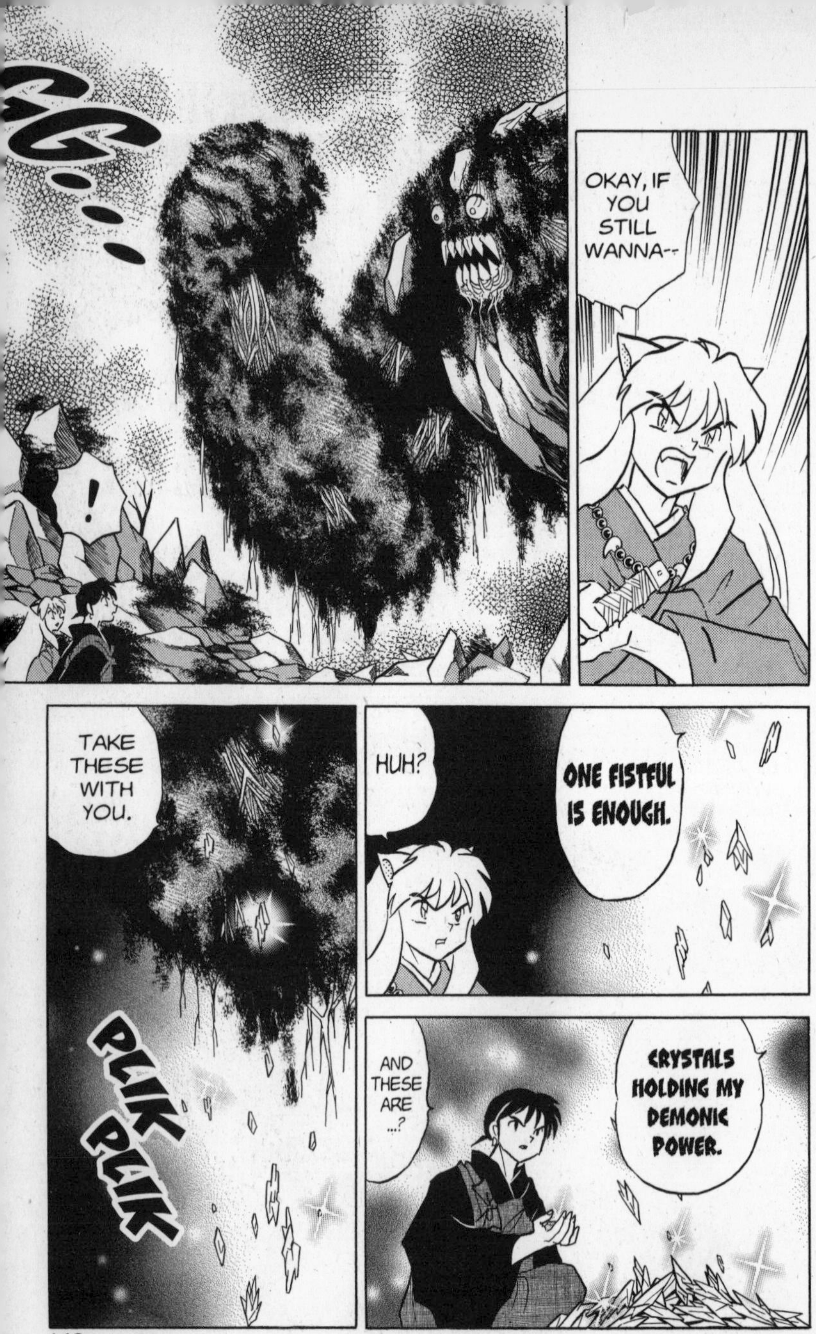
!
OKAY, IF YOU STILL WANNA--
TAKE THESE WITH YOU.
PLIK PLIK
HUH?
ONE FISTFUL IS ENOUGH.
AND THESE ARE ...?
CRYSTALS HOLDING MY DEMONIC POWER.

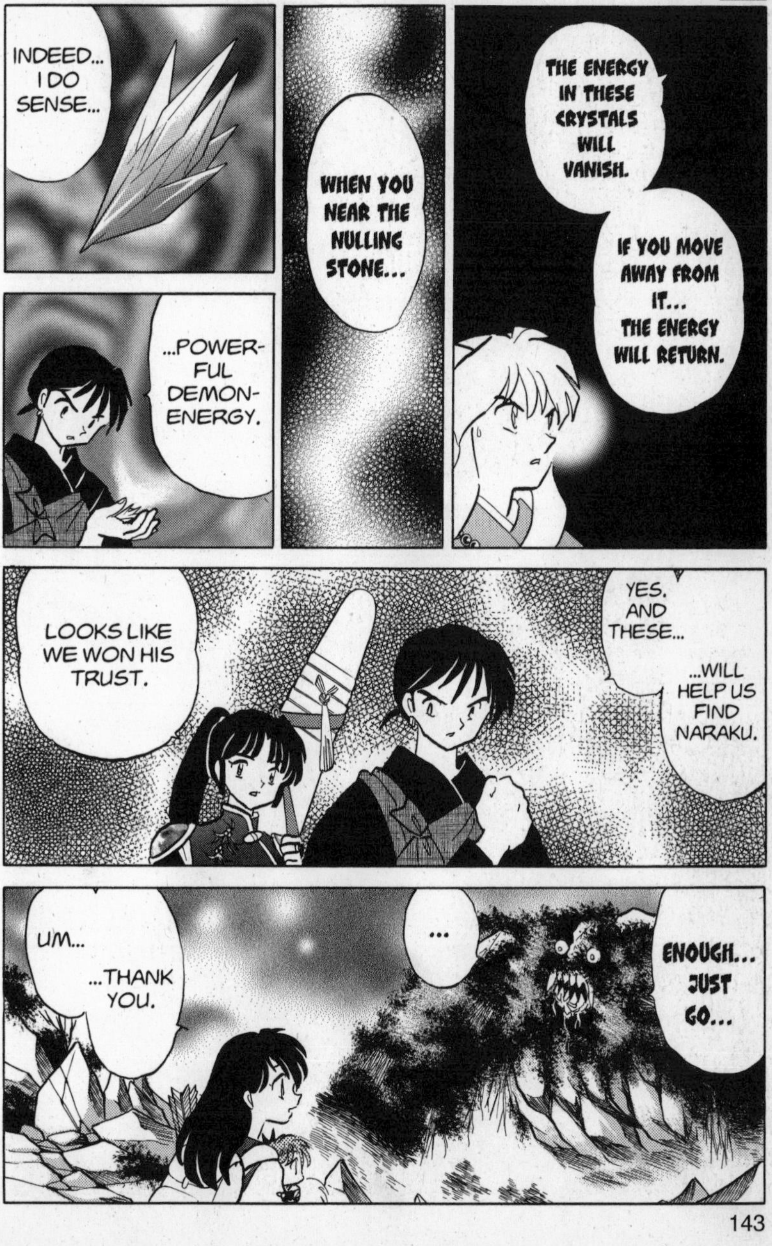
INDEED... I DO SENSE...
...POWER-FUL DEMON-ENERGY.
WHEN YOU NEAR THE NULLING STONE...
THE ENERGY IN THESE CRYSTALS WILL VANISH.
IF YOU MOVE AWAY FROM IT... THE ENERGY WILL RETURN.
LOOKS LIKE WE WON HIS TRUST.
YES. AND THESE...
...WILL HELP US FIND NARAKU.
UM...
...THANK YOU.
...
ENOUGH... JUST GO...

STILL, I WONDER...

WHY WOULD NARAKU STEAL A STONE LIKE THAT?

IT'S NOT LIKE HE'S EVER BEEN EASY TO TRACK DOWN.

IS HE ABOUT TO PULL SOMETHING THAT'LL REQUIRE HIM TO HIDE EVEN *MORE* ENERGY?

WSSH

I'M STARTING TO CATCH ON.

NARAKU MUST BE PLANNING TO USE THAT NULLING STONE...

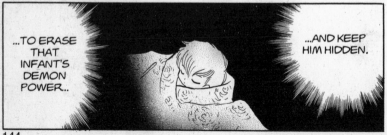

...TO ERASE THAT INFANT'S DEMON POWER...

...AND KEEP HIM HIDDEN.

144

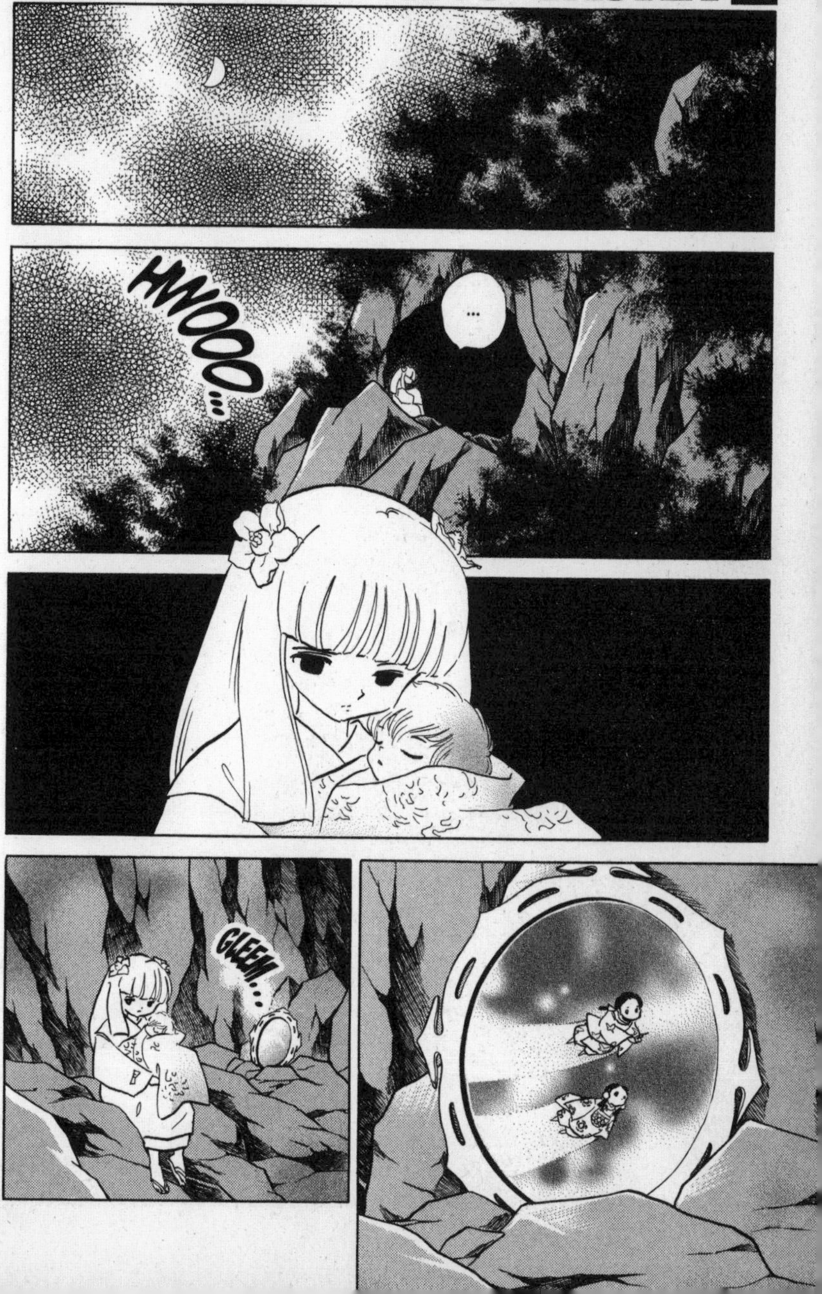
HWOOO...
...
GLEEM...

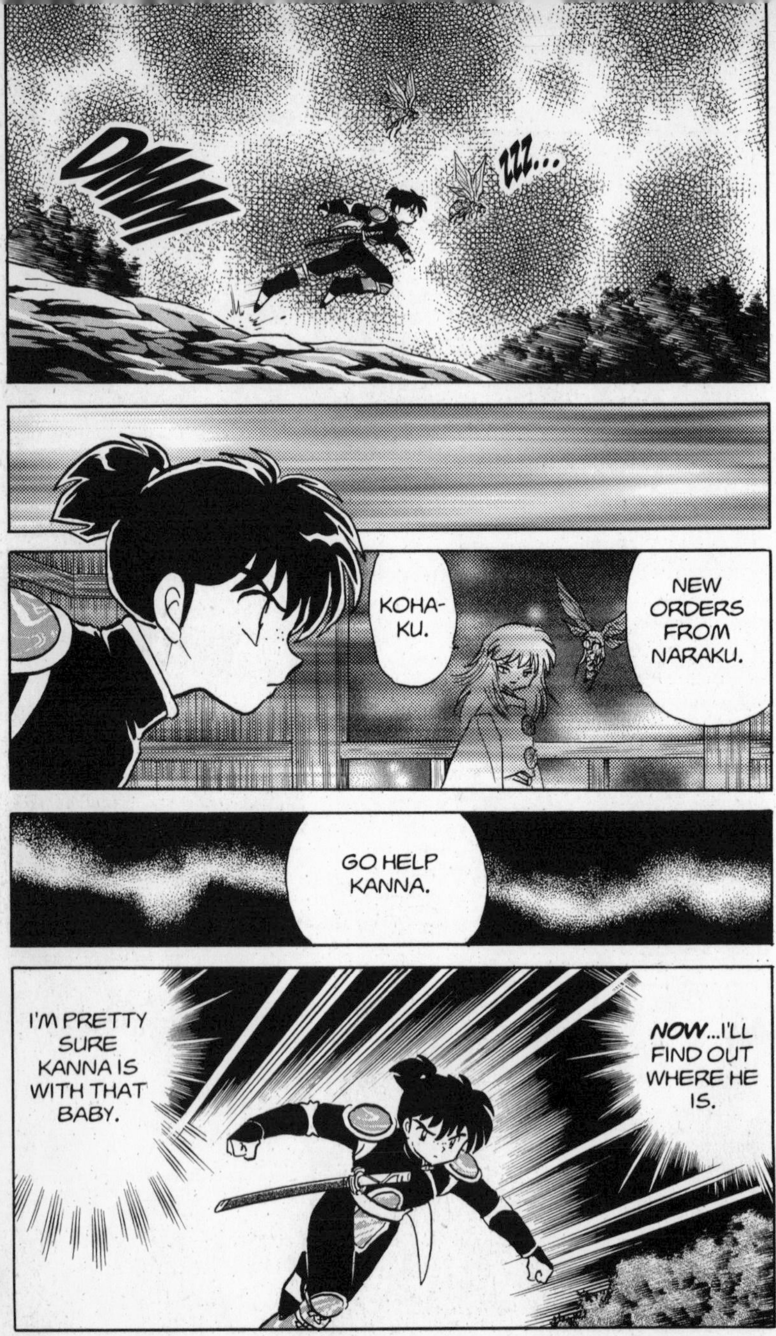
DMM
ZZZ...
KOHA-KU.
NEW ORDERS FROM NARAKU.
GO HELP KANNA.
I'M PRETTY SURE KANNA IS WITH THAT BABY.
NOW...I'LL FIND OUT WHERE HE IS.

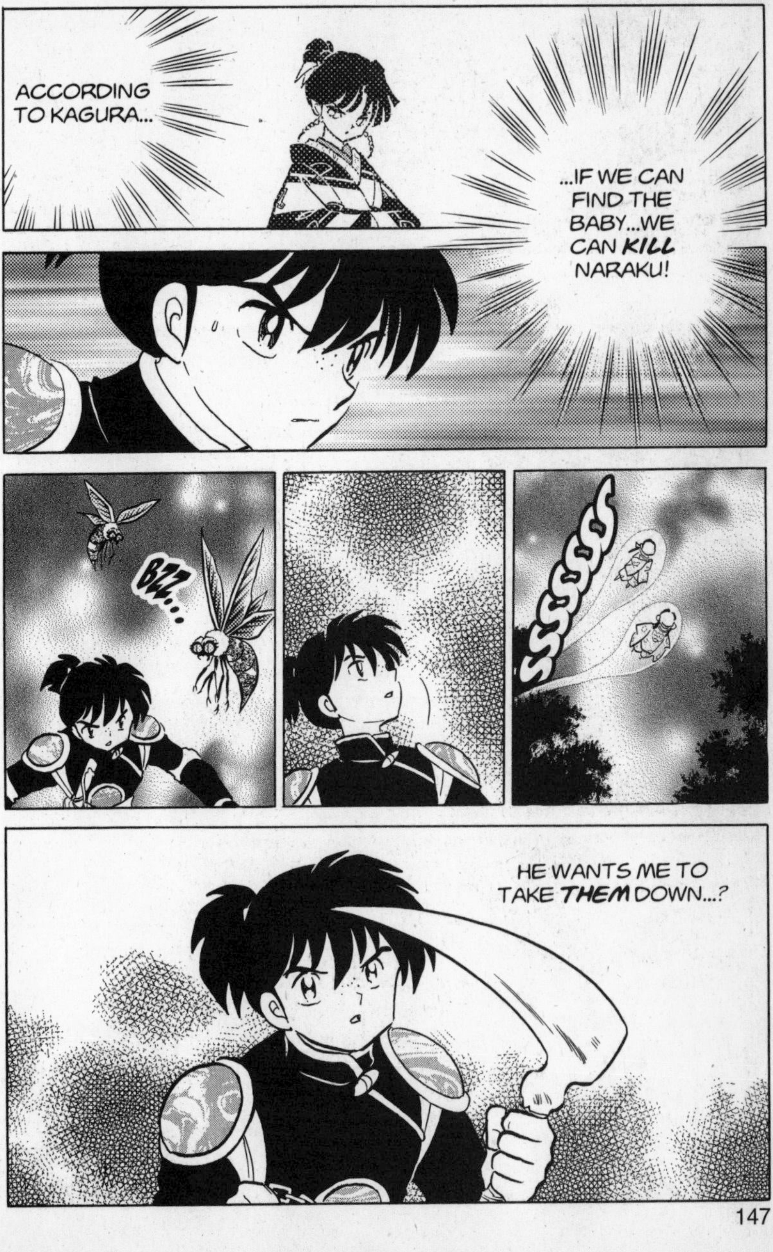
ACCORDING TO KAGURA...
...IF WE CAN FIND THE BABY...WE CAN KILL NARAKU!
BZZ...
SSSSSSS
HE WANTS ME TO TAKE THEM DOWN...?

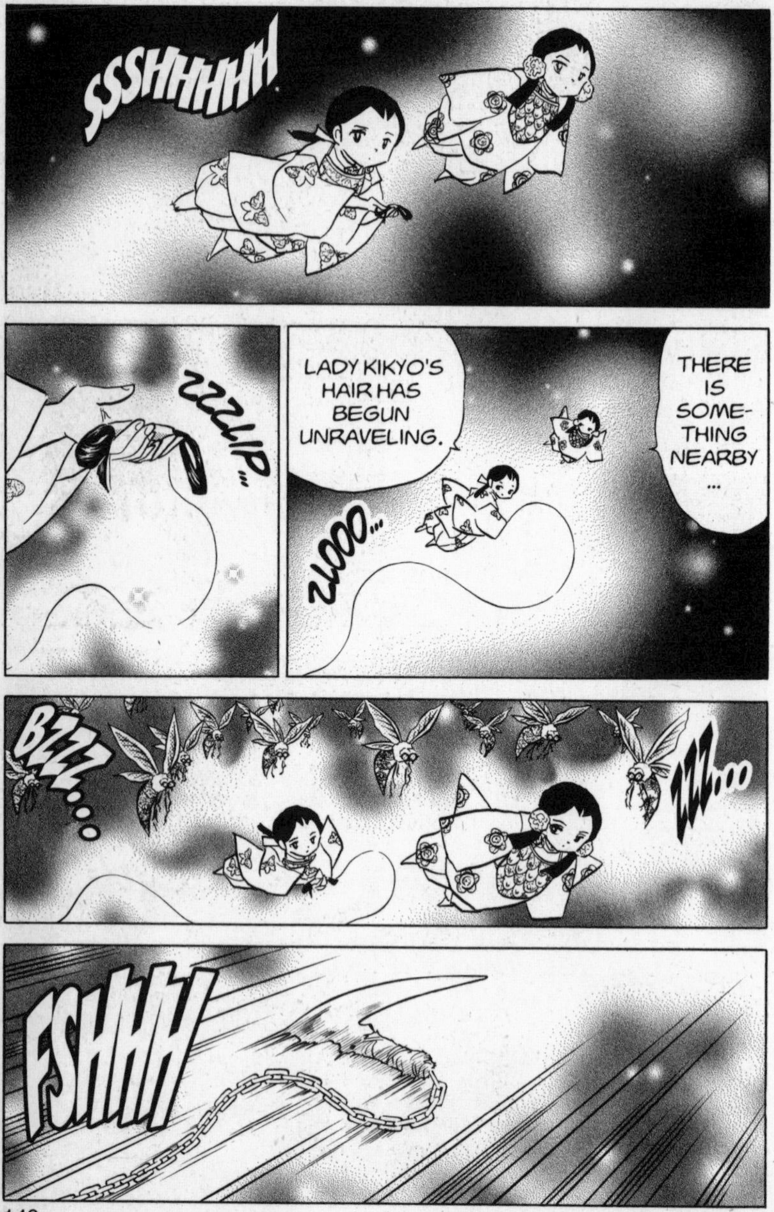
SSSHHHHH
ZZZLIP...
LADY KIKYO'S HAIR HAS BEGUN UNRAVELING.
ZLOOO...
THERE IS SOME-THING NEARBY ...
BZZZ...
ZZZ...
FSHHH

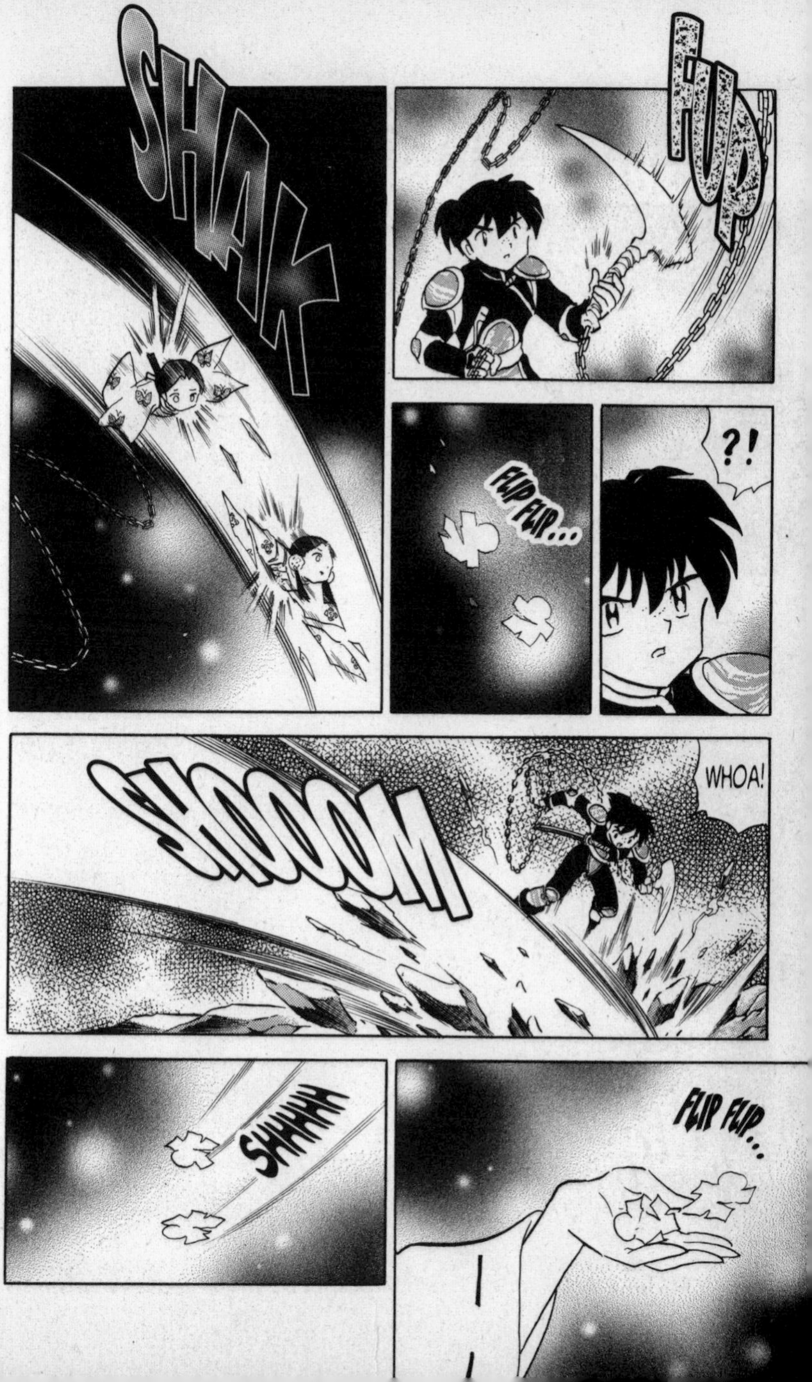
SHAK
FLIP
FLIP FLIP...
?!
SHOOOM
WHOA!
SHHHH
FLIP FLIP...

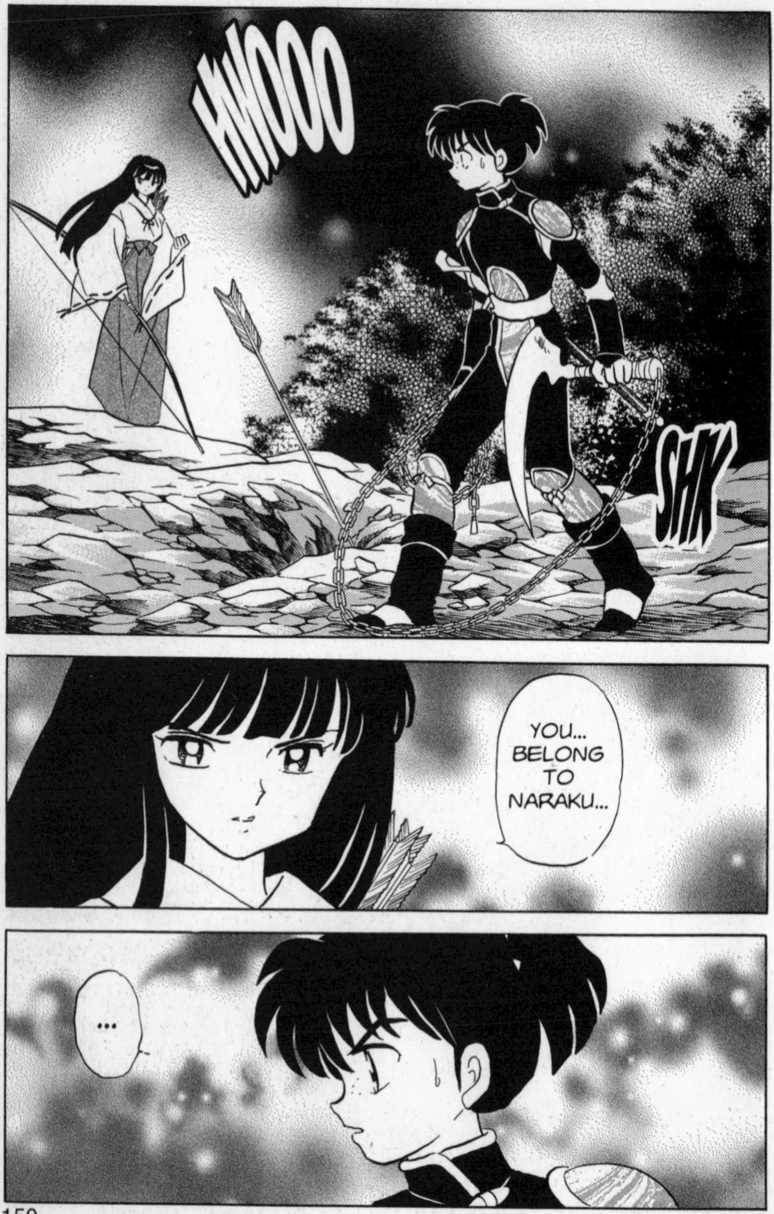
HWOOO
SHK
YOU... BELONG TO NARAKU...
...

SCROLL 9 THE NULLING STONE

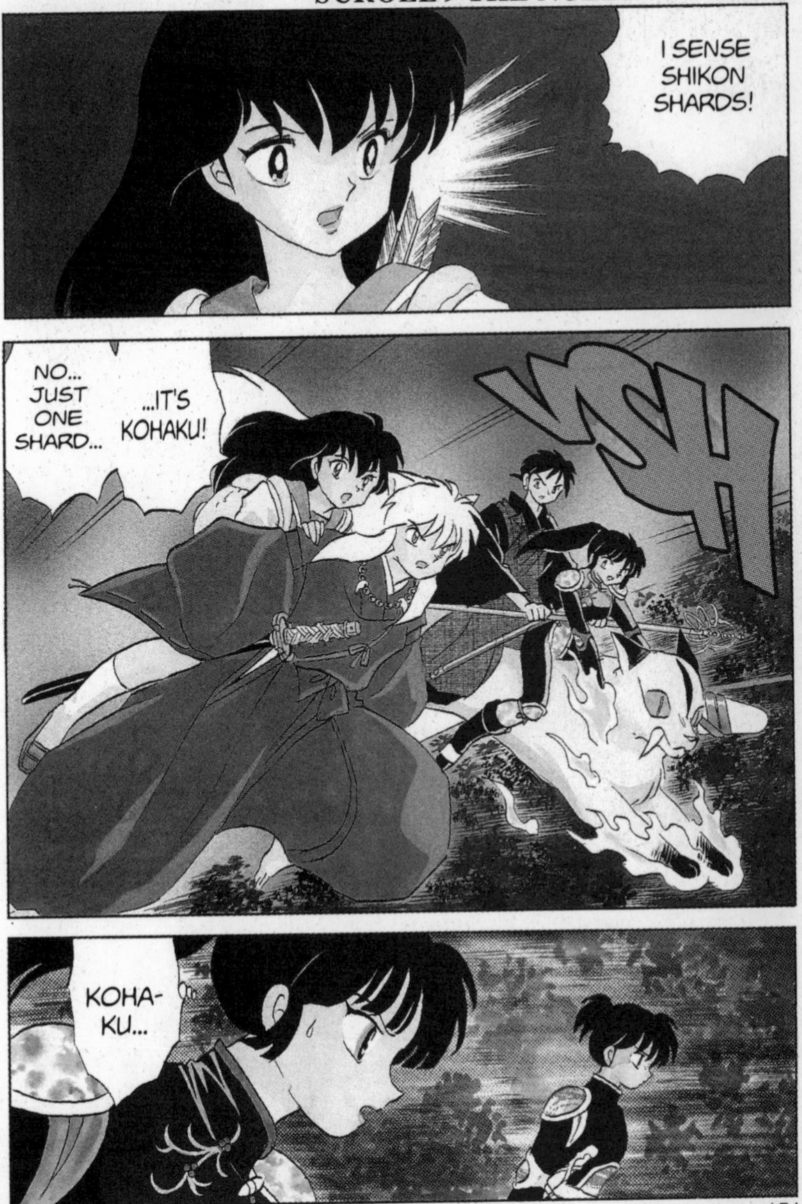
I SENSE SHIKON SHARDS!
NO... JUST ONE SHARD...
...IT'S KOHAKU!
VSH
KOHA-KU...

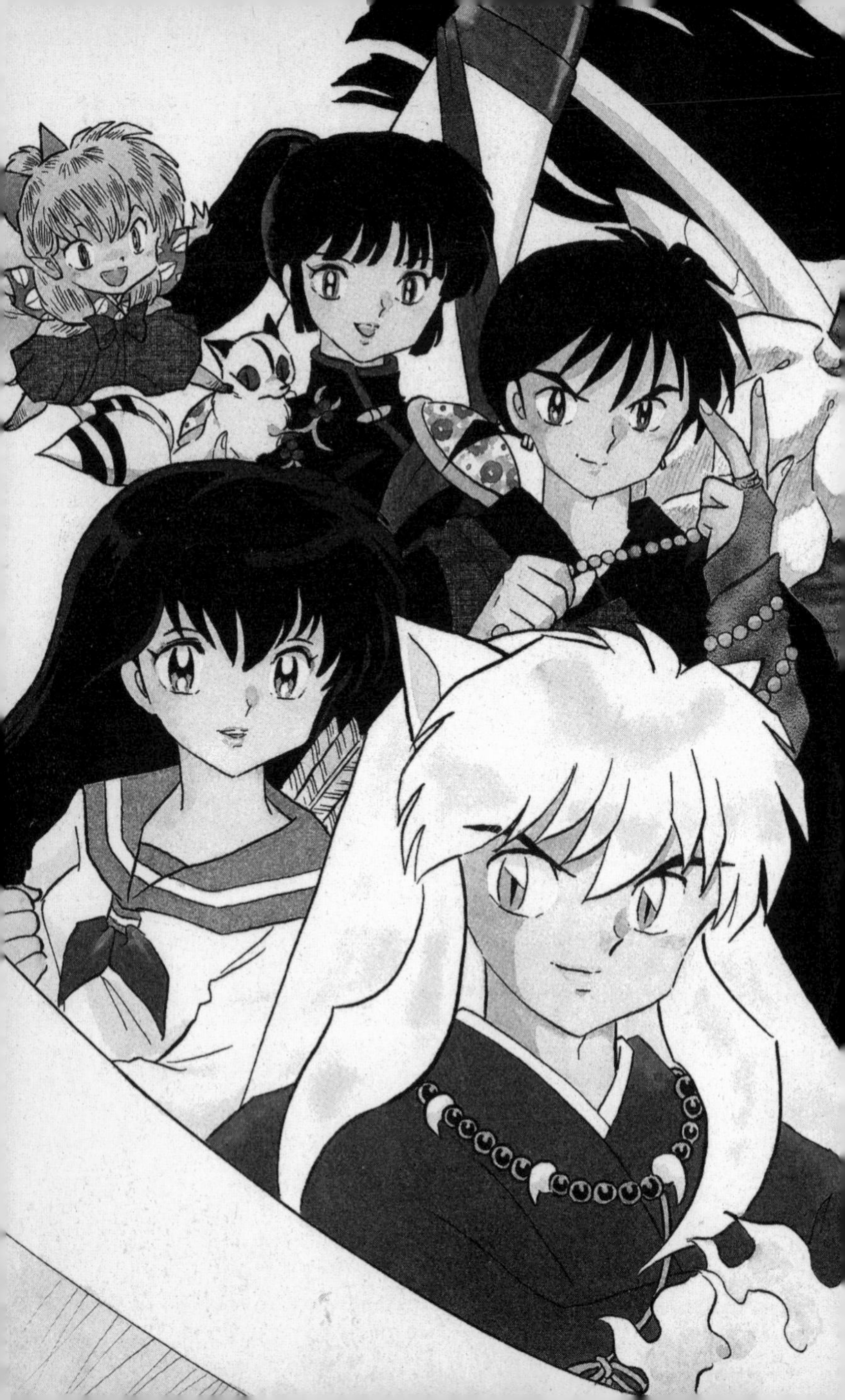

SCROLL 9

THE NULLING STONE

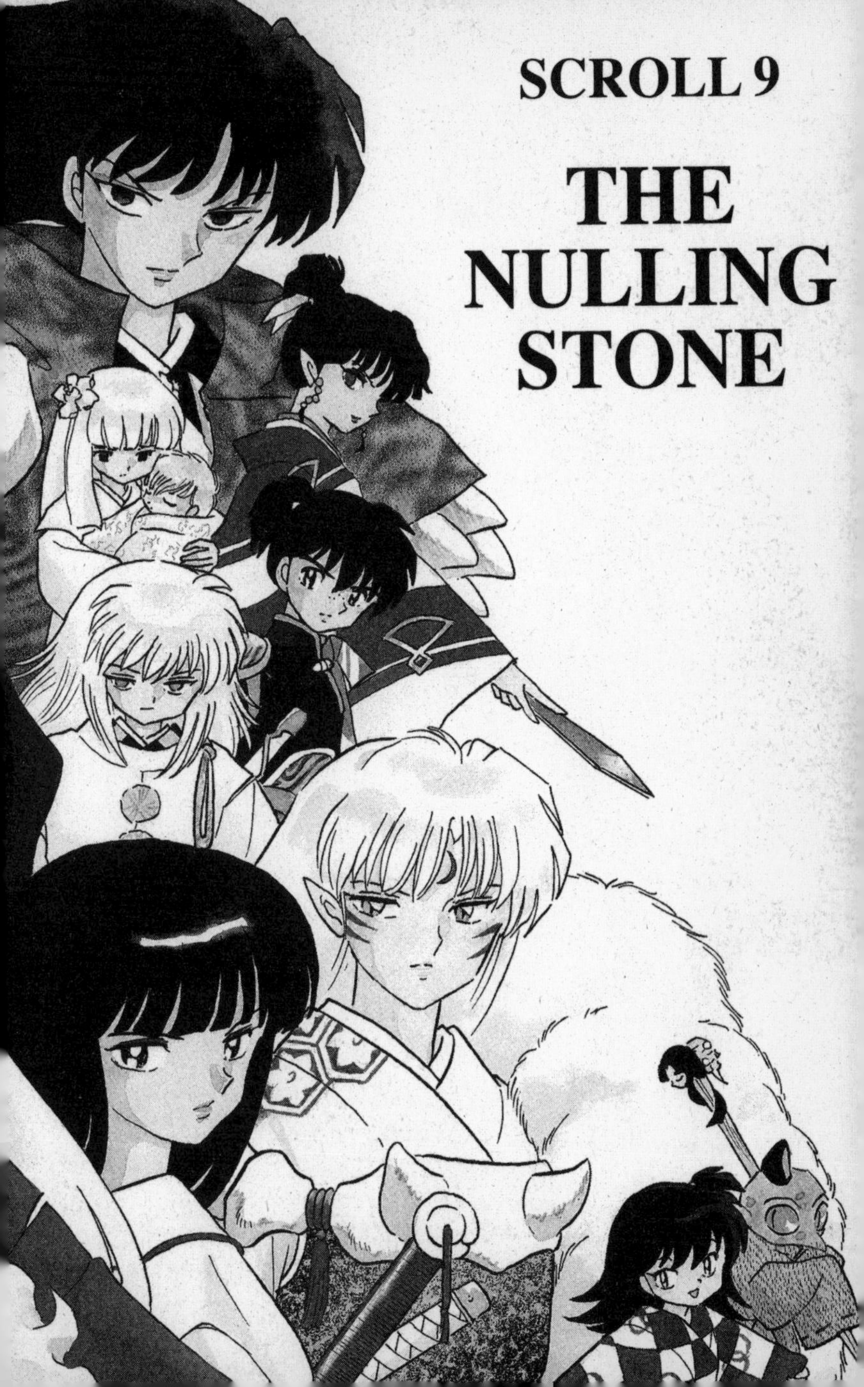

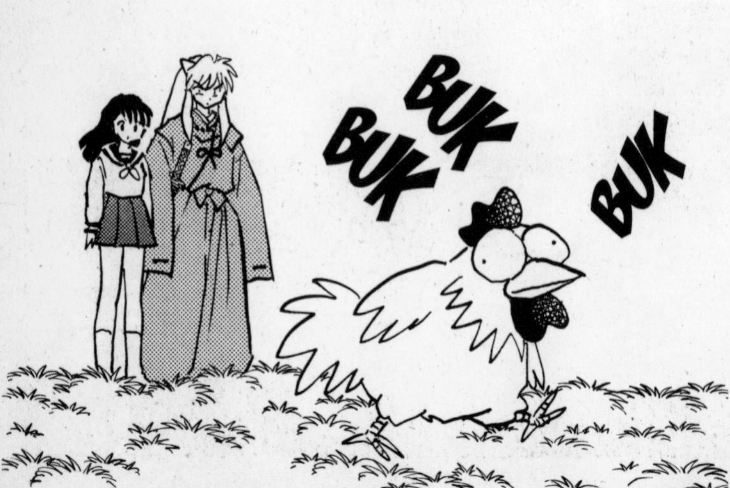
BUK
BUK
BUK

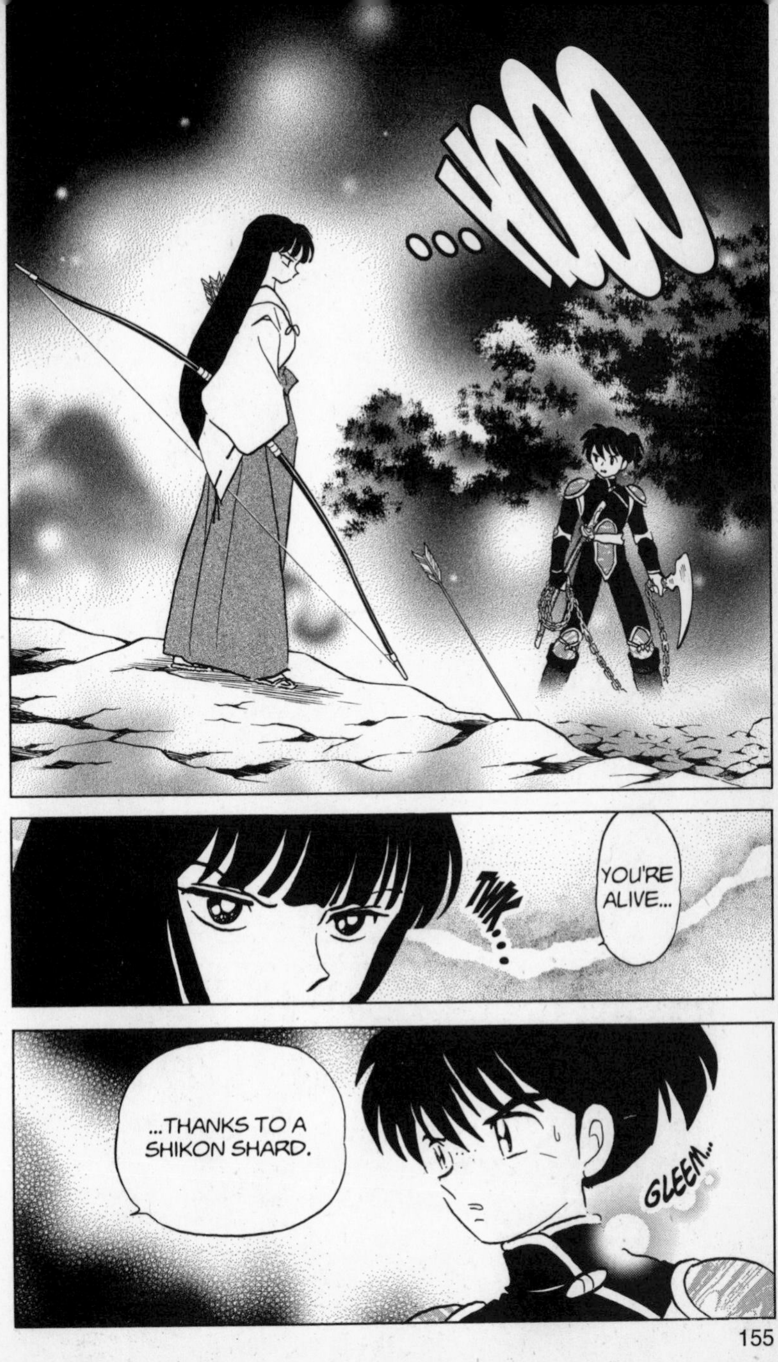
...WOOO
TWK...
YOU'RE ALIVE...
...THANKS TO A SHIKON SHARD.
GLEEM...

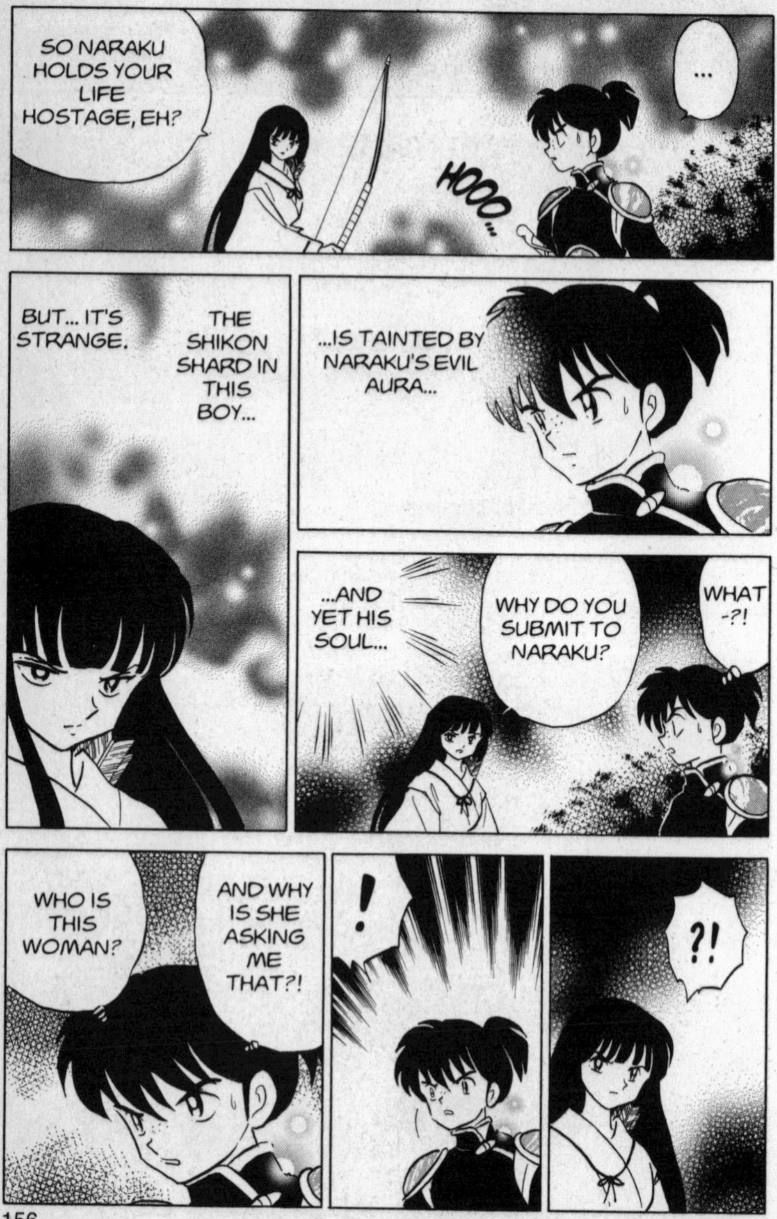
SO NARAKU HOLDS YOUR LIFE HOSTAGE, EH?
...
HOOO...
BUT... IT'S STRANGE.
THE SHIKON SHARD IN THIS BOY...
...IS TAINTED BY NARAKU'S EVIL AURA...
...AND YET HIS SOUL...
WHY DO YOU SUBMIT TO NARAKU?
WHAT -?!
WHO IS THIS WOMAN?
AND WHY IS SHE ASKING ME THAT?!
!
?!

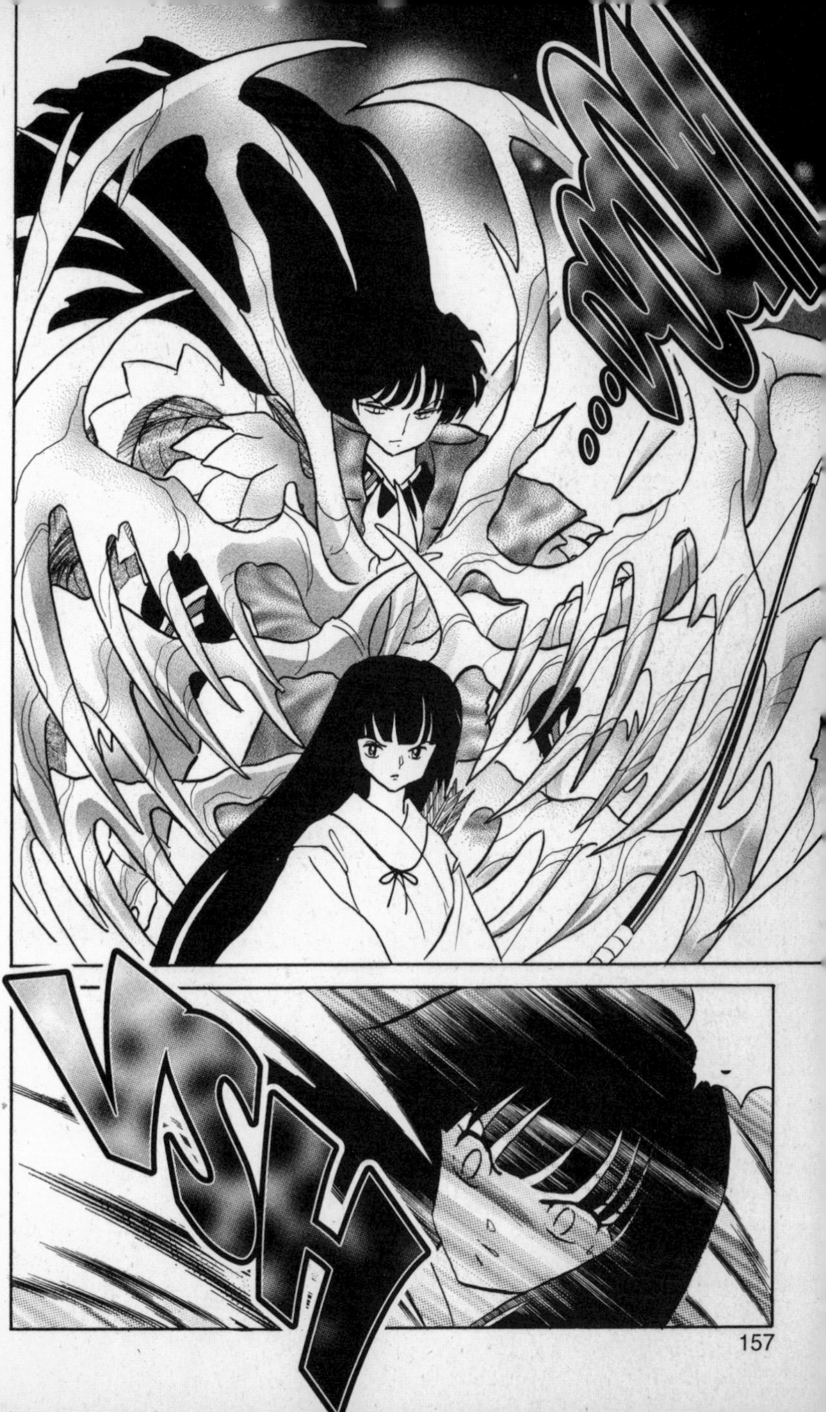
VSH

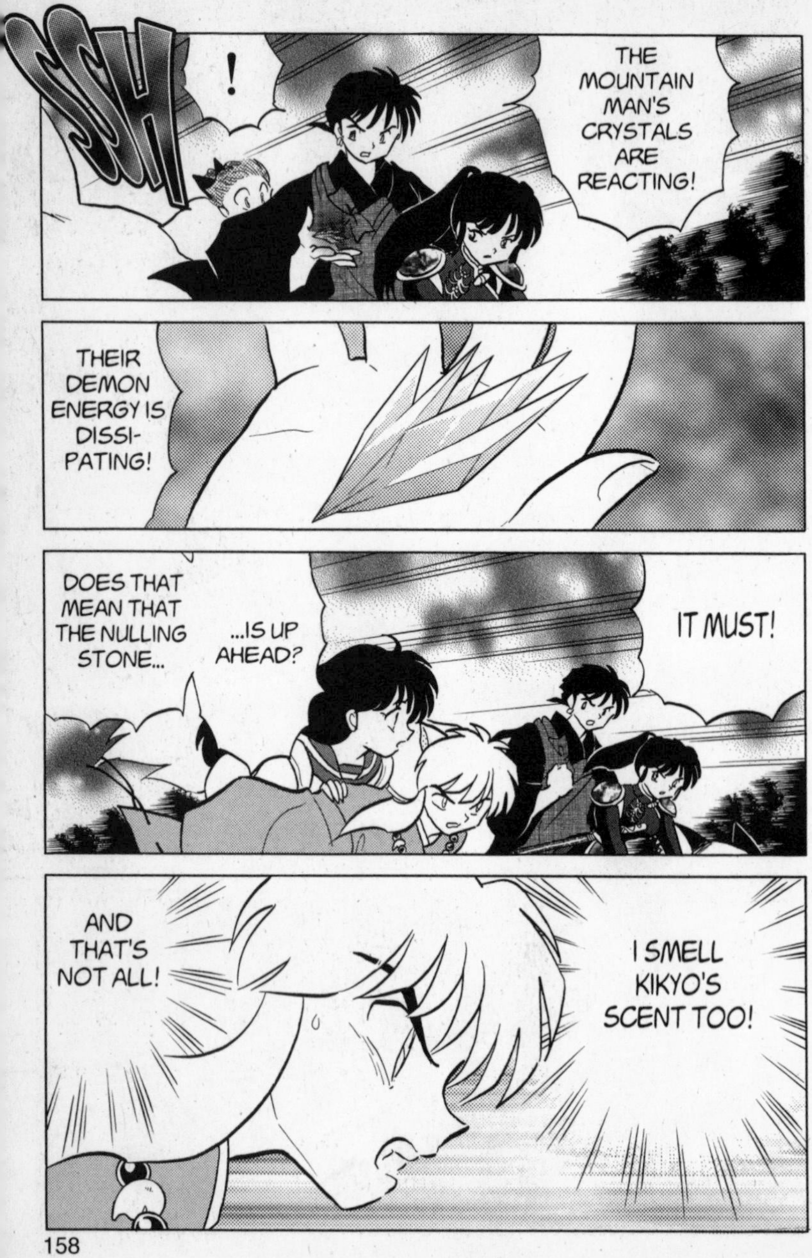
SSSH
!
THE MOUNTAIN MAN'S CRYSTALS ARE REACTING!
THEIR DEMON ENERGY IS DISSI-PATING!
DOES THAT MEAN THAT THE NULLING STONE...
...IS UP AHEAD?
IT MUST!
AND THAT'S NOT ALL!
I SMELL KIKYO'S SCENT TOO!

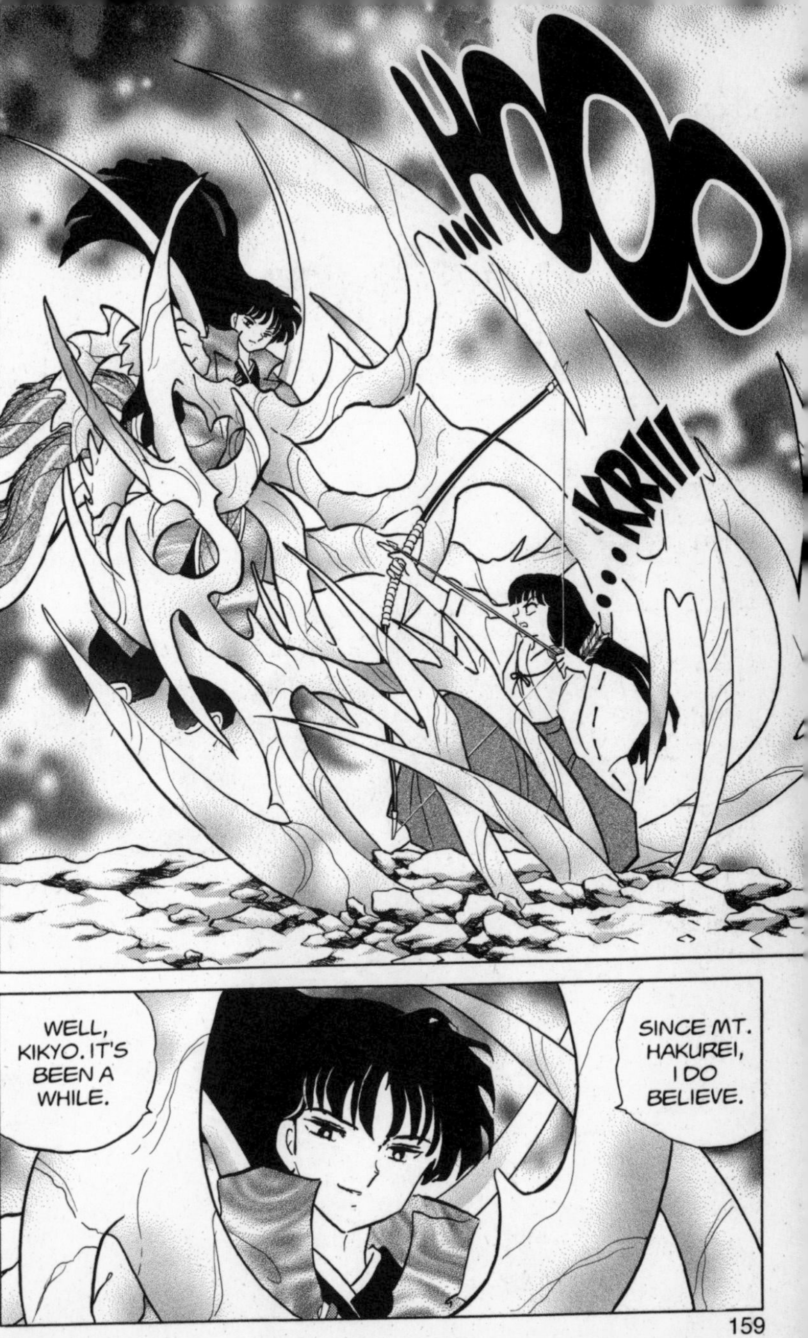
...HOOO
...KRIII
WELL, KIKYO. IT'S BEEN A WHILE.
SINCE MT. HAKUREI, I DO BELIEVE.

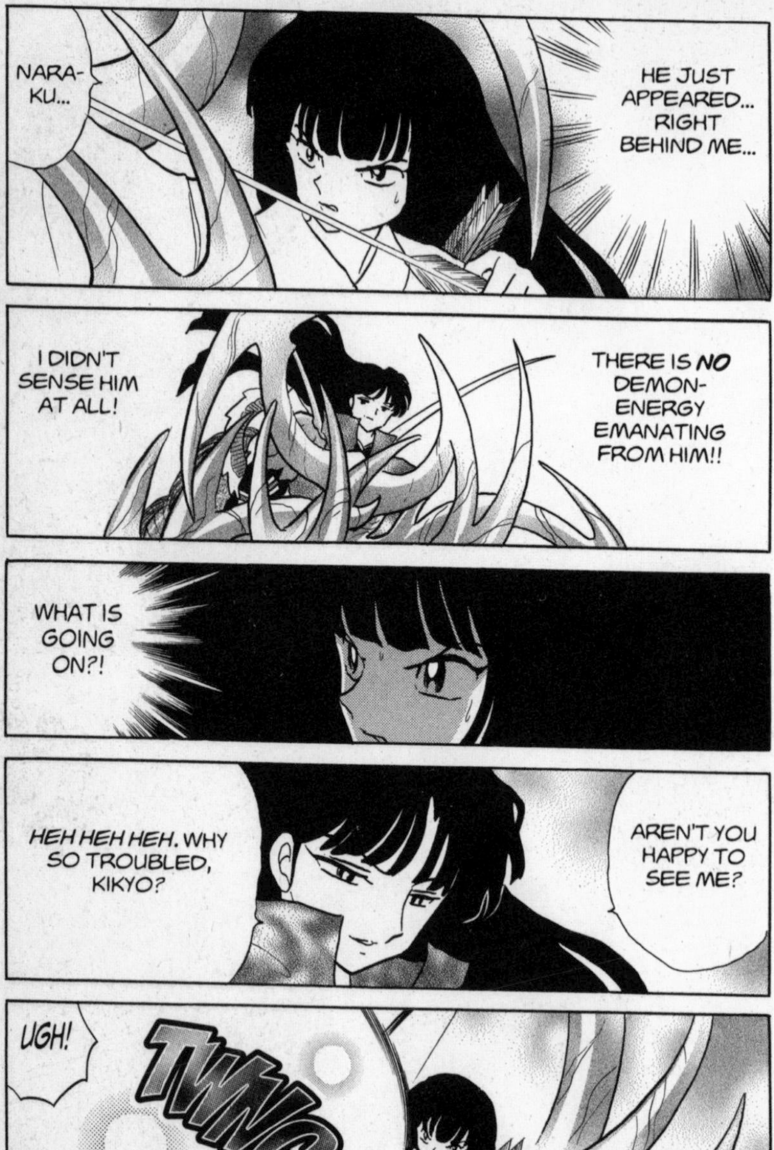
NARAKU...
HE JUST APPEARED... RIGHT BEHIND ME...
I DIDN'T SENSE HIM AT ALL!
THERE IS NO DEMON-ENERGY EMANATING FROM HIM!!
WHAT IS GOING ON?!
HEH HEH HEH. WHY SO TROUBLED, KIKYO?
AREN'T YOU HAPPY TO SEE ME?
UGH!
TWNG

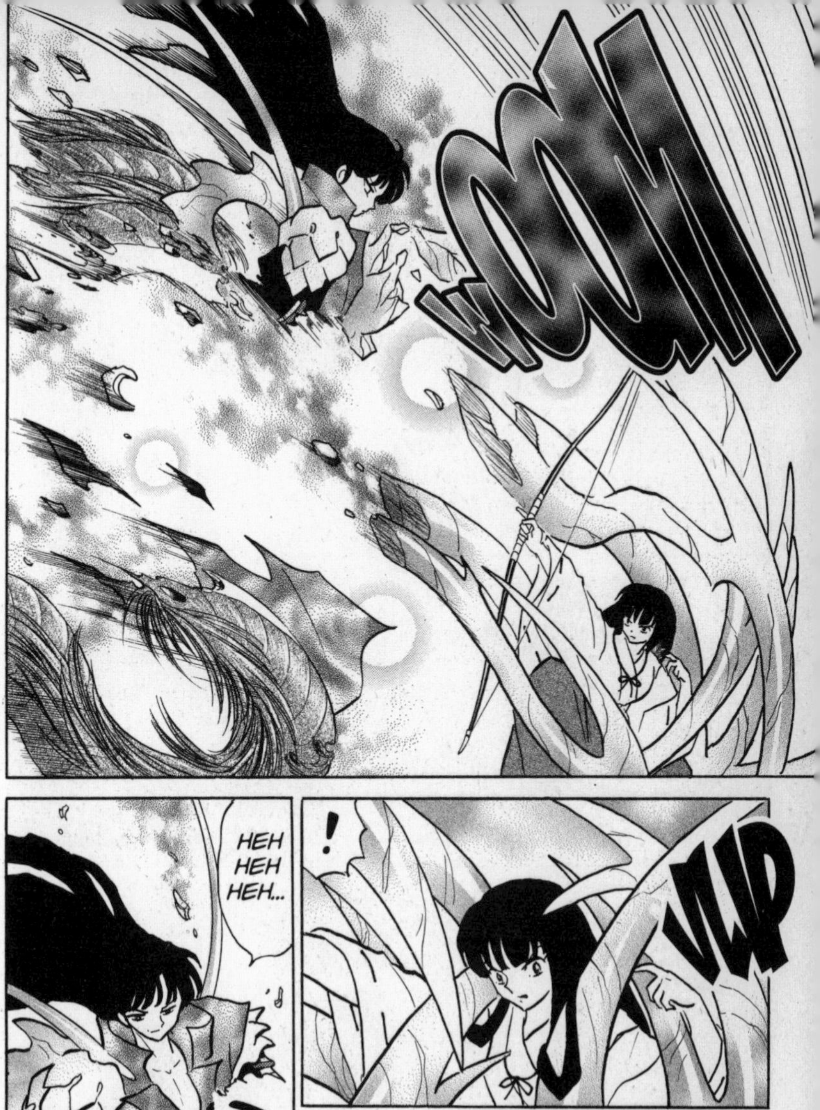
WOOM
HEH HEH HEH...
SHHHH
!
VWP
I CAN'T REACH MY ARROWS ...

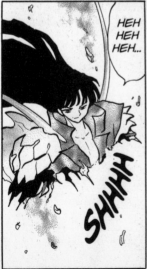

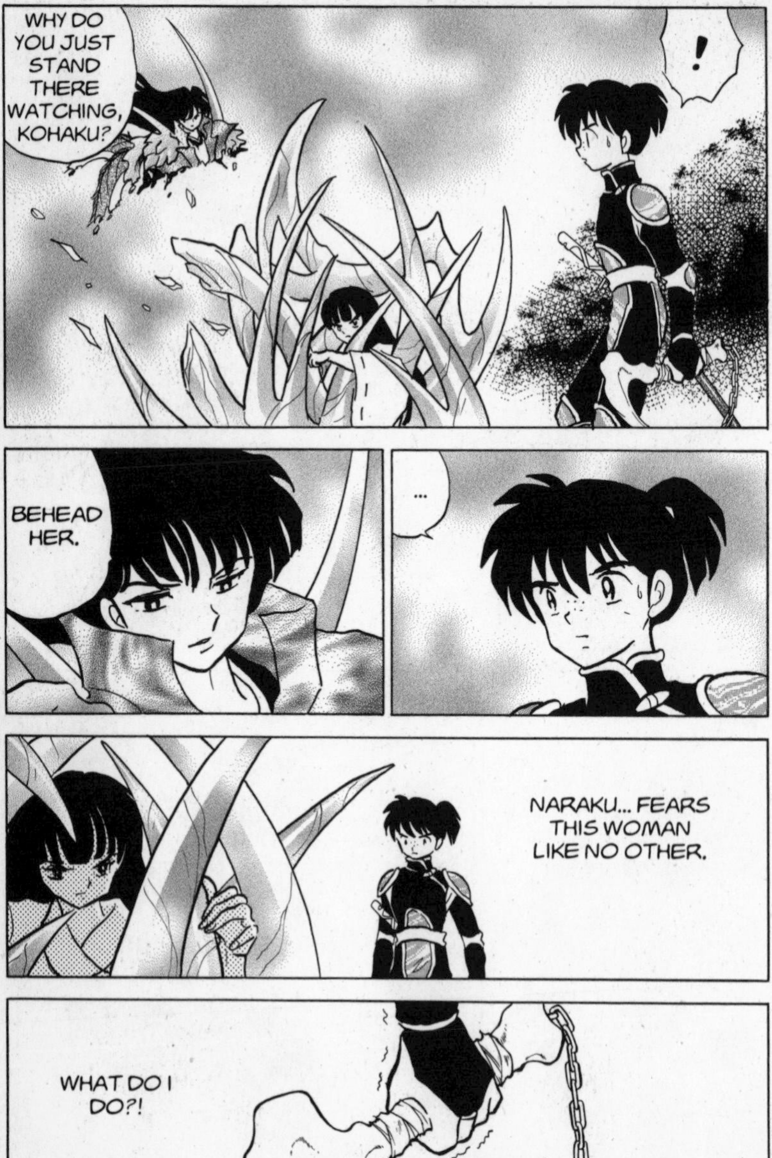
WHY DO YOU JUST STAND THERE WATCHING, KOHAKU?
!
BEHEAD HER.
...
NARAKU... FEARS THIS WOMAN LIKE NO OTHER.
WHAT DO I DO?!

HAVING A CRISIS OF **CONSCIENCE,** KOHAKU?

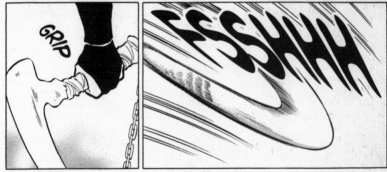

GRIP

SSSUHH

SHAK

!

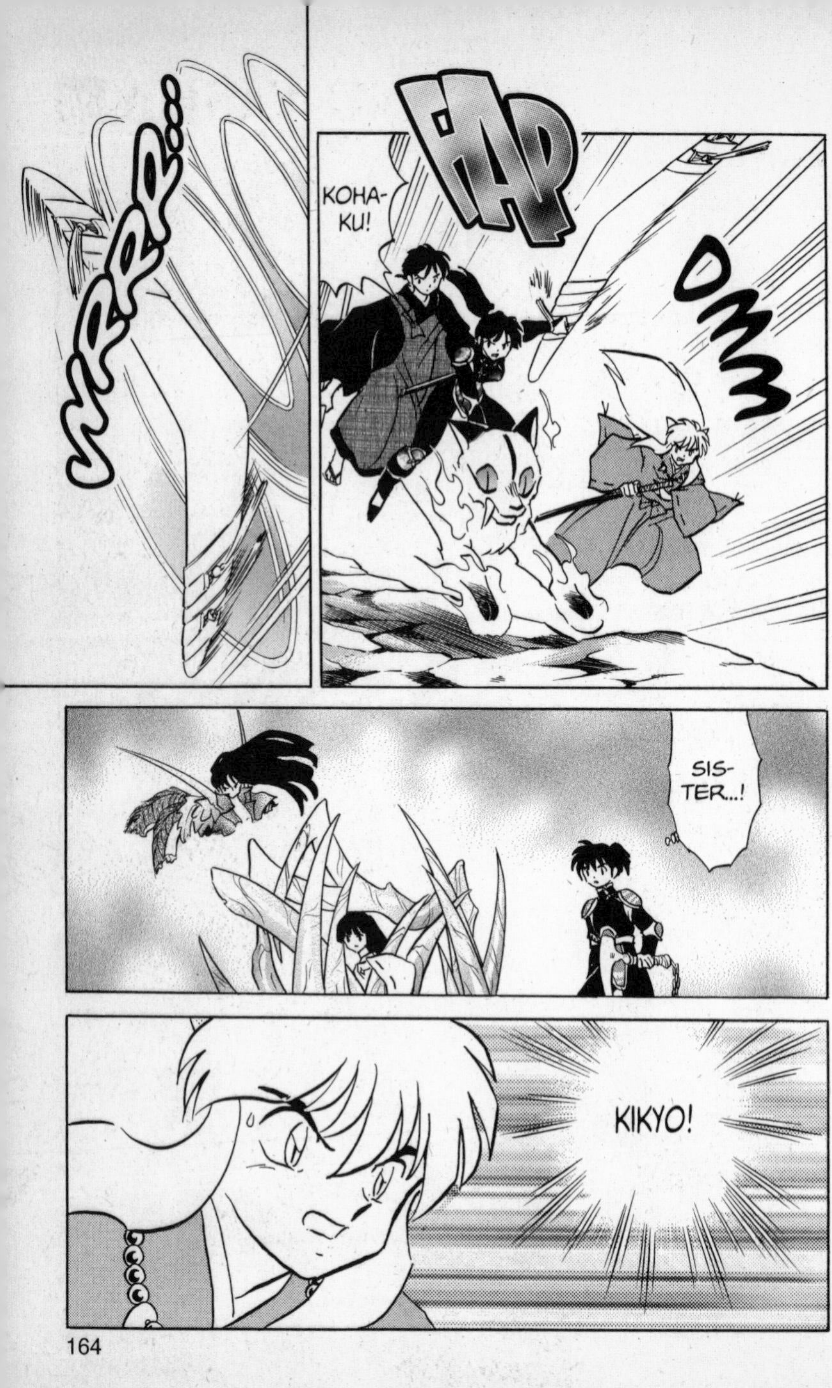
WHRR...
HAP
KOHA-
KU!
DMM
SIS-
TER...!
KIKYO!

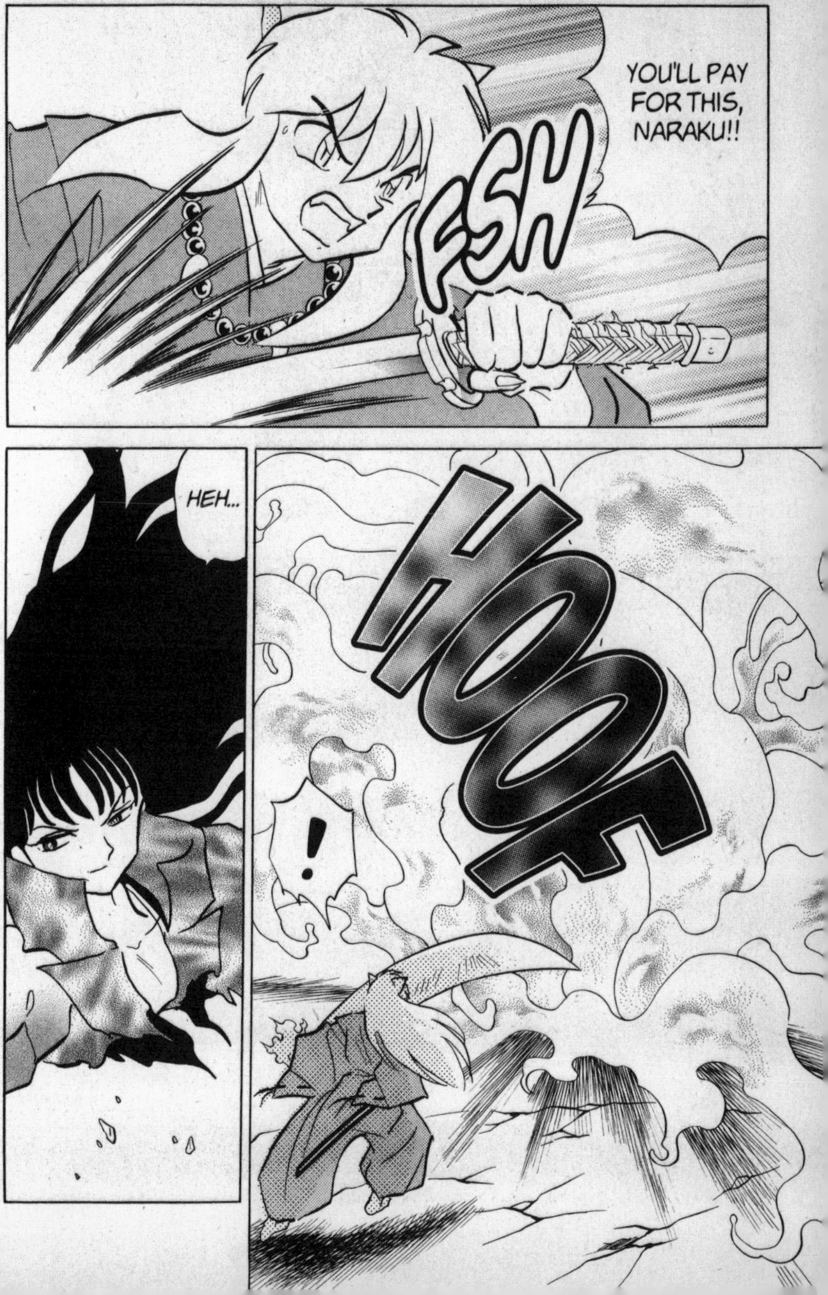
YOU'LL PAY FOR THIS, NARAKU!!
FSH
HEH...
HOOF
!

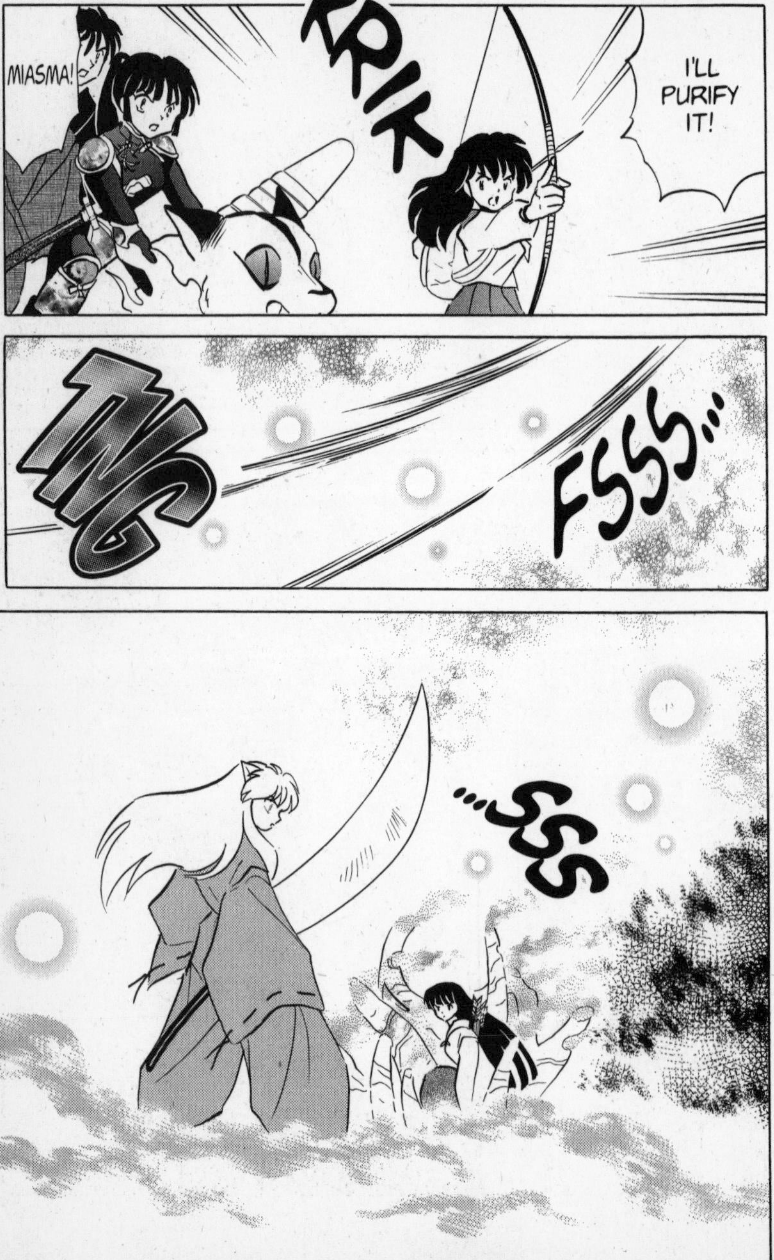

MIASMA!
KRIK
I'LL PURIFY IT!
TWNG
FSSS...
...SSS

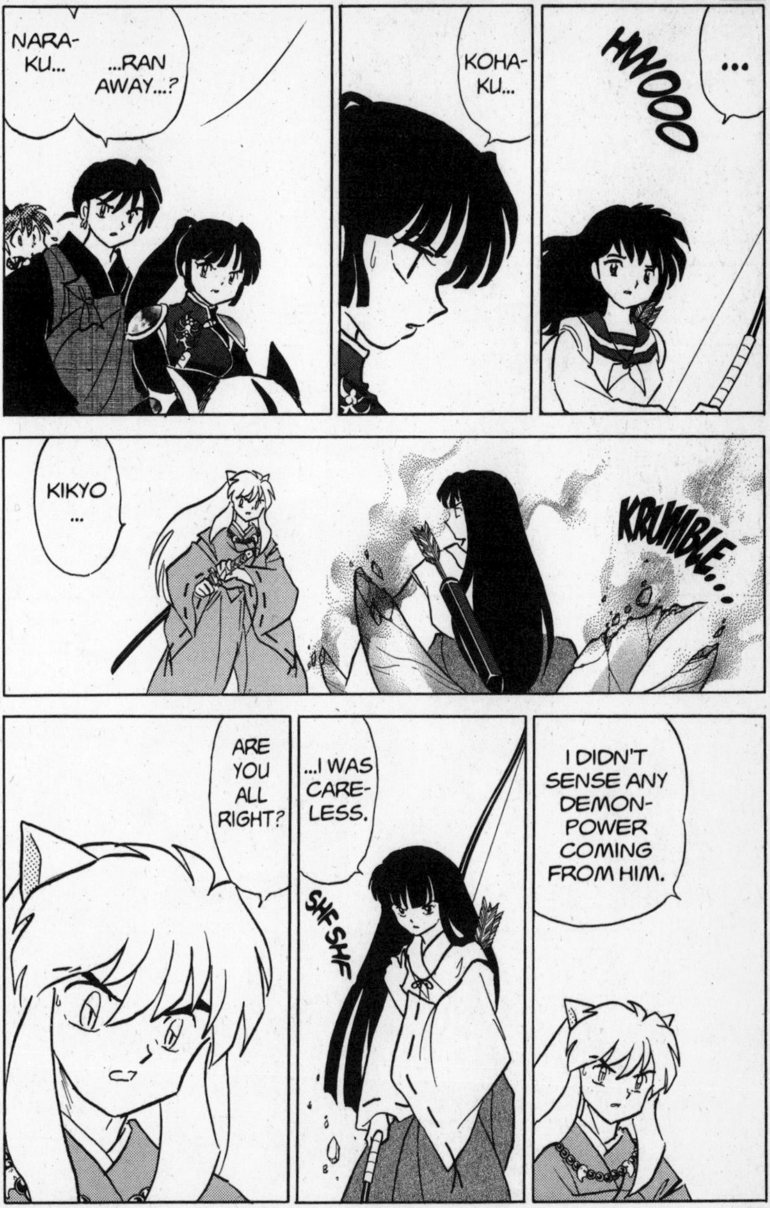
NARA-KU...
...RAN AWAY...?
KOHA-KU...
HWOOO
...
KIKYO ...
KRUMBLE...
ARE YOU ALL RIGHT?
...I WAS CARE-LESS.
SHF SHF
I DIDN'T SENSE ANY DEMON-POWER COMING FROM HIM.

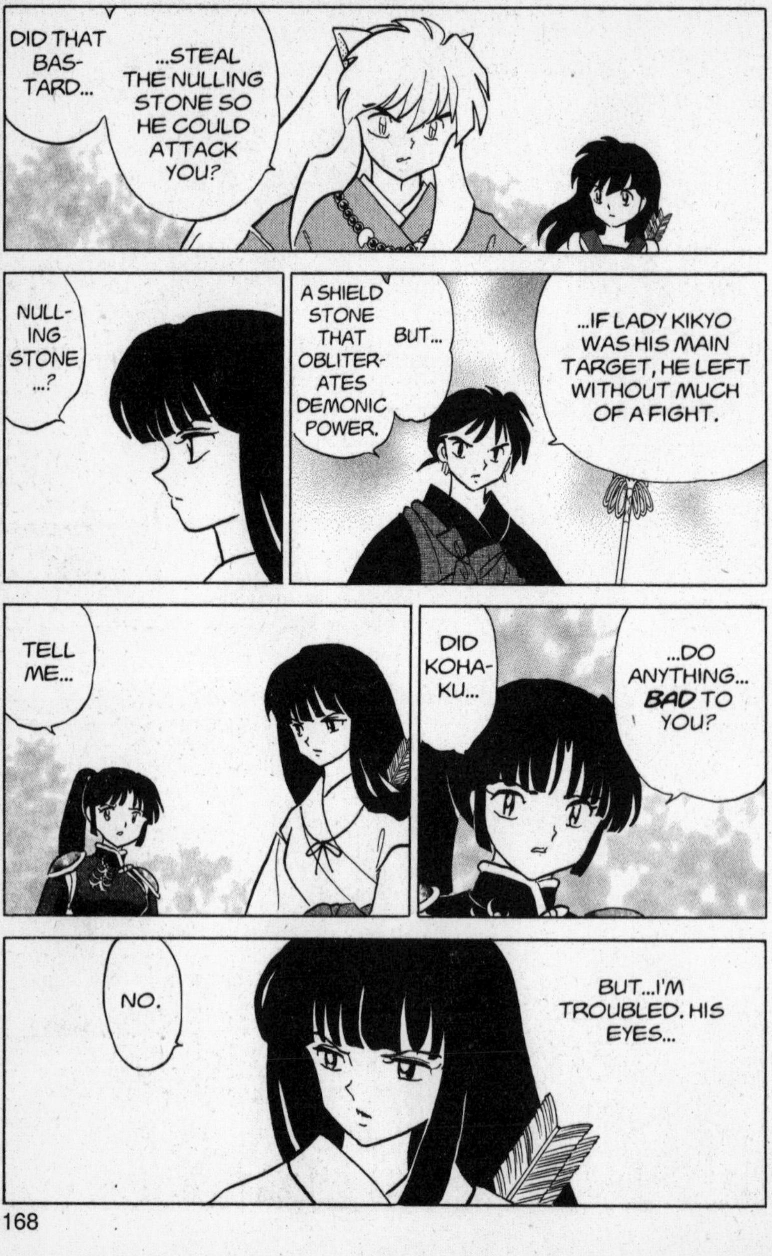
DID THAT BASTARD...
...STEAL THE NULLING STONE SO HE COULD ATTACK YOU?
NULLING STONE ...?
A SHIELD STONE THAT OBLITERATES DEMONIC POWER.
BUT...
...IF LADY KIKYO WAS HIS MAIN TARGET, HE LEFT WITHOUT MUCH OF A FIGHT.
TELL ME...
DID KOHAKU...
...DO ANYTHING... **BAD** TO YOU?
NO.
BUT...I'M TROUBLED. HIS EYES...

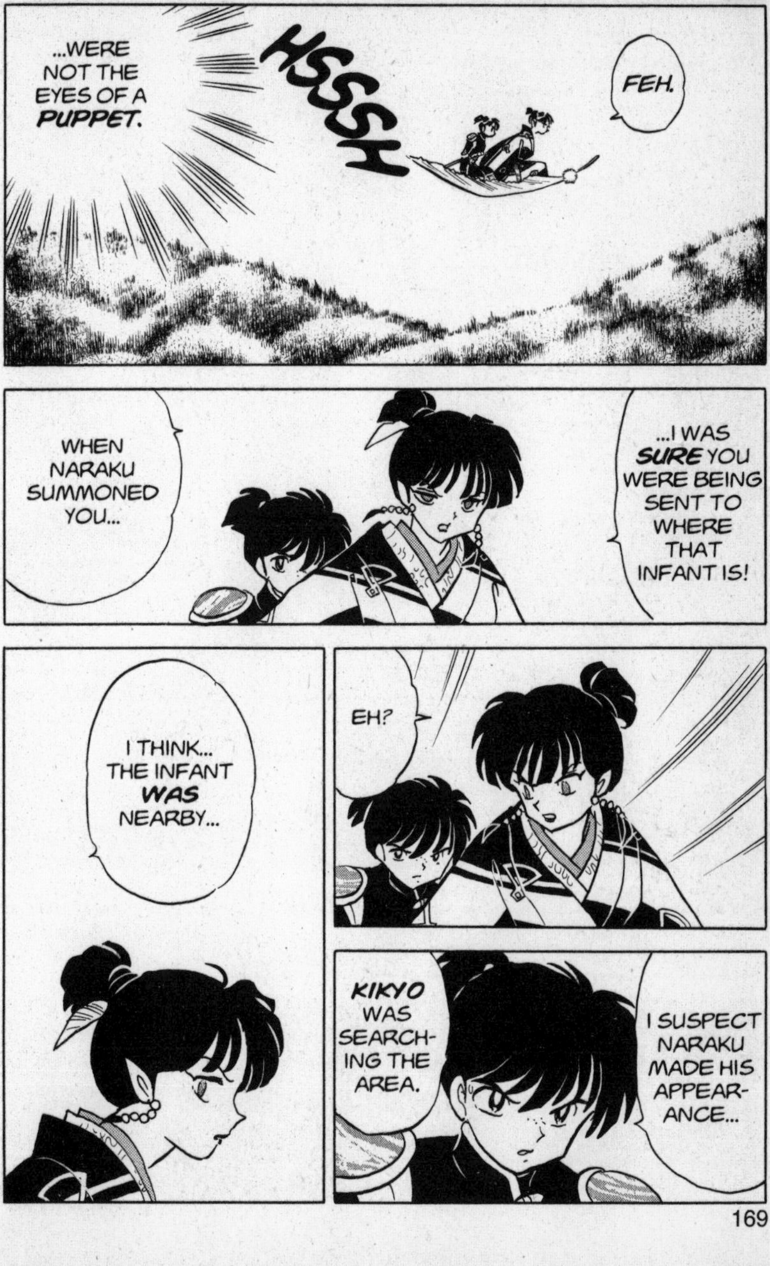
...WERE NOT THE EYES OF A *PUPPET*.
HSSSH
FEH.
WHEN NARAKU SUMMONED YOU...
...I WAS *SURE* YOU WERE BEING SENT TO WHERE THAT INFANT IS!
I THINK... THE INFANT *WAS* NEARBY...
EH?
KIKYO WAS SEARCH-ING THE AREA.
I SUSPECT NARAKU MADE HIS APPEAR-ANCE...

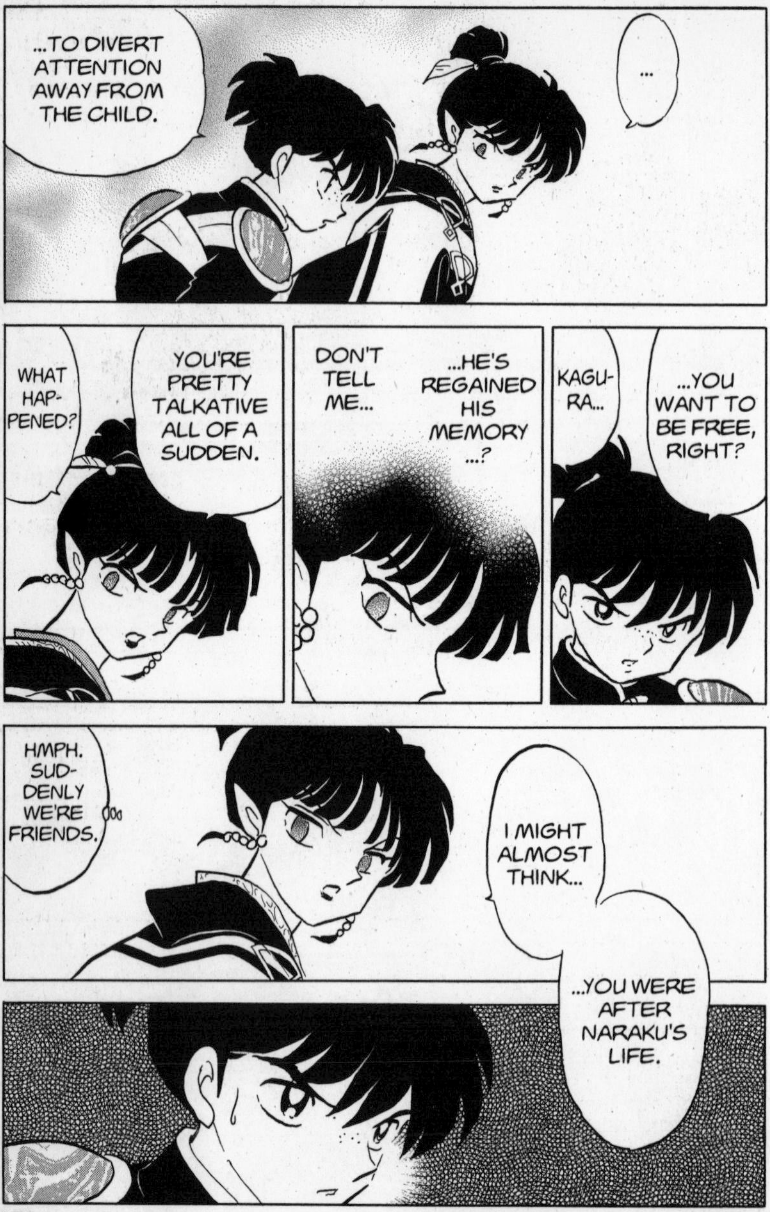
...TO DIVERT ATTENTION AWAY FROM THE CHILD.
...
WHAT HAP-PENED?
YOU'RE PRETTY TALKATIVE ALL OF A SUDDEN.
DON'T TELL ME...
...HE'S REGAINED HIS MEMORY ...?
KAGU-RA...
...YOU WANT TO BE FREE, RIGHT?
HMPH. SUD-DENLY WE'RE FRIENDS.
I MIGHT ALMOST THINK...
...YOU WERE AFTER NARAKU'S LIFE.

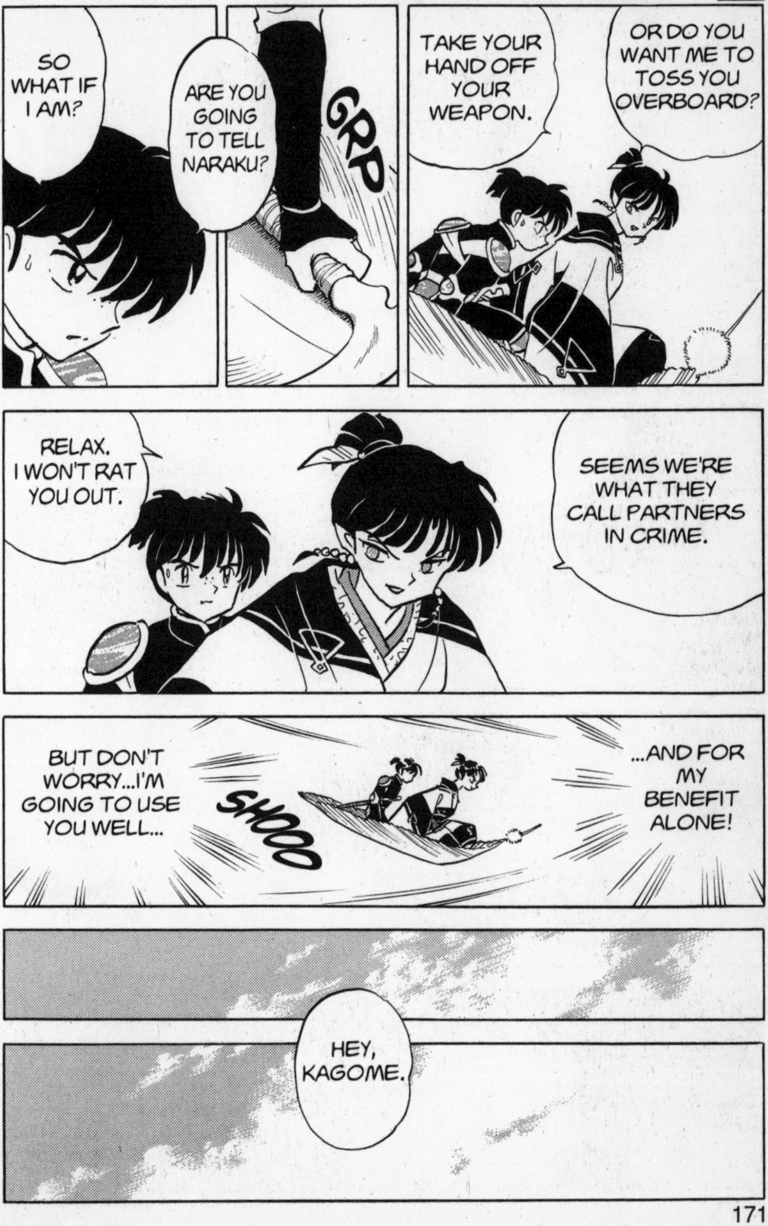
SO WHAT IF I AM?
ARE YOU GOING TO TELL NARAKU?
GRP
TAKE YOUR HAND OFF YOUR WEAPON.
OR DO YOU WANT ME TO TOSS YOU OVERBOARD?
RELAX. I WON'T RAT YOU OUT.
SEEMS WE'RE WHAT THEY CALL PARTNERS IN CRIME.
BUT DON'T WORRY...I'M GOING TO USE YOU WELL...
SHOOO
...AND FOR MY BENEFIT ALONE!
HEY, KAGOME.

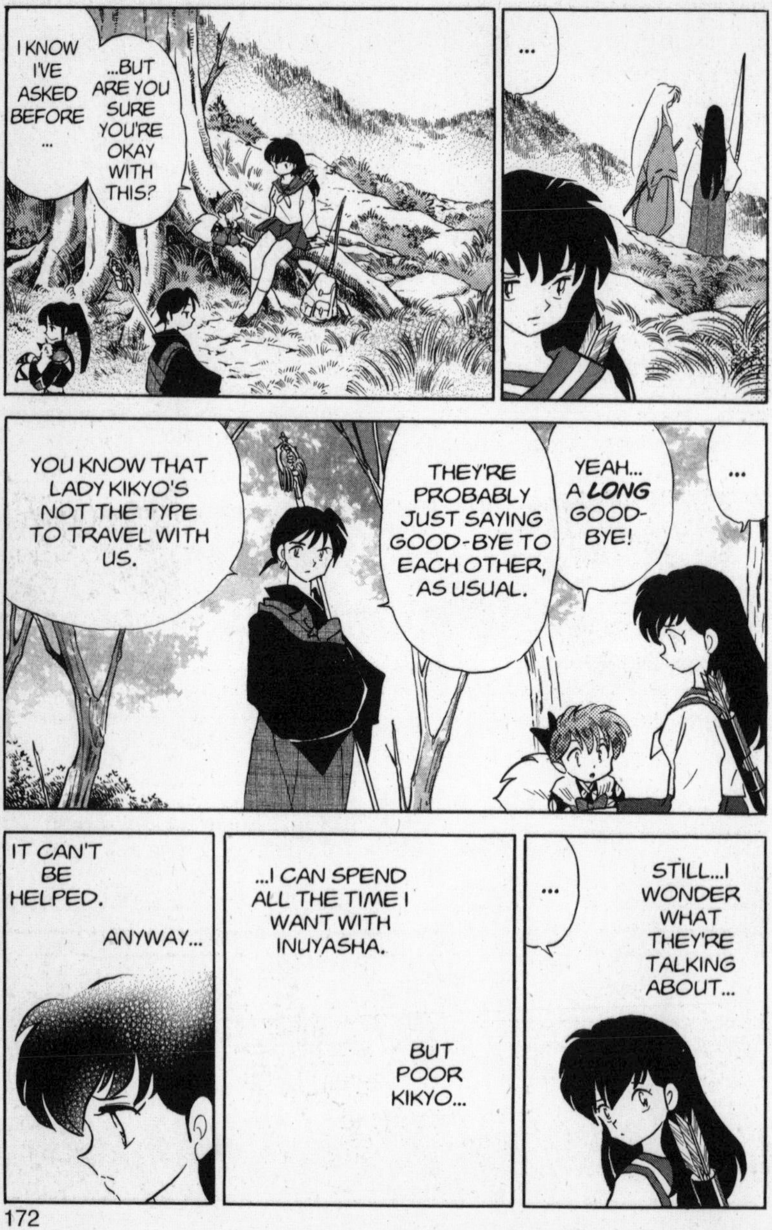
I KNOW I'VE ASKED BEFORE ...
...BUT ARE YOU SURE YOU'RE OKAY WITH THIS?
...
YOU KNOW THAT LADY KIKYO'S NOT THE TYPE TO TRAVEL WITH US.
THEY'RE PROBABLY JUST SAYING GOOD-BYE TO EACH OTHER, AS USUAL.
YEAH... A **LONG** GOOD-BYE!
...
IT CAN'T BE HELPED.
ANYWAY...
...I CAN SPEND ALL THE TIME I WANT WITH INUYASHA.
BUT POOR KIKYO...
...
STILL...I WONDER WHAT THEY'RE TALKING ABOUT...

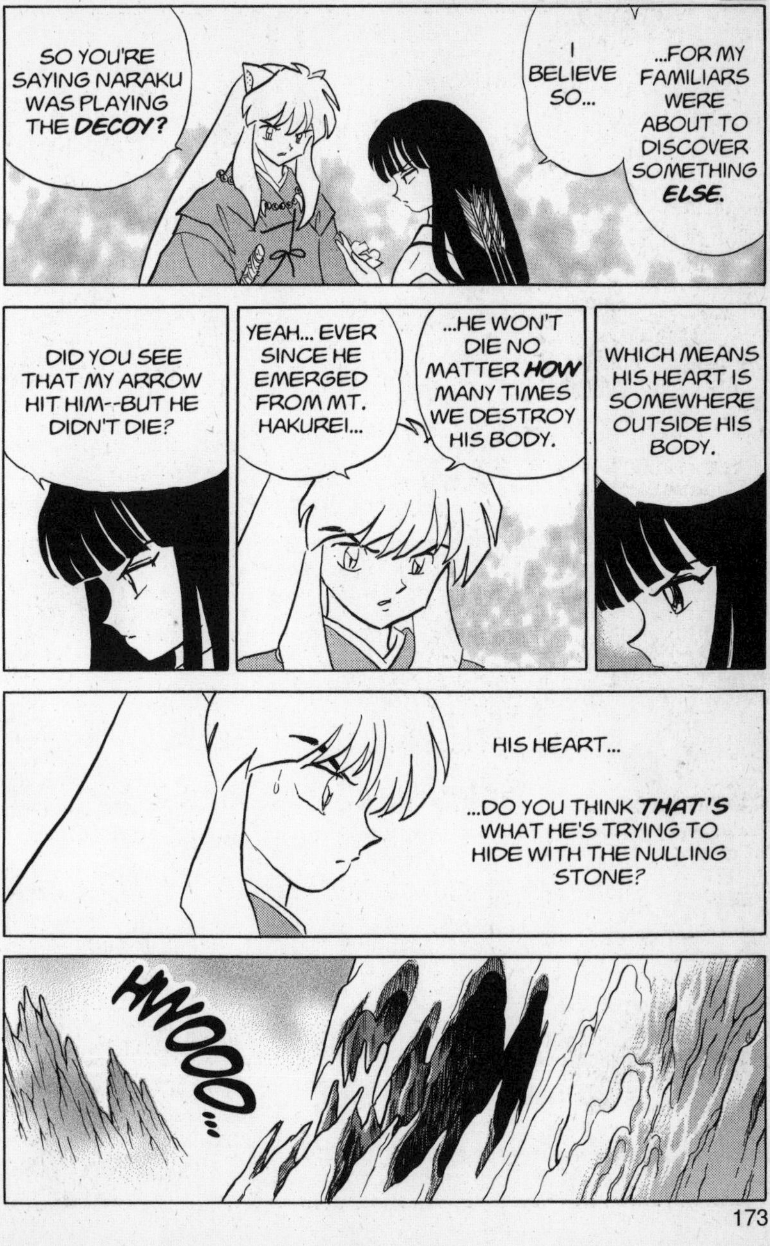
SO YOU'RE SAYING NARAKU WAS PLAYING THE *DECOY*?
I BELIEVE SO...
...FOR MY FAMILIARS WERE ABOUT TO DISCOVER SOMETHING *ELSE*.
DID YOU SEE THAT MY ARROW HIT HIM--BUT HE DIDN'T DIE?
YEAH... EVER SINCE HE EMERGED FROM MT. HAKUREI...
...HE WON'T DIE NO MATTER *HOW* MANY TIMES WE DESTROY HIS BODY.
WHICH MEANS HIS HEART IS SOMEWHERE OUTSIDE HIS BODY.
HIS HEART...
...DO YOU THINK *THAT'S* WHAT HE'S TRYING TO HIDE WITH THE NULLING STONE?
HWOOO...

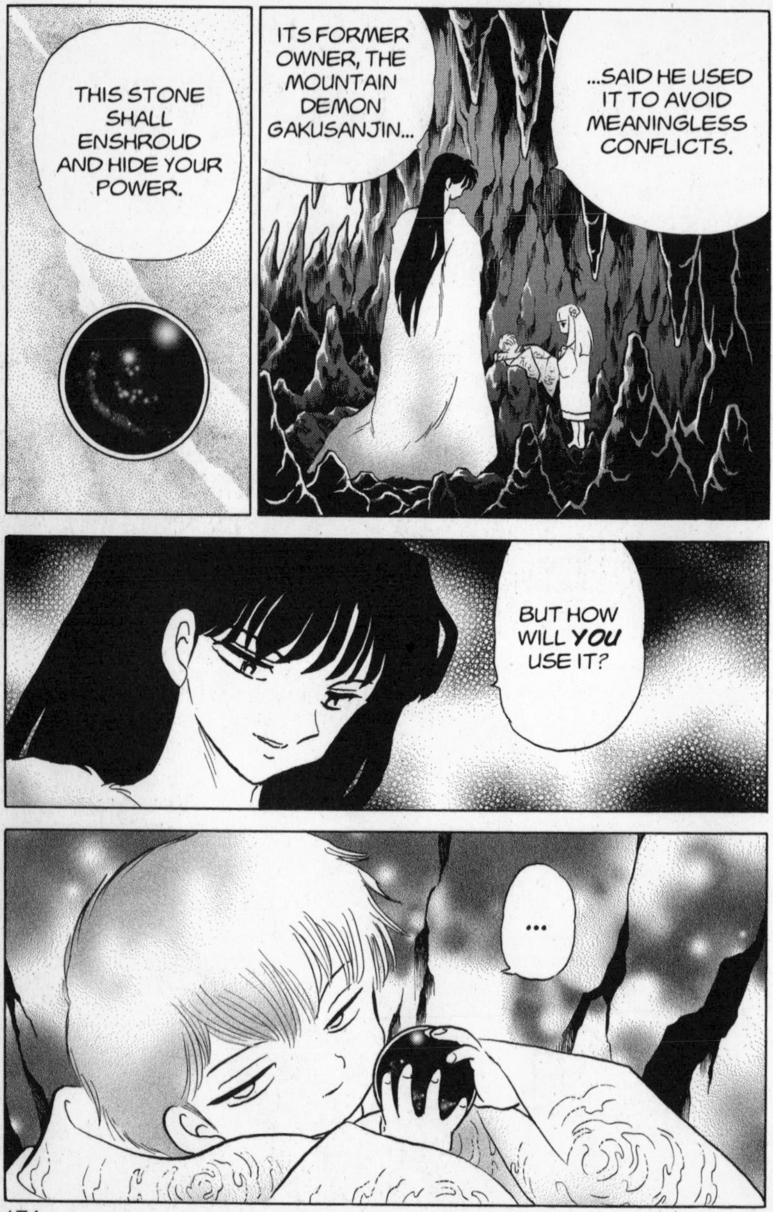
THIS STONE SHALL ENSHROUD AND HIDE YOUR POWER.
ITS FORMER OWNER, THE MOUNTAIN DEMON GAKUSANJIN...
...SAID HE USED IT TO AVOID MEANINGLESS CONFLICTS.
BUT HOW WILL ***YOU*** USE IT?
...

SCROLL 10
HARVESTING SOULS

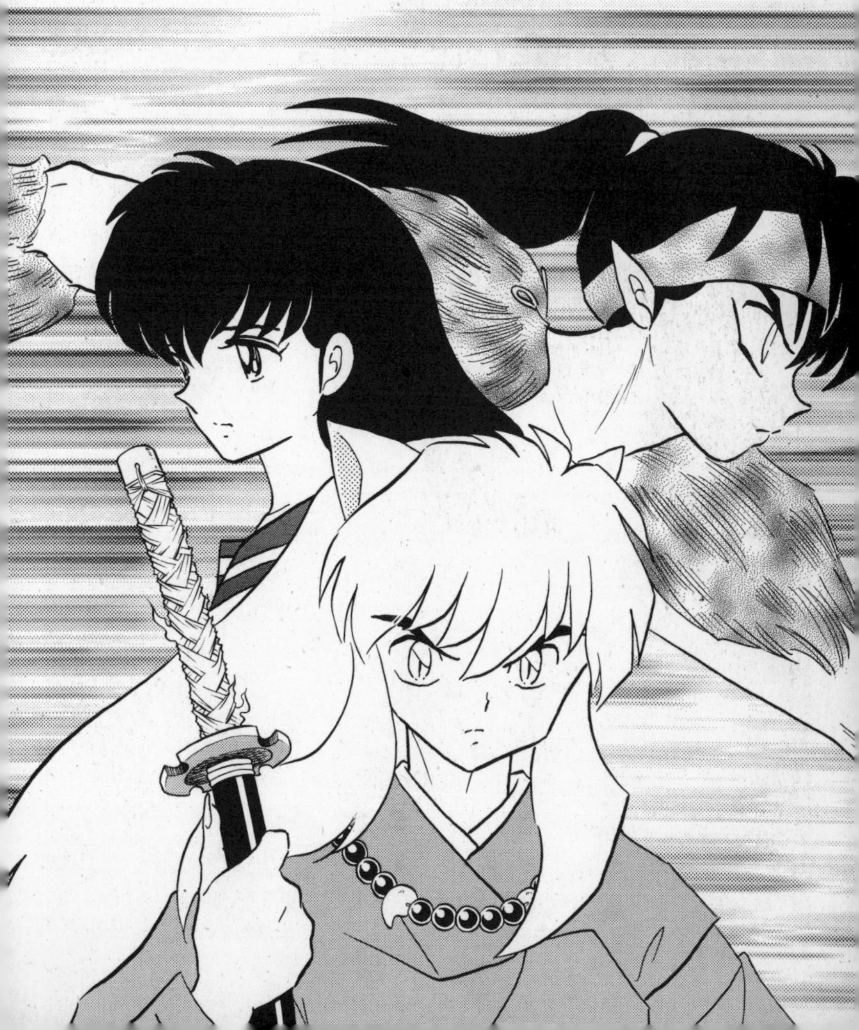

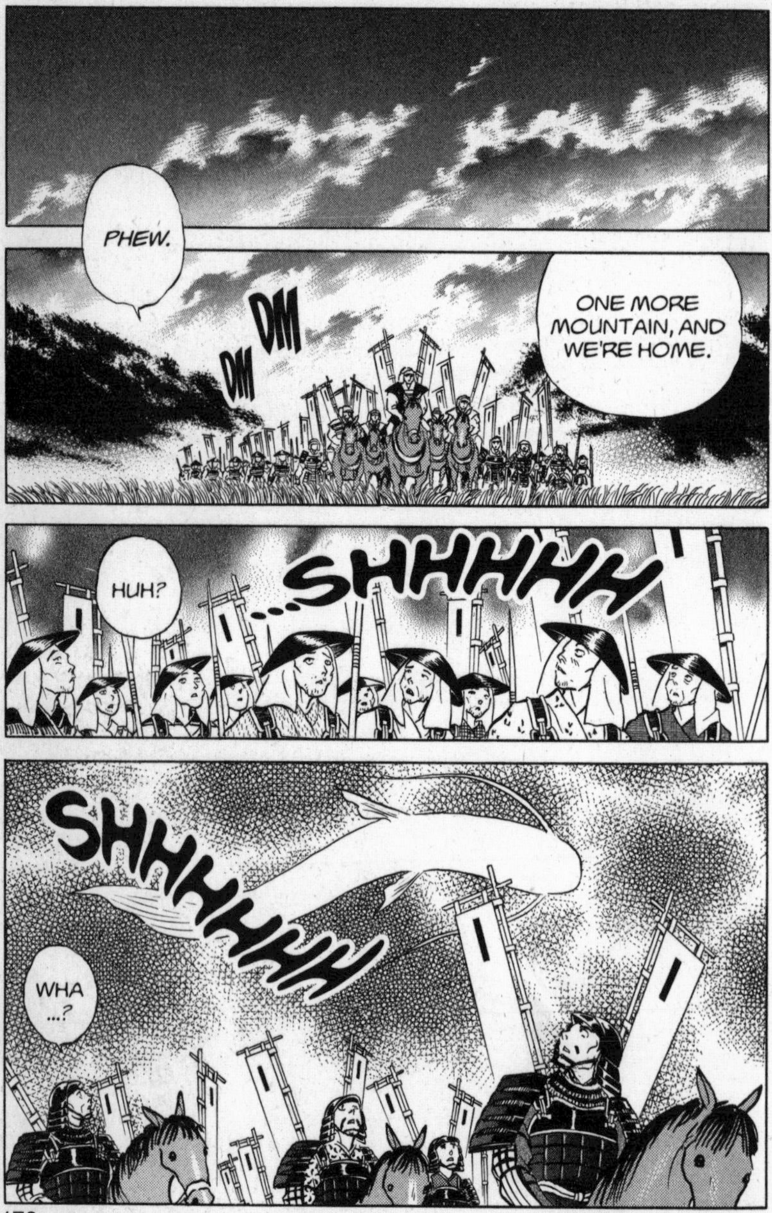
PHEW.
DM DM
ONE MORE MOUNTAIN, AND WE'RE HOME.
HUH?
...SHHHHH
SHHHHHHH
WHA ...?

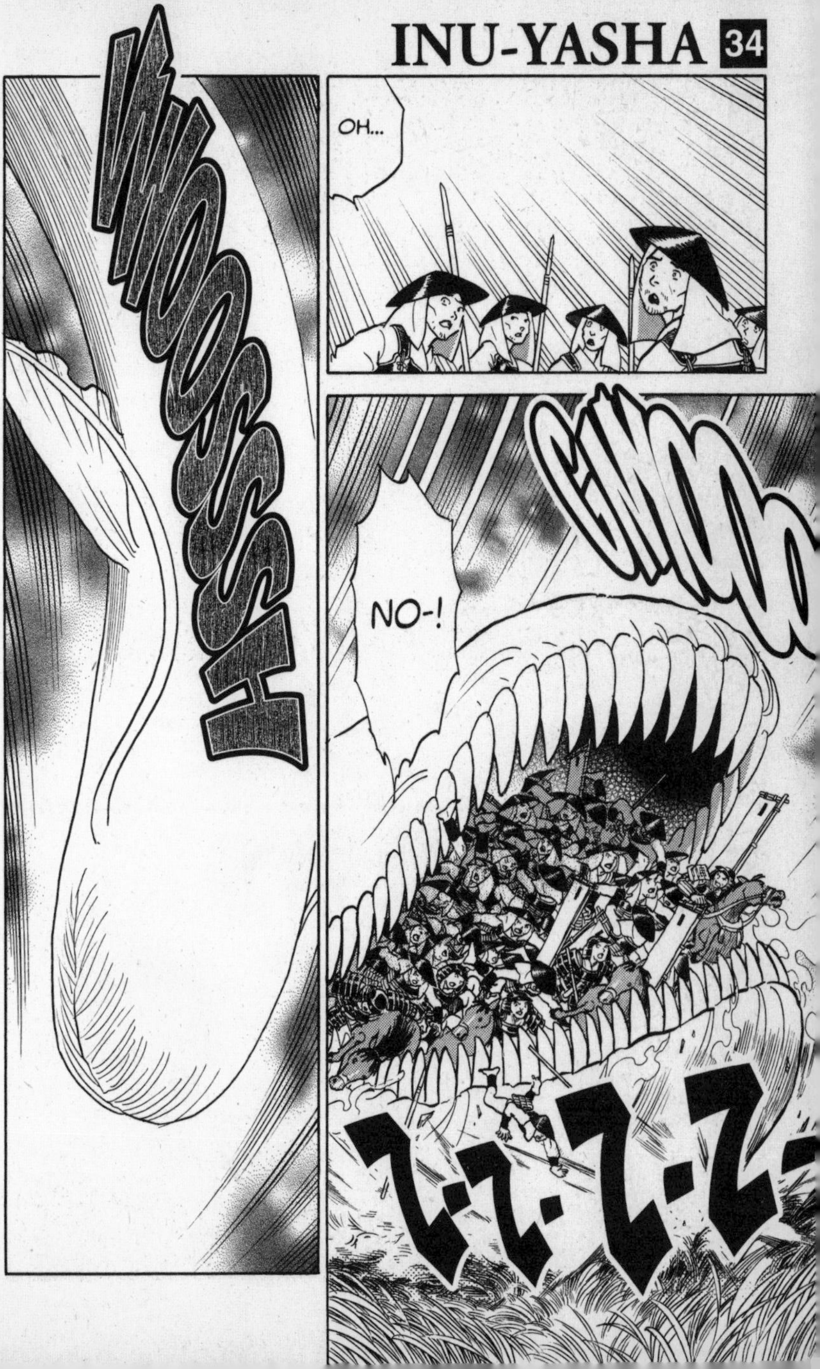
WOOSSH!
OH...
NO-!
GWOO
Z-Z-Z-Z

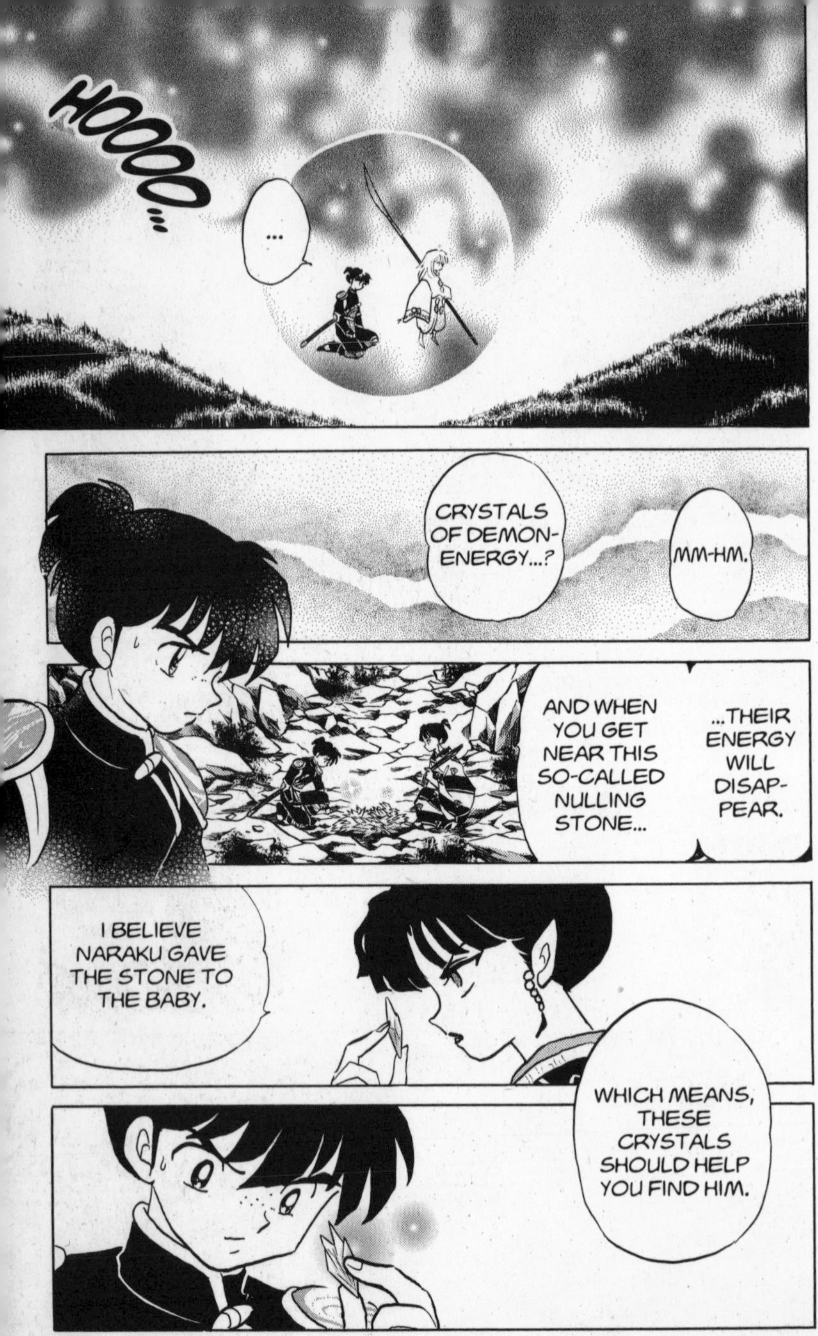
HOOOO...
...
CRYSTALS OF DEMON-ENERGY...?
MM-HM.
AND WHEN YOU GET NEAR THIS SO-CALLED NULLING STONE...
...THEIR ENERGY WILL DISAP-PEAR.
I BELIEVE NARAKU GAVE THE STONE TO THE BABY.
WHICH MEANS, THESE CRYSTALS SHOULD HELP YOU FIND HIM.

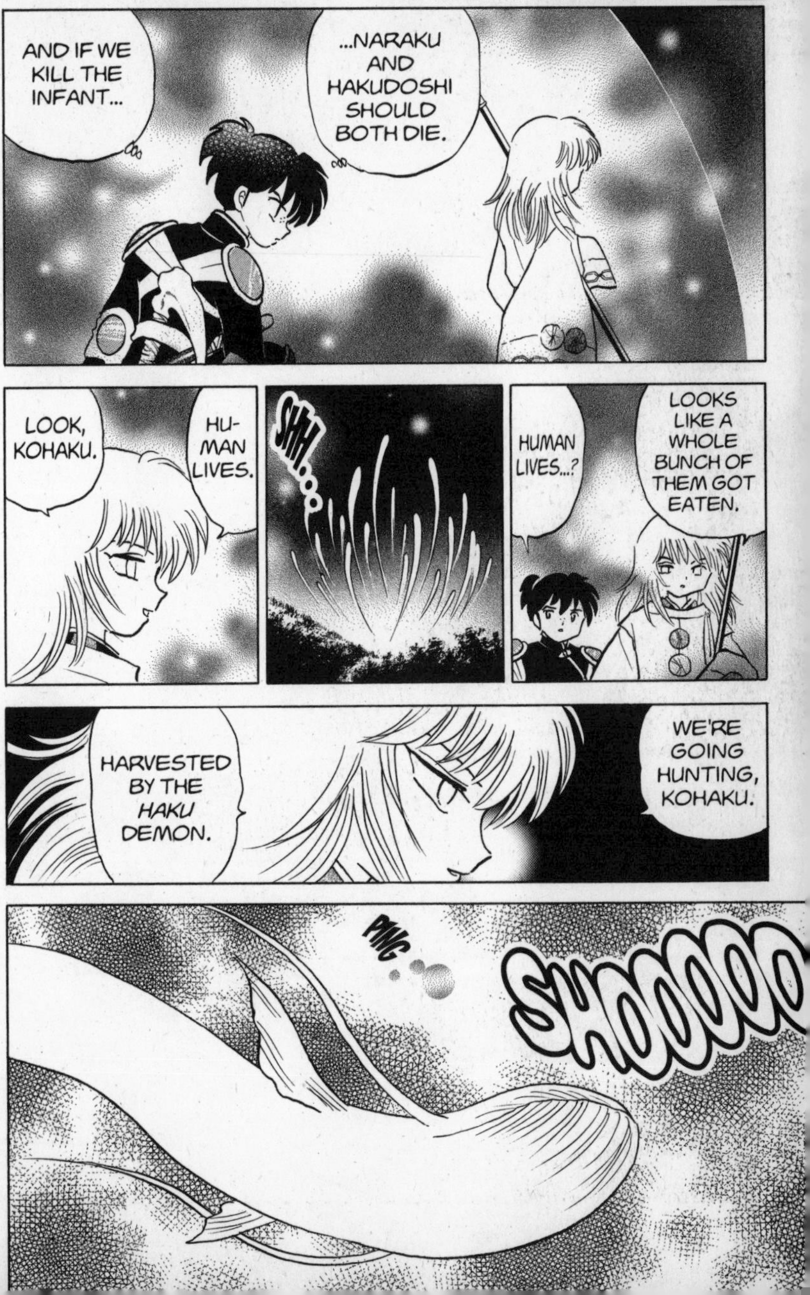
AND IF WE KILL THE INFANT...
...NARAKU AND HAKUDOSHI SHOULD BOTH DIE.
LOOK, KOHAKU.
HU-MAN LIVES.
SHH...
HUMAN LIVES...?
LOOKS LIKE A WHOLE BUNCH OF THEM GOT EATEN.
HARVESTED BY THE HAKU DEMON.
WE'RE GOING HUNTING, KOHAKU.
PING...
SHOOOOO

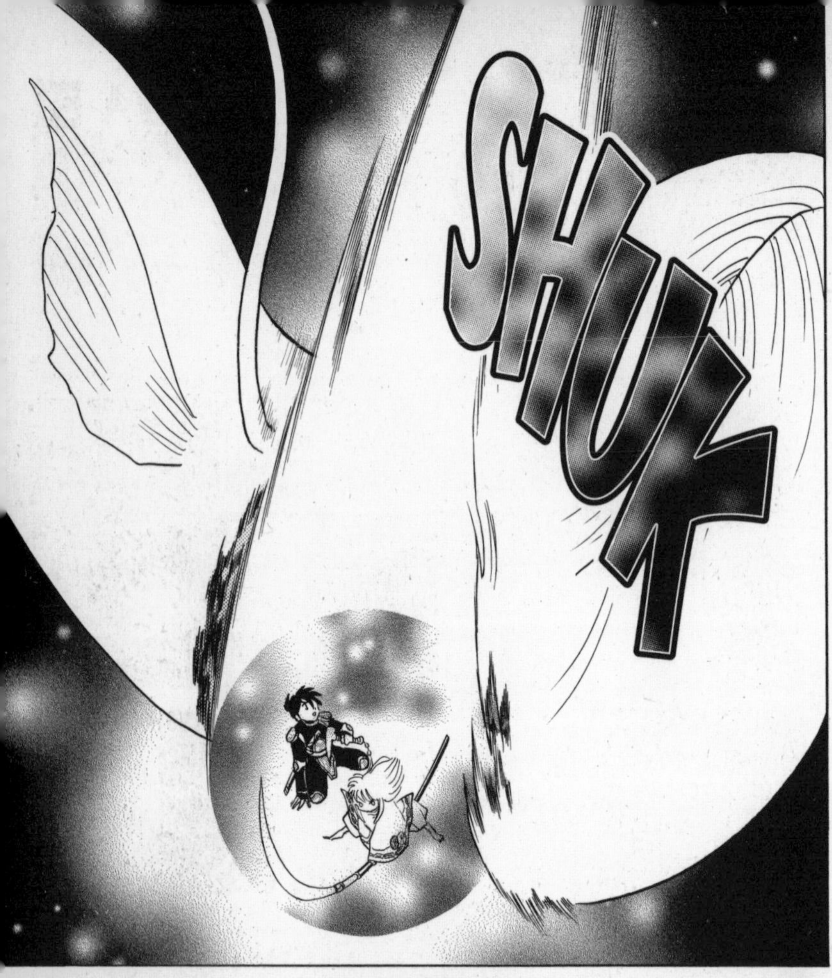
SHUK
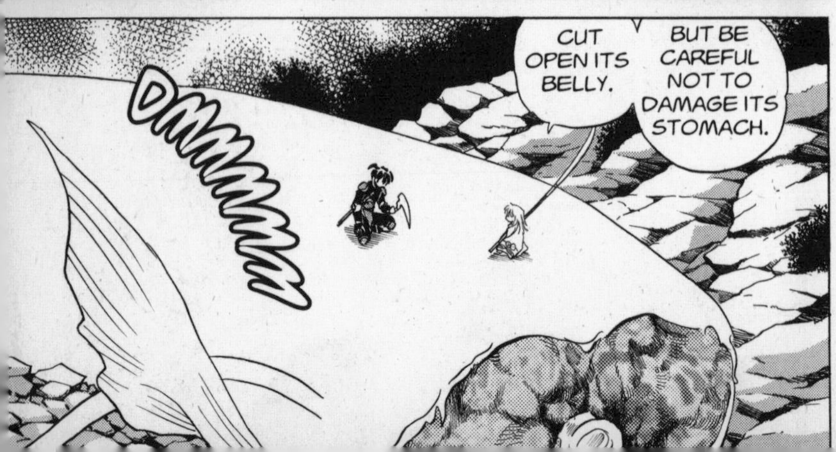
DMMMM
CUT OPEN ITS BELLY.
BUT BE CAREFUL NOT TO DAMAGE ITS STOMACH.

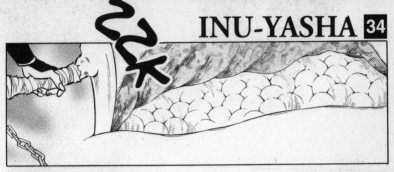

ZZK

WHAT IN...? IT'S FULL OF SHINY SPHERES...

LIFE FORCES. HAKU.

THE FOOD OF THE **HAKU** DEMON.

HAKU ...?

HEH HEH HEH...

HMM, NOW WHAT **SHALL** I USE THEM FOR...?

VSSSSSH

KOGA, WAIT!

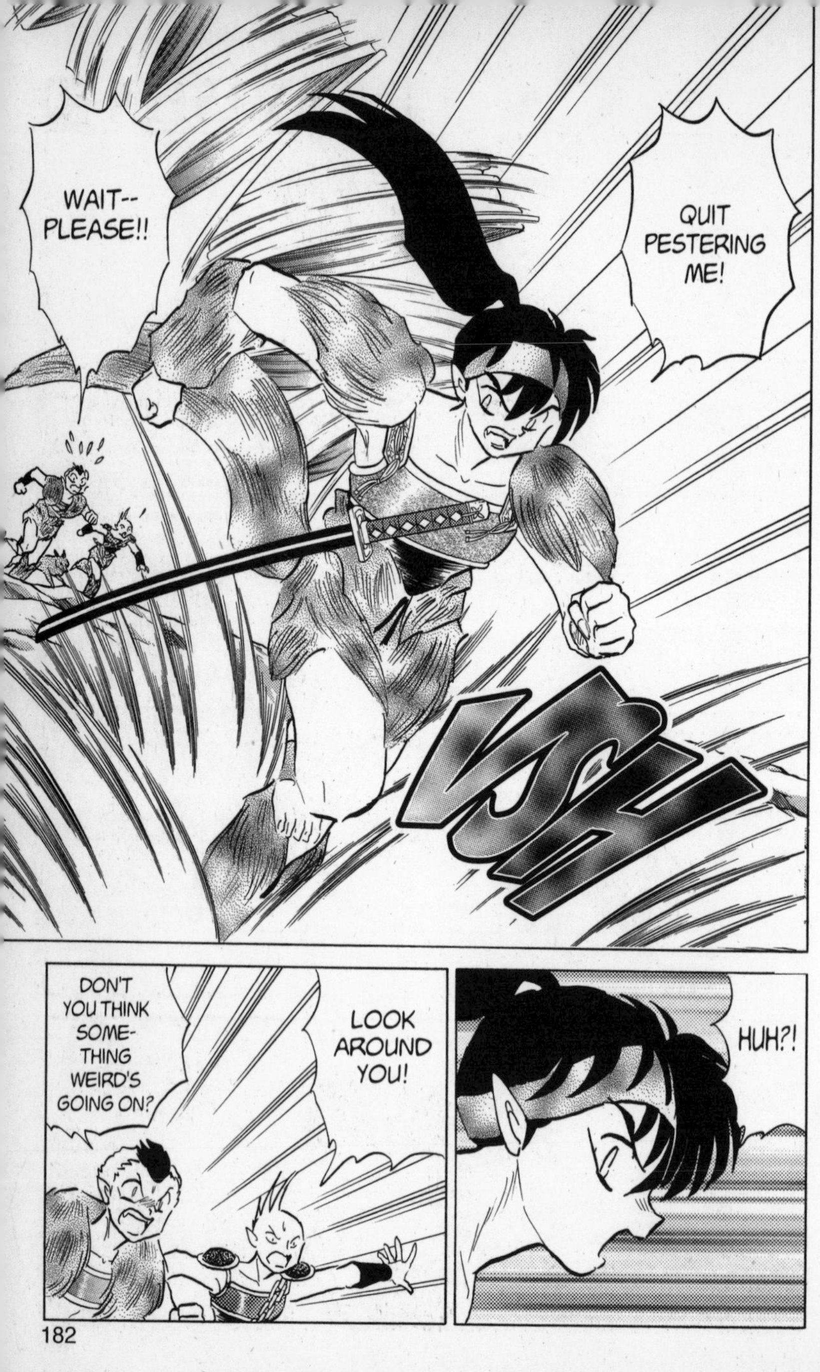
WAIT--
PLEASE!!
QUIT PESTERING ME!
VSH
DON'T YOU THINK SOME-THING WEIRD'S GOING ON?
LOOK AROUND YOU!
HUH?!

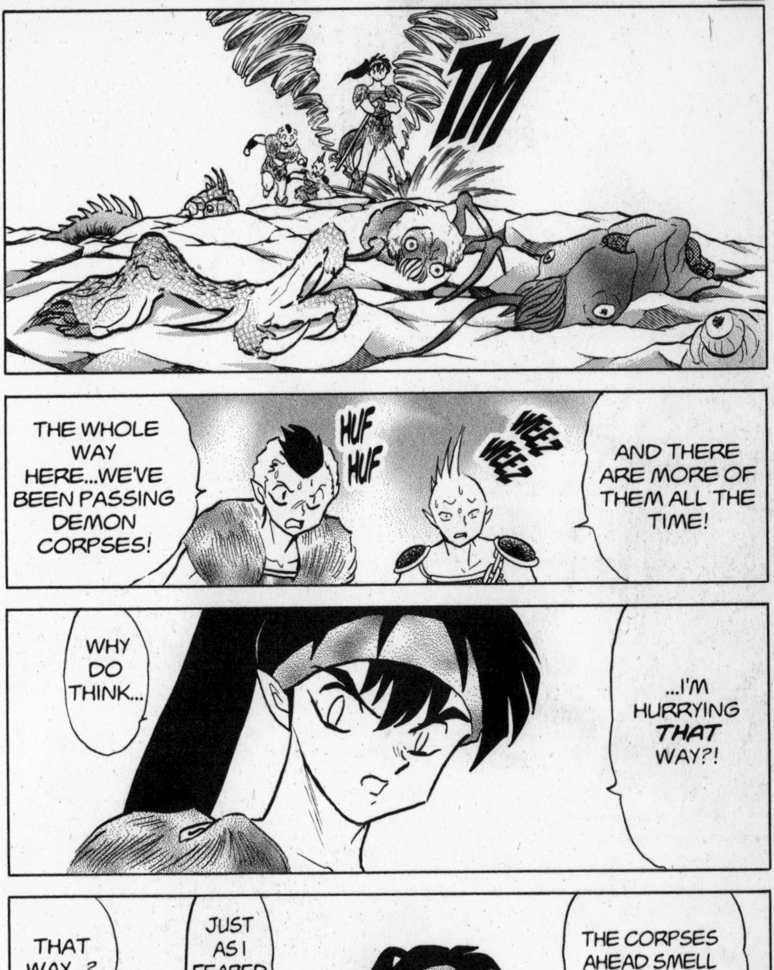
TM
THE WHOLE WAY HERE...WE'VE BEEN PASSING DEMON CORPSES!
HUF HUF
WEEZ WEEZ
AND THERE ARE MORE OF THEM ALL THE TIME!
WHY DO THINK...
...I'M HURRYING THAT WAY?!
THAT WAY...?
JUST AS I FEARED ...
THE CORPSES AHEAD SMELL FRESHER...
WHICH MEANS WE'RE GETTING CLOSER TO THE KILLER.

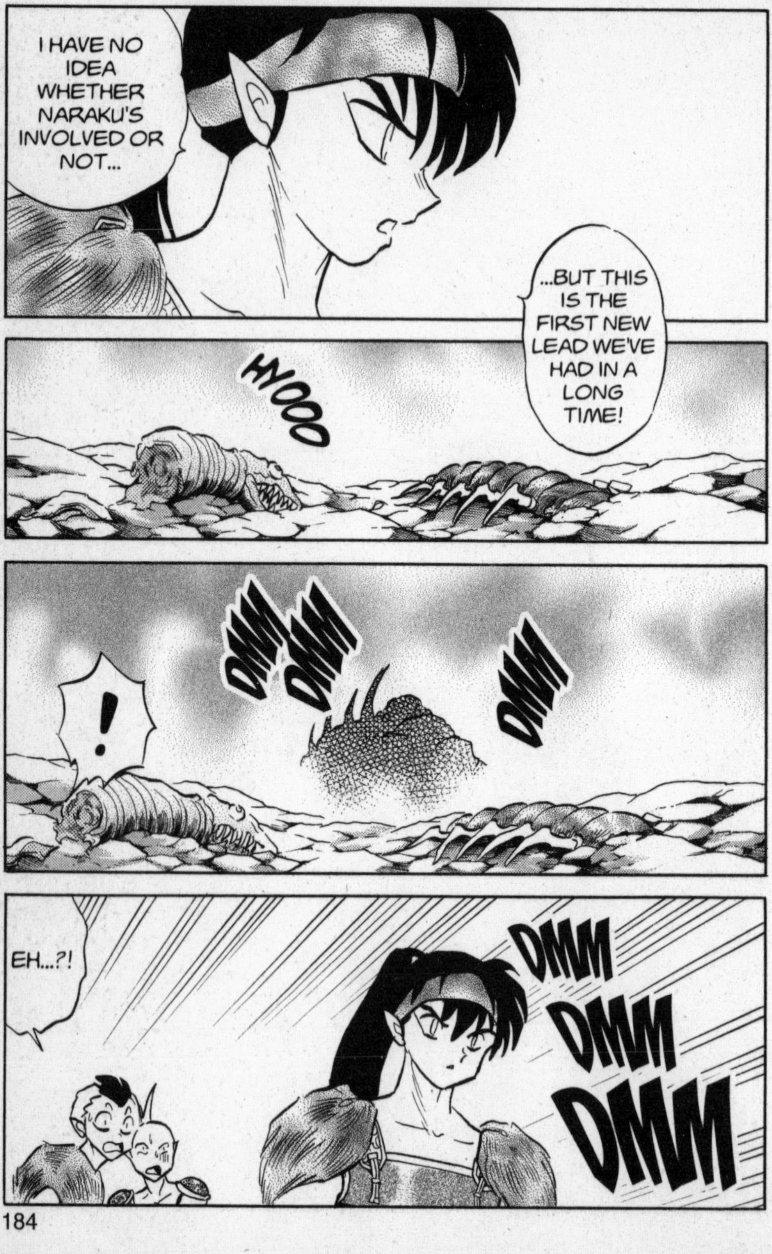
I HAVE NO IDEA WHETHER NARAKU'S INVOLVED OR NOT...
...BUT THIS IS THE FIRST NEW LEAD WE'VE HAD IN A LONG TIME!
HYOOO
!
DMM DMM
DMM
EH...?!
DMM DMM DMM

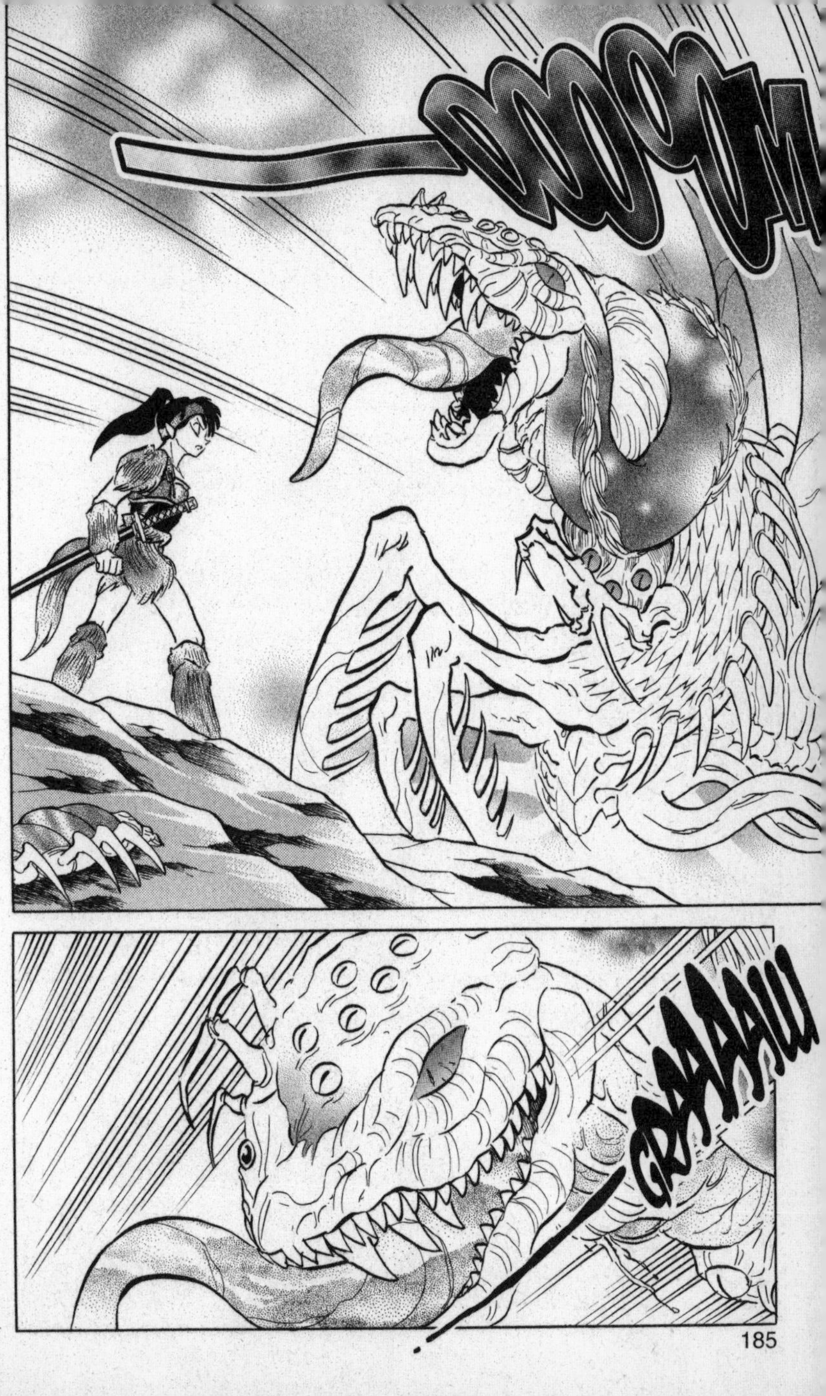
GRAAAU

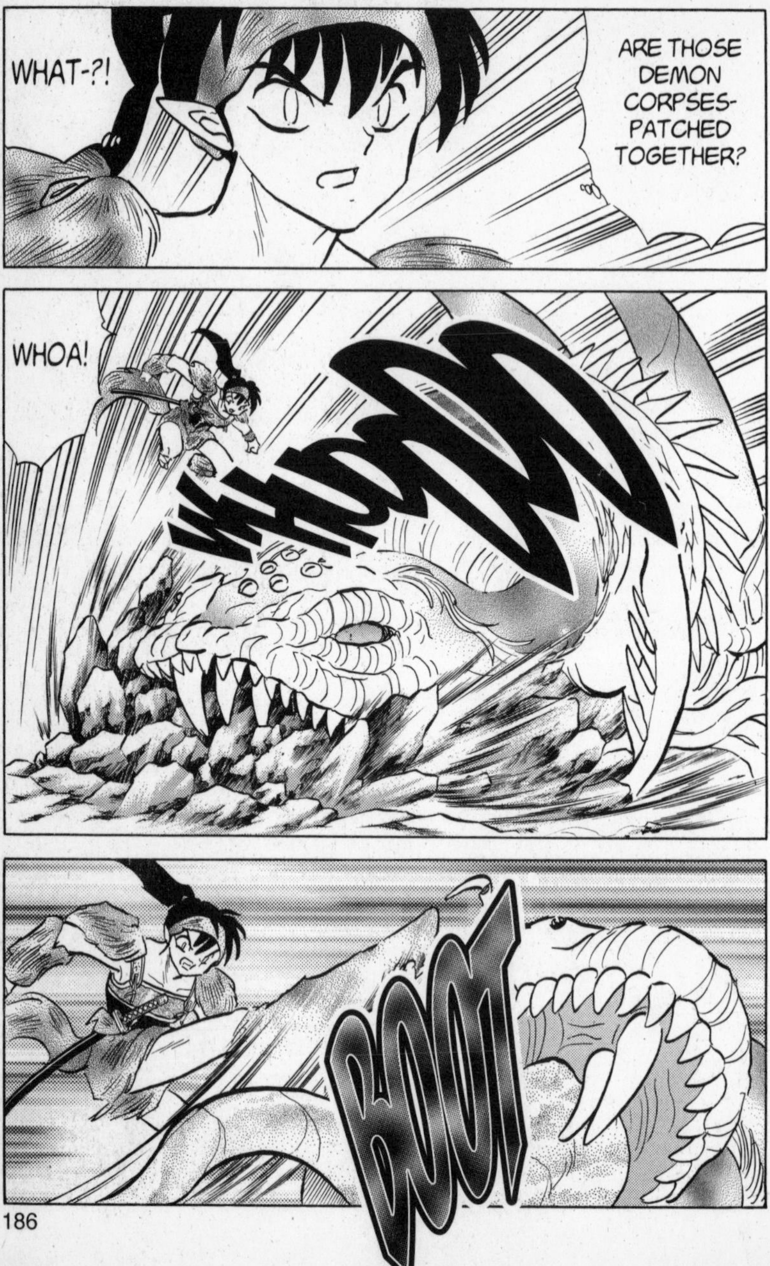
WHAT-?!
ARE THOSE DEMON CORPSES- PATCHED TOGETHER?
WHOA!
WHOMM
BOOOT

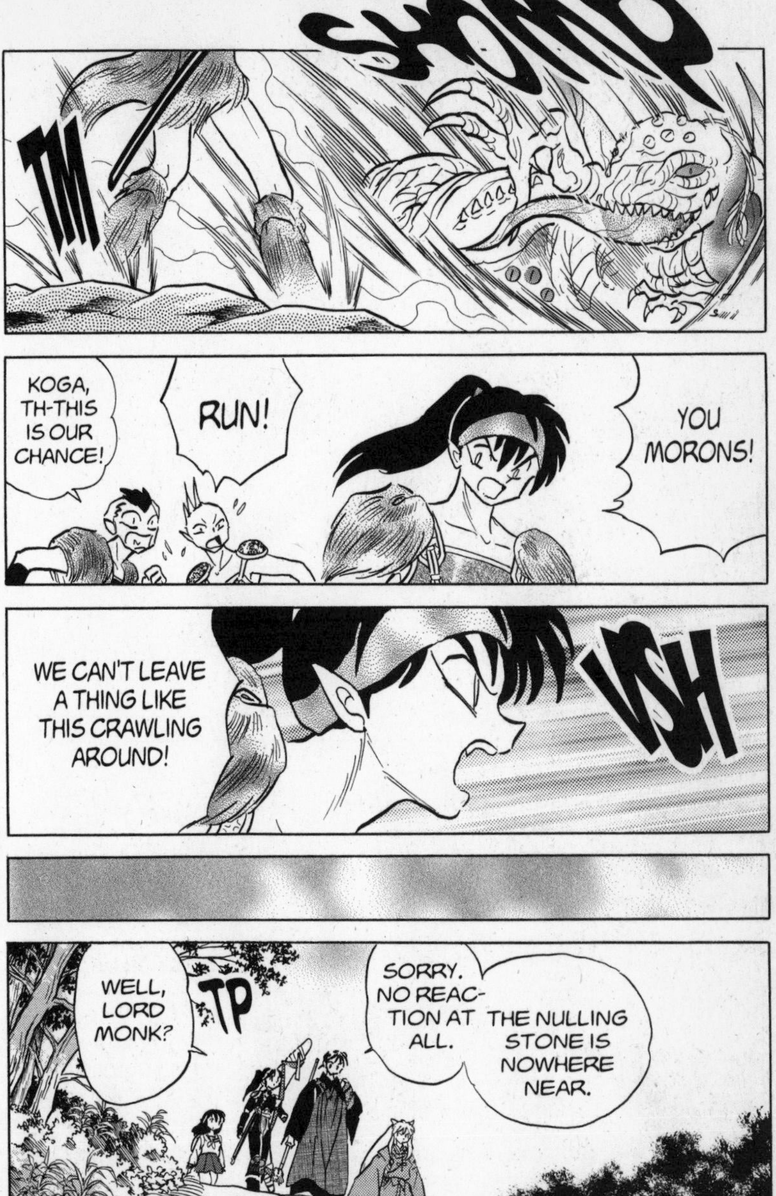
SHOMP
TM
KOGA, TH-THIS IS OUR CHANCE!
RUN!
YOU MORONS!
WE CAN'T LEAVE A THING LIKE THIS CRAWLING AROUND!
VSH
WELL, LORD MONK?
TP
SORRY. NO REAC-TION AT ALL.
THE NULLING STONE IS NOWHERE NEAR.

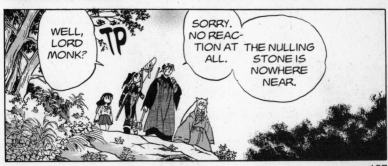

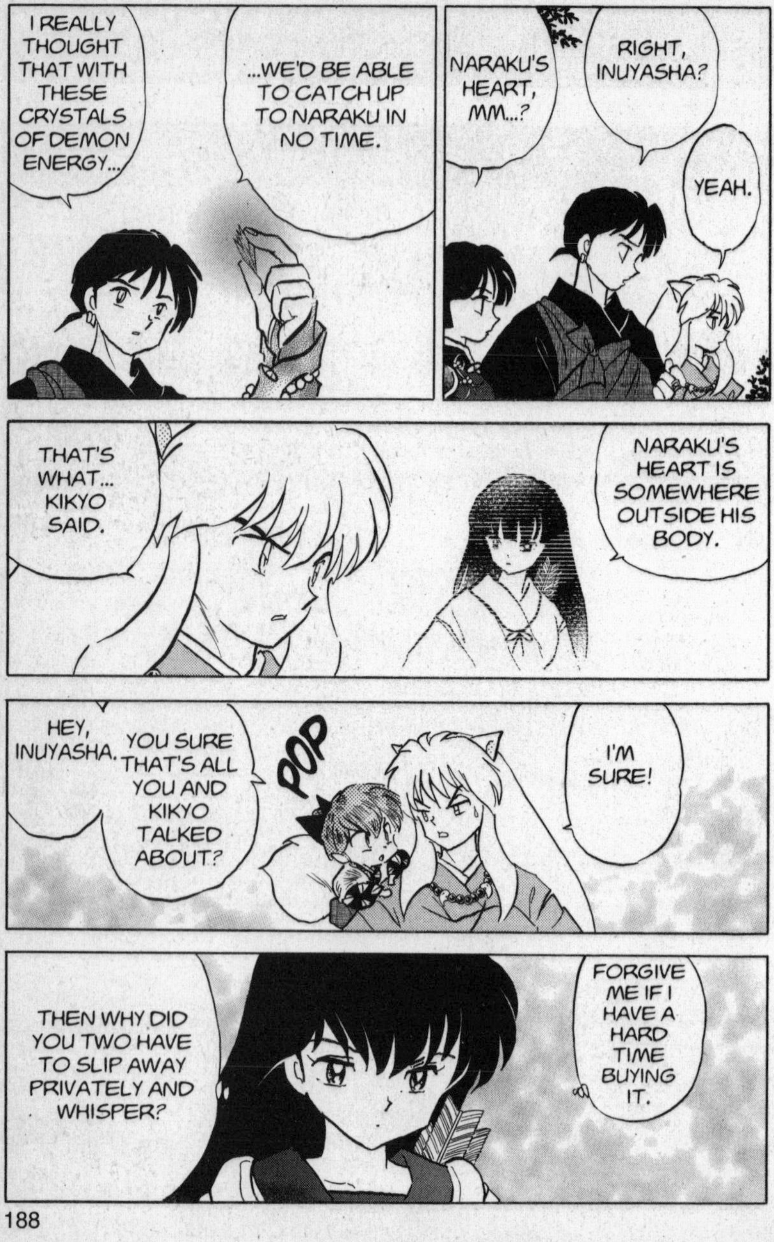

I REALLY THOUGHT THAT WITH THESE CRYSTALS OF DEMON ENERGY...
...WE'D BE ABLE TO CATCH UP TO NARAKU IN NO TIME.
NARAKU'S HEART, MM...?
RIGHT, INUYASHA?
YEAH.
THAT'S WHAT... KIKYO SAID.
NARAKU'S HEART IS SOMEWHERE OUTSIDE HIS BODY.
HEY, INUYASHA.
YOU SURE THAT'S ALL YOU AND KIKYO TALKED ABOUT?
POP
I'M SURE!
THEN WHY DID YOU TWO HAVE TO SLIP AWAY PRIVATELY AND WHISPER?
FORGIVE ME IF I HAVE A HARD TIME BUYING IT.

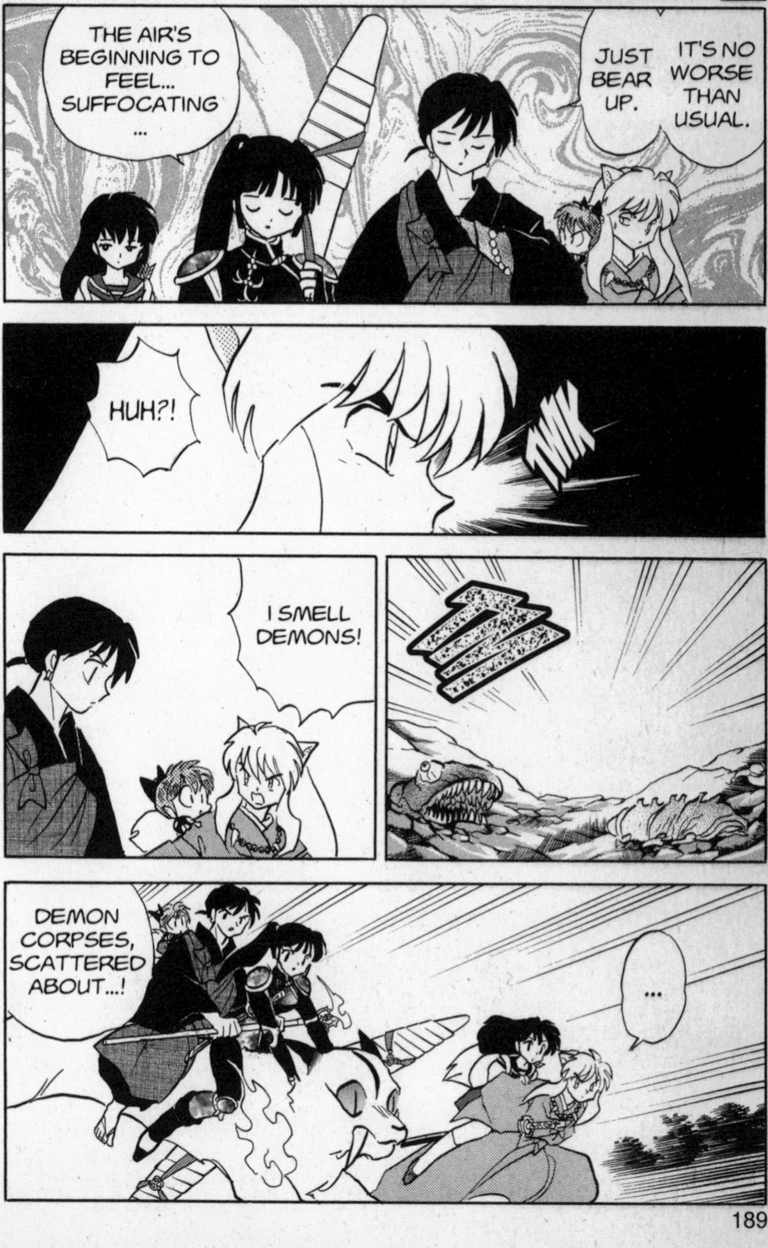
THE AIR'S BEGINNING TO FEEL... SUFFOCATING ...
JUST BEAR UP.
IT'S NO WORSE THAN USUAL.
HUH?!
TWK
I SMELL DEMONS!
DEMON CORPSES, SCATTERED ABOUT...!
...

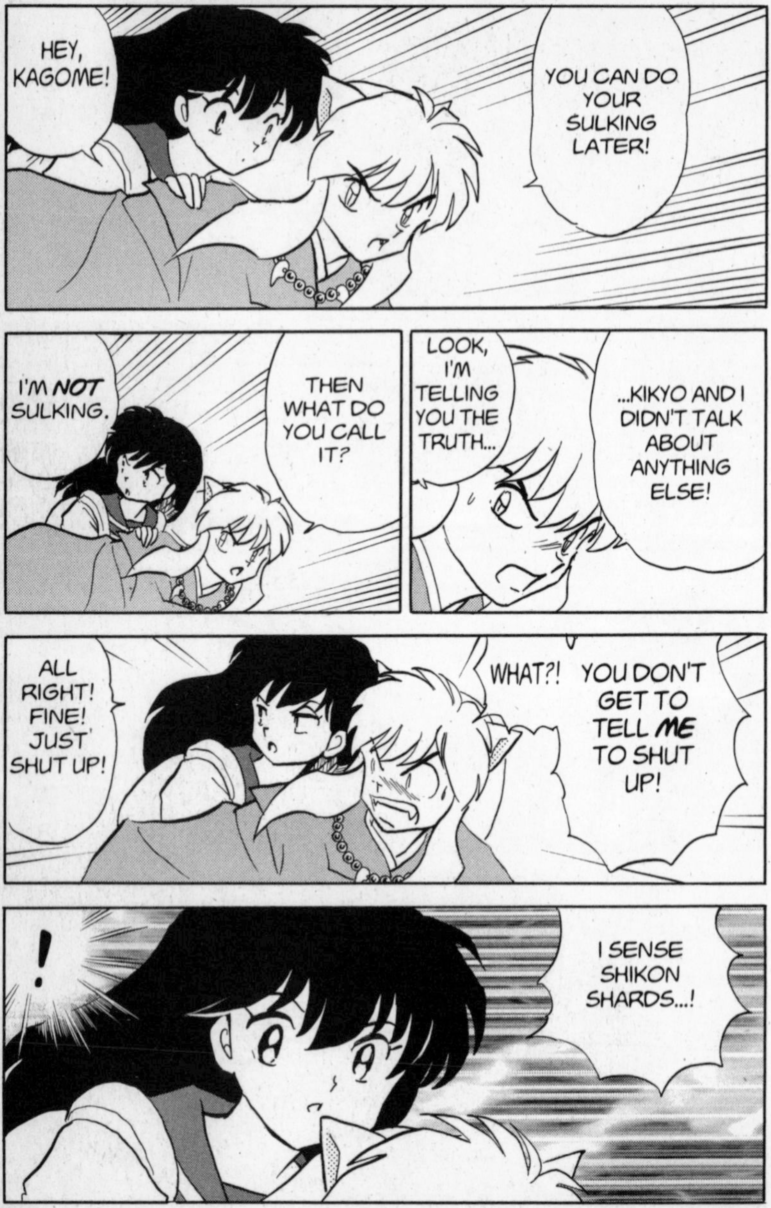

HEY, KAGOME!
YOU CAN DO YOUR SULKING LATER!
I'M **NOT** SULKING.
THEN WHAT DO YOU CALL IT?
LOOK, I'M TELLING YOU THE TRUTH...
...KIKYO AND I DIDN'T TALK ABOUT ANYTHING ELSE!
ALL RIGHT! FINE! JUST SHUT UP!
WHAT?!
YOU DON'T GET TO TELL **ME** TO SHUT UP!
!
I SENSE SHIKON SHARDS...!

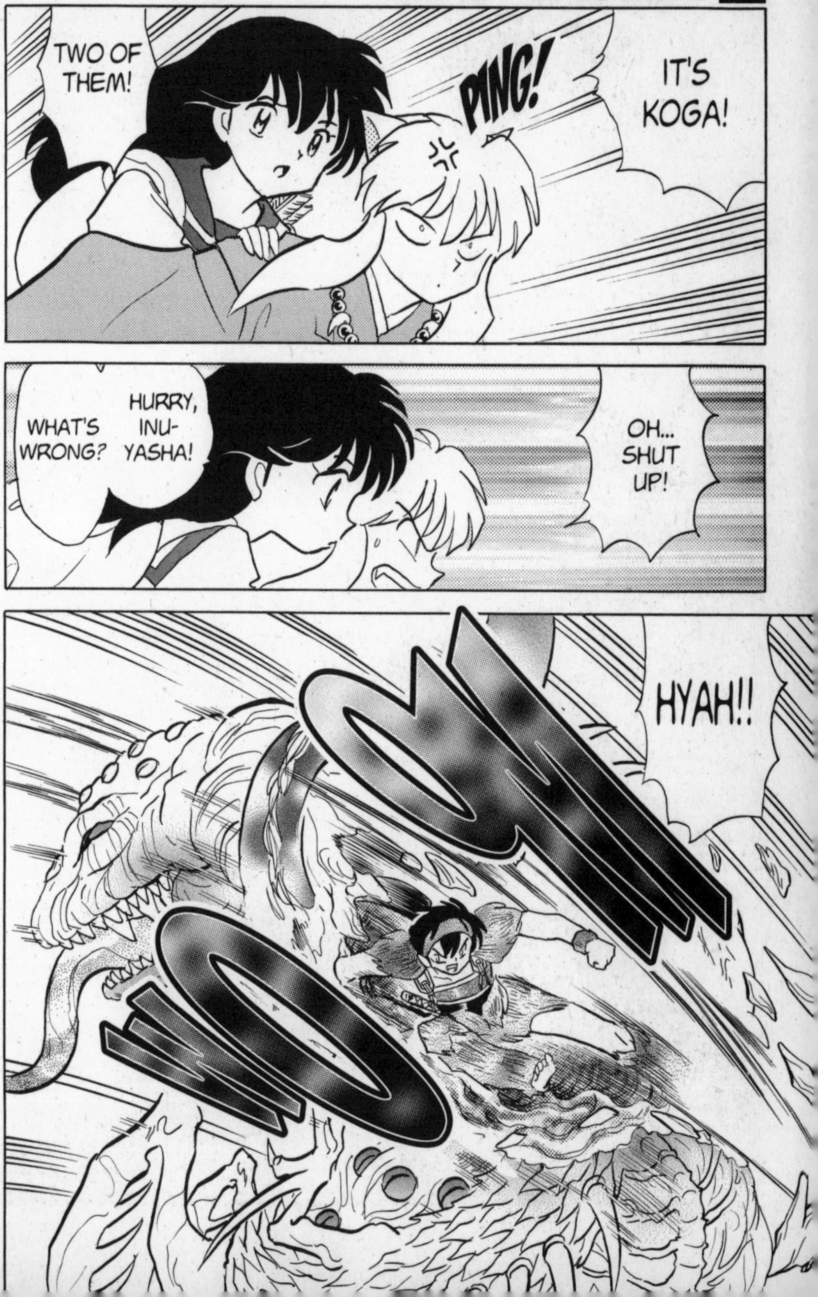
TWO OF THEM!
PING!
IT'S KOGA!
WHAT'S WRONG?
HURRY, INU-YASHA!
OH... SHUT UP!
HYAH!!

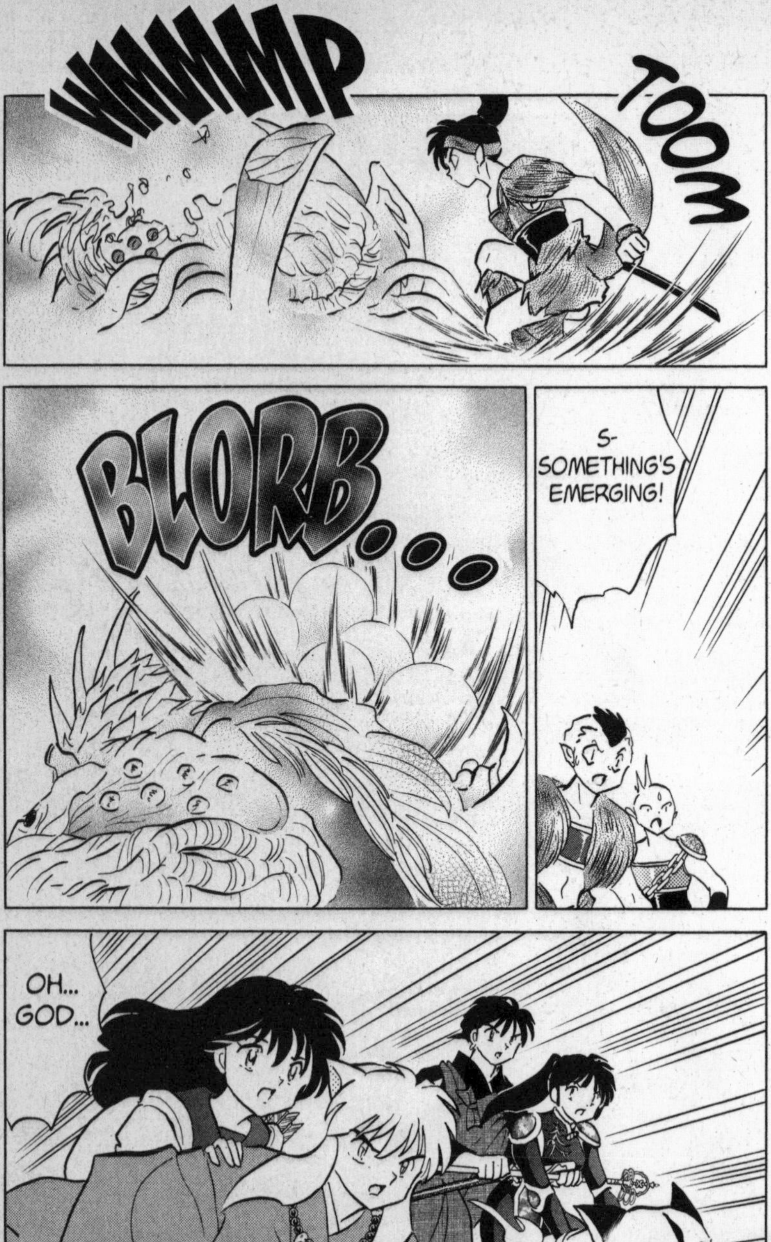
WMMMP
TOOM
BLORB...
S- SOMETHING'S EMERGING!
OH... GOD...

INUYASHA 34 - END --

INUYASHA

Read the action from the start with the original manga series

Full color adaptation of the popular TV series

Art book with cel art, paintings, character profiles and more

The popular anime series now on DVD—each season available in a collectible box set

TV SERIES & MOVIES ON DVD!

See more of the action in *Inuyasha* full-length movies

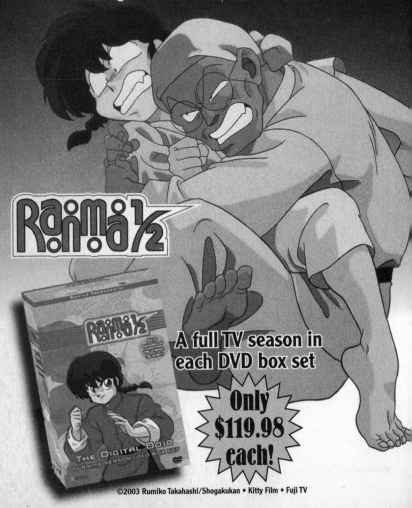

LOVE MANGA?
LET US KNOW WHAT YOU THINK!

OUR MANGA SURVEY IS NOW
AVAILABLE ONLINE. PLEASE VISIT:
VIZ.COM/MANGASURVEY

HELP US MAKE THE MANGA
YOU LOVE BETTER!

viz
media